FLY-FISHING GUIDE
TO THE

Upper
Delaware
River

FLY-FISHING GUIDE
TO THE

Upper
Delaware
River

Paul Weamer

STACKPOLE
BOOKS

To Charles R. Meck and to the memory
of my grandfather, Paul F. McConnell—
two great men who have given me
more than I could ever repay.

Copyright © 2007 by Stackpole Books

Published by
STACKPOLE BOOKS
5067 Ritter Road
Mechanicsburg, PA 17055
www.stackpolebooks.com

Printed in Singapore

First edition

10 9 8 7 6 5 4 3 2 1

Cover design by Wendy A. Reynolds
Cover photographs by Paul Weamer
Maps designed by Caroline Stover, with Martha Tyzenhouse

Library of Congress Cataloging-in-Publication Data

Weamer, Paul.
    Fly-fishing guide to the upper Delaware River / Paul Weamer. — 1st ed.
        p. cm.
    Includes bibliographical references and index.
    ISBN-13: 978-0-8117-3408-0
    ISBN-10: 0-8117-3408-0
    1. Fly fishing—Delaware River Watershed (N.Y.-Del. and N.J.)—Guidebooks. 2. Fly fishing—Pennsylvania—Guidebooks. I. Title.
SH456.W34   2007
799.12′409749—dc22
                                     2006037814

CONTENTS

ACKNOWLEDGMENTS

Thanks to Jim "Coz" Costolnick, Joe Demalderis, Lee Hartman, Ben Rinker, Tony Ritter, and Steve Taggert. I originally intended to include full-length interviews with each of these fantastic Upper Delaware guides, and I spent a great deal of time talking with them about the fishery for that purpose, but to do so would have required a much longer book. I deeply appreciate the time these fine anglers spent with me. I also had the privilege of interviewing two Upper Delaware legends—Al Caucci and Ed Van Put—during my research. Few anglers will ever know the Upper Delaware as intimately as these men do. The time I spent discussing the river system with them was one of the highlights of this project. The maps and New York State Department of Environmental Conversation studies that Mr. Van Put shared with me were invaluable.

Thanks to Mary Dette Clark for her friendship, advice, and insight into the history of the Upper Delaware's reservoirs.

Thanks to John Miller for providing the green caddis, little sister sedge, and golden drake photos.

Thanks to Upper Delaware guide Pat Schuler and to Bob Laubauch for assisting me with the pool and riffle names included in the maps, and to Jeff White, manager of the Delaware River Club, for sharing his historical books about the Upper Delaware.

Thanks to Craig Findley, president of Friends of the Upper Delaware River, for proofreading my answers to the complex questions of Upper Delaware flow issues.

Thanks to Walt Mercencavic for sharing his thoughts on the development of the East Branch fishery and to Jack Mynarski for sharing his about night fishing.

Thanks to my good friends and fly-shop cohorts Walter "Wally" Falkoff, Ron "Curly" Huber, Tim Olyphant, and Chris Pappas for their help—and to the "social outcasters," "shop monkeys," and all the other customers of the two Upper Delaware fly shops that I've been associated with. Your support and friendship are as important to me as the rivers and the trout.

Thanks to Monte Burke and Charles Meck, two great writers who inspired me and aided my development as a writer, before and during the work on this book.

Thanks to John Randolph and the staff at *Fly Fisherman* for giving me my first opportunity to write about the Upper Delaware.

Thanks to Judith Schnell at Stackpole for taking a chance and giving me the opportunity to write this book.

Thanks to Jay Nichols, who served as editor, photography instructor, and manager for this project. Many of the things that are good about this book are thanks to Jay.

Thanks to my mother for encouraging and nurturing my interest in the outdoors and to my father for sharing his love of hunting and fly fishing with me. And thanks to my brothers—Sean, Ryan, and Chris—who have always been my favorite hunting and fishing companions.

Thanks most of all to my wife, Ruthann. Without her patience, understanding, support, and willingness to help, I never could have written this book. Ruthann's love, optimism, and strong faith in God—and in me—have been some of the few constants during our turbulent life together, living and obsessing with trout in the Catskills.

INTRODUCTION

I'll never forget the first time I saw the Delaware River. I was traveling from my former home near Altoona, Pennsylvania, to spend a weekend fishing the Beaverkill when I crossed the Delaware's Main Stem at Port Jervis, New York. The river was huge compared with the small Pennsylvania limestone creeks I usually fished. I formed an opinion about the Delaware in the first second I saw it—it was too big for me, and it didn't look like a trout river.

I eventually learned that the Delaware isn't a trout river near Port Jervis. It's too far from the Delaware system's reservoirs and their cold bottom releases, and therefore too warm in the summer for trout. But even some of the Upper Delaware's trout water, the sections nearer the dams, is vast and nearly as wide as the river I first saw at Port Jervis. The river's size probably deters more anglers than it attracts. After spending nearly a decade talking to Upper Delaware fly fishermen, I realized that I wasn't alone in my initial impression. New anglers are often apprehensive about the big water, and few of them understand the dynamics of the Delaware River system's water releases, which have a tremendous impact on aquatic hatches and trout.

Several years after my first glimpse of the Lower Delaware, my wife and I decided to take a year away from real life to run a fly shop and fishing lodge on the Upper Delaware's Main Stem. For weeks I watched the expansive river through the lodge's windows as late winter melted into early spring, wondering whether we had made the right decision to move here and whether I would ever catch an Upper Delaware trout. One day I saw something that I should have noticed weeks earlier: a large island divides the river just above the deep pool in front of the lodge, and the island's right river channel didn't look so big; in fact, it wasn't as big as some stretches I had already fished on the Beaverkill.

I put on my fishing vest, strung my rod, and left the lodge to get a taste of the Upper Delaware's trout fishery. I caught two large rainbows that day— trout that would have been trophies on the limestone creeks back home. They were wild and they fought like it, pulling my fly line deep into the pool and stretching it down to the backing. The rainbows weren't the only things hooked that day. The Upper Delaware system captivated me unlike any other trout water I had fished before.

Large wild rainbows, rare in the eastern United States, live in all the Upper Delaware branches, but they are most prolific in the Main Stem and Lower East Branch. Rainbows are one of the river system's biggest attractions.

When I returned to the river the next day for my second Upper Delaware fishing experience, I was confident that I could catch its trout. I fished the same riffle along the same island with the same flies at the same time of day—and I didn't catch a thing. But I learned something about the river that day: as soon as you think you've uncovered a secret about the Delaware, it changes. That's why there are no Upper Delaware River experts. Even after fishing the river at least 150 days a year for most of the last decade, it can still throw me curve balls, and some nights I leave the river shaking my head in frustration. Experts catch trout every time they fish, but I don't know anyone who does that here.

You have to work at becoming a good Upper Delaware angler. This river and its fish don't surrender their secrets easily. The Upper Delaware stretches anglers. If the Upper Delaware doesn't humble you or teach you something new, then you're either not paying attention or not trying hard enough. I didn't know it at the time, but my first two days of Upper Delaware trout fishing were fairly typical of this complex river system.

The Delaware River System

The Delaware may be the most important river system in the United States. Its watershed supplies New York City with half its drinking water and also provides drinking water and sewage transport for many other cities and towns along its course. The Delaware's Main Stem travels 321 miles from its source near Hancock, New York, to the Delaware Bay and, ultimately, the Atlantic Ocean—making it the longest undammed river east of the Mississippi and providing Philadelphia with a port and a fishing industry. A quarter of all the people in the United States live within a six-hour drive of the Delaware watershed. The river is a wild oasis amidst the greatest localized center of American civilization.

The Upper Delaware system consists of approximately 78 miles of identified trout water, not including small feeder creeks and its largest tributary, the Beaverkill. The Upper Delaware system comprises three distinct yet interdependent rivers: the West Branch, the East Branch, and the Main Stem. Each of these rivers is a fantastic fishery in its own right, and taken as a whole, they provide more angling opportunities than one fisherman can enjoy in a lifetime. The close proximity of the branches to Hancock, New York, allows mobile anglers to fish one branch in the morning and another at night, just for a change of scenery or to chase different hatches and follow the best water conditions.

The legendary Beaverkill unites with the Upper East Branch to form the Lower East Branch and contributes a significant amount of water to the system. The Beaverkill impacts river conditions throughout the Lower East Branch and the Main Stem, and it even shares its migrating trout with these rivers. But the Beaverkill receives little attention in this book. Several great books written by the legendary fly fishermen Mac Francis, Eric Peper and Gary LaFontaine, and Ed Van Put explore the Beaverkill fishery with depth and passion. The vastness and complexity of the three Upper Delaware branches provide more than enough discussion for this volume.

Most of the Upper Delaware's trout are large, wild, and highly selective, with fighting abilities so legendary that many well-traveled anglers consider them to be among the hardest fighting and most athletic trout in the world. Because of the heavy hatches, the presence of trophy trout, and the ability to fish the river from a drift boat, the Upper Delaware is heavily fished by eastern anglers looking for a more western experience without the cost and travel time of a trip to Montana. But easterners aren't the only fishermen who pursue the Upper Delaware's bounty. Anglers from all over the world, including the western United States, travel to the river each year. Some come to find out for themselves why the Upper Delaware is beloved by so many. Some come just to pay homage to the fabled Catskill rivers. Some come because they know that the Upper Delaware system is one of the best trout fisheries anywhere in the world.

The Upper Delaware System

NEW YORK

PENNSYLVANIA

to Margaretville

to Delhi

to Sidney

to Binghamton

to NYC

Walton 206

10

206

30

Pepacton Reservoir

Bear Spring Mountain

Cannonsville Reservoir

West Branch

Trout Brook

Downsville

Corbett

Campbell Brook

Shinhopple 30

Upper East Branch

East Branch 17

Peakville

Harvard

Baxter Brook

Read Creek

Cadosia Creek

Roods Creek

268

Cold Spring Brook

8

10

Deposit

Oquaga Creek

FUTURE 86

17

West Branch

Hale Eddy

Sherman Creek

Balls Eddy

Balls Creek

Hancock

Main Stem

Lower East Branch Eddy

Fishs Eddy

Peas Eddy Creek

Abe Lord Creek

Lordville 191

97

Equinunk

Long Eddy

Kellams

Bouchouxville Brook

Hoolihan Creek

Basket Brook

Hankins Creek

Hankins

Callicoon 97

Callicoon Creek

Horton Brook

Russell Brook

Horton

Trout Creek

Cook's Falls

Beaverkill

Roscoe

Willowemoc

Livingston Manor

DeBruce

Little Beaver Kill

17

FUTURE 86

Alder Creek

Turnwood

Lewbeach

Mongaup Creek

Beaverkill

Fir Brook

Willowemoc

Using This Guide

To simplify the river system, I discuss each branch separately in a general river description and then subdivide them according to boat launches or access areas. Each general river description contains three charts: floats, distances, and durations; flows; and fishing regulations.

The charts on floats, distances, and durations provide important information for individuals planning to float the river. Float times are calculated for canoes and are slightly longer for those using drift boats and pontoon or float tubes. River levels, wind, anchoring durations, and individual rowing and paddling skills also influence float times. The charts include rowing and drifting time only, not fishing time. Always give yourself enough time to complete a float trip without rushing, especially if it's your first time on a particular river section. Boat launches look different after dark and can be missed by those unfamiliar with the river. The river mileages included in the charts are approximate.

The flow charts are intended to provide a basic understanding of fishing conditions and options at various water levels. These charts are based on my own ideals; your individual wading and boating skills will have a tremendous impact on what you consider low, ideal, safe, and dangerous conditions. Use the charts as a baseline, but always err on the side of caution and your own personal safety. People have lost boats and equipment and even drowned in the Upper Delaware system. Never underestimate the power of the river. The flow charts contain stricter classifications for ideal pontoon boat and canoe conditions than for drift boats, because it's easier to fish from a drift boat. Many Upper Delaware pontoon boat and canoe anglers use their boats predominately as transportation to wading areas, and I have factored that use into the charts.

The fishing regulation charts are based on the 2006 New York and Pennsylvania fishing digests. Regulations change, so always consult a current digest before fishing. Both states require all anglers aged 16 and older to have a current fishing license. Trout harvest size and limits are included in these charts, but you should strongly consider releasing all your catch. The Upper Delaware system hosts a tremendous number of anglers each season, and if each of these fishermen kept just one fish, it wouldn't be long before the river's trout population would be decimated. Remember, most of the fish you catch aren't stocked. If we deplete the Upper Delaware's wild trout population, we may never get it back.

I've included descriptions of public-access areas, directions for reaching them, and their corresponding GPS coordinates within the river subsections. The descriptions have two purposes. First, they tell first-time wading anglers what fishing options are available within easy walking distance of the access areas. Second, they provide a general description of boat launches and takeouts, so inexperienced boaters will know whether they need four-wheel drive to use an access and how to find a takeout at night. I use the terms *right*

Two drift boat anglers search for rising trout in the riffles above Pennsylvania's Upper Game Lands. Anglers can use either a New York or a Pennsylvania fishing license in the West Branch's and Main Stem's border water.

side and *left side* of the river in the access area descriptions. These terms refer to a position standing in the middle of the river and facing upriver or downriver, as noted.

Anglers are permitted to wade within the West Branch and Main Stem riverbeds as long as they stay within the high-water mark. These rivers form the border between New York and Pennsylvania and are bound by federal and state navigability laws. The right to wade within the high-water mark does not give anglers permission to trespass across private property to reach these rivers; anglers must initially access the rivers from public property. The East Branch lies entirely within New York State, so the same state and federal navigability laws may not pertain to it. To read more about the high-water mark, see chapter 8.

Many anglers access the rivers along railroad tracks. A few of these areas are legal, but many others are not. Parking along the railroad tracks is probably not a good idea. Tires can be punctured by driving over sharp pieces of metal embedded in the gravel along the tracks, and parking tickets area possibility too. You'll have to decide for yourself whether the risks outweigh the benefits. No railroad parking areas are included in this book because of their inherent liabilities.

Other private access points are available only through landowner permission. However, to protect the rights and goodwill of the property owners, I have omitted explicit directions to most of these areas. Also, access to some of these areas is unreliable—some are closed each year, and occasionally a new one is opened. Courteous, respectful anglers may discover and procure their own private property fishing access simply by asking permission of the landowner. Always respect private property when you are fishing: don't litter, and don't trespass through farmers' fields or people's yards. Say hello to those who live along the river. Tell them that you appreciate the beauty of their river and that you release the fish you catch. Offer to teach them what you know about fishing if they show interest. Talk long enough to be polite, but don't overstay your welcome. In addition to finding your own private-land fishing access, you may even make a few new friends. I have.

Maps are also included for each river section. I originally intended to provide a name for every pool and riffle, but I discovered that was impossible. Some of the river's pools and riffles have never been named, or their names have been lost to history; some locations have been called by many different names. I've always believed that the Upper Delaware has been shortchanged by the lack of a standardized list of names for its users to follow. Other Catskill rivers have signs denoting famous fishing spots, such as the Hendrickson's or Wagon Tracks pools on the Beaverkill. These names give identity to the river and allow anglers to talk intelligently with one another about specific locations. Discussions with longtime residents and anglers and with other fishing guides helped me procure the most common and relevant names for each of the pools and riffles listed in this book. The maps are not drawn to scale and are designed to be used with the detailed directions in the text.

Rivers live in a constant state of change, so it's impossible to provide completely current information, in permanent written form, for fishing them. A pool can be created or partially filled with gravel; islands may form or be obliterated after floods such as those that occurred in September 2004, April 2005, and June 2006. Seasonal trout migration, drought, floods, and other effects of extreme weather all impact the river system. But the Upper Delaware has survived these occurrences many times in the past. Some river sections have held trout for hundreds of years and will continue to do so in the future.

Chapter 1 examines the history and current status of the Cannonsville and Pepacton Reservoirs, as well as the rivers they dammed. Without these impoundments, there would be no reason to write this book. Their cold-water releases are the lifeblood of the Upper Delaware's trout fishery.

Some of what I've written about the management of the Upper Delaware's reservoirs is critical of the New York City Department of Environmental Protection (the DEP is really just the city's water authority). I realize that these reservoirs were never intended to create or enhance wild trout fisheries, and I wholeheartedly believe that New York City's water supply is far more valuable than all the trout in the Upper Delaware system. I take issue with the decisions of DEP officials only when they have had the opportunity to both maintain the highest priority for their water supply and protect the wild trout fishery and have failed to do the latter. It's the responsibility of all Upper Delaware anglers to make our voices heard when the trout fishery's viability is completely disregarded by those in power.

Chapters 2 through 4 provide detailed information about the three tailwater branches that constitute the Upper Delaware system. It's these rivers, below the dams, that most people associate with the Upper Delaware's trout fishery. Each branch has its own trout population, physical characteristics, and fly-fishing quirks that individualize it. Because all the rivers are connected, they do share some similarities. But they can also differ greatly, so it's important to think of them as separate, self-contained entities.

Chapter 5 begins with a brief look at the fish species that call the Upper Delaware River their home: the three trout species—browns, rainbows, and brookies—and a few other gamefish that one might encounter with a fly rod. The rest of the chapter examines equipment; fly patterns; and dry-fly, nymph, and streamer techniques that are vital to productive Upper Delaware trout fishing. Finally, it addresses night fishing and fish etiquette—two of the river's most overlooked topics.

Most Upper Delaware fly anglers prefer to fish hatches, usually with dry flies. Chapters 6 and 7 examine the most important mayfly, caddis, and stonefly hatches that occur during the spring, summer, and fall, respectively. I've included hatch charts for each of the seasons, but it's difficult to give a specific time line for how these hatches will progress within the Upper Delaware system during any given year. In the East, hatches typically begin in the warmer, bottom section of a river and slowly progress upriver, but it doesn't always happen that way in the Upper Delaware system. The Upper Delaware branches can have widely varying temperatures, depending on their water levels. It's not uncommon for a hatch to begin in one branch a week to several weeks before it begins in another. And the hatches can sometimes occur haphazardly, without an orderly progression—in the top section of one river, and in the bottom of another. A change in reservoir releases or spill or an isolated rainstorm can also retard a hatch in one section without affecting the same hatch in another section. The best way to learn whether a particular hatch is occurring in an individual river branch is to call one of the fly shops listed in the appendix of this book.

The hatch chapters are not meant to be a discourse on entomology. But the information and photographs they contain are intended to provide basic knowledge of the most important hatches. Many Upper Delaware anglers choose to sit on the riverbank, waiting for a fish to rise. Those who would rather spend their time fishing subsurface between hatches will find the physical descriptions and habitat requirements of the various nymphs and larvae beneficial. Knowing what the nymphs look like and how, when, and where to fish them ensures that nymphing and wet-fly fishing will be more productive.

The often crowded Upper Delaware River system is largely ignored during the winter. Many of the river's angler paths, which are heavily traveled during the hatch season, are abandoned once the hatches end and the mountains fill with snow. I realized years ago that Upper Delaware trout will still take flies, run, and sometimes even jump during the winter. The end of chapter 7 discusses the winter fly-fishing options available to Upper Delaware anglers.

The final chapter provides a series of questions and answers about Upper Delaware water issues based on the most commonly asked questions in my fly shop. It's important for all Upper Delaware anglers to understand how the system works so that we can better protect it in the future. Chapter 8 also discusses the high-water mark, catch and release, and the ethics of fishing during periods of thermal stress, all of which will impact the river's future as a trout fishery. I end the chapter with some brief thoughts about why the Upper Delaware is worth protecting. It's a perilous time in the history of the

John Hurley casts to a bank feeder at the head of the last Wulff Pool. Legendary fly anglers Lee and Joan Wulff used to own this section of the Upper East Branch, but their land has been sold and subdivided to create seasonal homes. Issues related to development and private property will continue to impact the river system in the future.

Upper Delaware River. Issues related to private property, development, reservoir management, and competition among fishermen will all impact the river system. The river has no voice. It is up to those of us who love the Delaware to ensure that it continues to flow cold, clean, and full of trout.

The Upper Delaware is a famous river with an army of anglers who feel connected to it. The very mention of its name provokes intense feelings and opinions from many of these loyal fishermen. This book is not intended to be the last word on the subject. Many volumes could be filled with information about the Upper Delaware River system, and there is no way to include it all in one book.

If you are unfamiliar with the river system, this book will get you started. The maps will give you an idea of the layout of the river's branches and help you find exact fishing locations. The fly pattern photographs and recipes will arm you with a selection of Upper Delaware trout-tested flies so that your fly boxes will be up to the challenge of the river's legendary fish. If you're already acquainted with the fishery, then hopefully this book will help you catch a few more trout, introduce you to an access you may have overlooked, or encourage you to become involved in the river's stewardship.

I feel inadequate, in many ways, to be the writer of this book. My fly-fishing and writing abilities pale in comparison to the Upper Delaware's greatness. Writing this book has made me examine my own understanding of the system in a new, more thorough way. I believe it has made me a better angler. I hope it improves your Upper Delaware fly fishing as well.

CHAPTER 1

Creation of the Upper Delaware's Tailwater Trout Fishery

Cannonsville Reservoir and the West Branch above the Dam

The history of the photographs recording the construction of Cannonsville Reservoir is almost as interesting as the history of the reservoir itself. Many of these photos, which are now displayed in local Delaware County historical societies and in the New York City DEP offices, were taken by Catskill fly-tying legend and fly-shop owner Walt Dette. Walt's daughter, Mary Dette Clark, is the heir to her father's work and may be the greatest living Catskill fly tier. My friendship with Mary and her husband, Gene, began when I started tying flies for the Dette Fly Shop, now owned and cared for by Mary. (Sadly, Gene Clark passed away in early 2006. His smile and gentle nature will be dearly missed by all who knew him.) It was Mary who relayed this story to me.

Walt's career as a photographer began when Mary was a child. And it happened by accident—a truck accident. A tractor trailer was traveling very fast along Route 17 near Roscoe, New York, when its driver tried to navigate the sharp turn near town. He lost control, the truck rolled over, and its cargo—a load of cameras—went plummeting down a bank and into the Beaverkill. Local residents aided in the cleanup by walking along the river and collecting the debris. Most believed it to be improper to keep all of the cameras they found. So they each gathered several—enough to return one or two to their rightful owners and to retain one as payment for their efforts. Walt was one of the lucky residents who wound up with a camera that was only slightly damaged. He repaired it and began to teach himself the art of photography, just as he had taught himself to tie flies.

It must have been as financially unrewarding to own a Catskill fly shop in the 1940s, 1950s, and 1960s as it is today. Walt's wife, Winnie, worked at a local bank and still found time to tie flies, run the shop, and raise the children. Walt left the shop each day to try to bring in extra income for the family. One of his jobs was to shoot photographs (with the camera he found near the Beaverkill) of the construction of Cannonsville Reservoir project that began in 1955.

The 16-mile-long, approximately half-mile-wide reservoir was completed by 1967, although some limited use began in 1965. Cannonsville's earthen dam, measuring 2,800 feet long and 175 feet high, cost $140 million to build. The lake created by the dam lies 1,150 feet above sea level, covers 4,568 acres of land, and is surrounded by 53 miles of forested shoreline. It has an average depth of 61 feet and a maximum depth of 140 feet. The 98 billion gallons of water held by the full Cannonsville Reservoir buries the remains of five former Catskill communities: Beerston, Cannonsville, Granton, Rock Rift, and Rock Royal. The total New York City–owned Cannonsville Reservoir property swallowed 19,910 acres of land in New York's Delaware County, including 94 family owned farms. A total of 941 residents from the submerged communities were forced to leave their homes. And 2,150 of their ancestors were moved from their initial resting places and reinterred in 11 Delaware County cemeteries (Galusha 1999).

The loss of the five Catskill communities and the displacement of their residents and cemeteries engendered anger and mistrust toward the New York City DEP that continue to be felt today among many upstate New Yorkers. But the wounds of past property seizures aren't the only reminder of what the New York City water authority has forcefully taken from the Catskills and the power it continues to wield over the region. A severe drought in 2001 prompted the DEP to lower Cannonsville's water level to 2.5 percent to maintain the Montague, New Jersey, flow target (see chapter 8). The bones of the old towns—the roads and bridges that connected them— were visible in the soupy hole that used to contain a lake. Many of the reservoir's sport fish and alewives (a prolific species of baitfish that lives in the reservoir) died. The West Branch tailwater stood at the precipice of destruction as the reservoir level fell to a one-week supply of water. If Cannonsville went dry, the West Branch's riverbed would have dried up too, especially near Stilesville. At the last possible moment, waves of rainstorms swept over the region and saved the reservoir and tailwater fisheries.

Some may argue that the DEP only did what it had to do during the drought. But these people miss the larger picture. The other Delaware reservoirs maintained water levels well above 50 percent during the drought. Releases could have been made equitably, from all the dams, to save enough water in Cannonsville to protect the West Branch fishery. But the DEP seldom considers the fisheries when it makes its water management decisions. Upstate New York residents realize that the city owns their dams. They just want the DEP to consider the needs of the upstate population and its fisheries as part of a regionwide plan. But the DEP seldom does that, either. Instead, it often treats upstate New York communities as an annoying child, unworthy of attention. A January 2006 article in the *Times Herald-Record* of Middletown,

New York, reported that a dam inspector working on behalf of the New York City DEP had falsified Catskill reservoir inspection reports—potentially jeopardizing the human populations living below the dams. Instead of completing actual physical inspections of the reservoirs, previous reports were allegedly photocopied and passed off as current inspections (Bruno and Gardner 2006).

This revelation was made in the wake of the devastating flooding of the Delaware River basin in the fall of 2004 and the spring of 2005—floods that killed two people and destroyed countless homes and properties. Many local residents believe that the flooding could have been mitigated if the DEP cared about the well-being of the communities that surround and in many ways protect the city's water supply. They believe that the reservoirs should never be full enough to cause flooding in the event of a hurricane or sudden snowmelt. I don't believe that the floods were entirely the DEP's fault. Rivers sometimes flood—it's a well-known fact of nature. But it's difficult to defend any of the DEP's water management decisions when its own dam inspectors provide ammunition to those who believe that the DEP simply wants the Upper Delaware's wild trout and human populations to quietly disappear.

There are at least two sides to every story. Despite everything New York City has taken from the region to build its reservoirs, in some ways, it has returned even more. The city provides reservoir stipend monies to some Catskill communities—money that is desperately needed to fund local school districts—and it pays taxes on the land it owns. The deep Delaware reservoirs also create thriving tailwater trout fisheries that lure tourists to the region who spend money at local businesses.

The Cannonsville Reservoir created a good lake fishery for perch, bass, and brown trout. The lake's brown trout can grow to over 10 pounds by consuming its vast population of alewives. These browns are so big that the only comparable fish in the East are the salmonoids in the Great Lakes—fish that also grow large from consuming alewives. And the anglers who pursue them have created a lake fishing industry for the upstate New York communities of Deposit and Walton—a town that does not benefit financially from the tailwater fishery created below the dam.

The Cannonsville Reservoir also dramatically improved the Upper Delaware's West Branch trout fishery. Before the dam, much of the river was a put-and-take stocked trout fishery. In fact, the 40 miles of free-flowing West Branch above the dam remains largely a stocked trout fishery today. The West Branch above the dam warms very quickly in the summer, and most of the trout fishing there occurs in the spring for freshly stocked fish. But the river does maintain a small population of holdovers and wild brown and brook trout that find refuge in areas of groundwater infiltration during periods of high thermal stress. The river also hosts a significant number of fallfish that are sometimes so populous that it's hard to catch any trout at all because every fly is attacked by these simple minnows.

Cannonsville Reservoir's breast and spillway. Cannonsville often spills in the spring, sweeping alewives and huge brown trout into the West Branch.

Physically, the West Branch above the dam looks very similar to the river below it. It's dominated by flat, slow-moving pools connected by short riffles of medium depth. Many of its pool bottoms are covered with silt, due in large part to the extensive farming that occurs in the region. The aquatic hatches above the dam remain impressive. In fact, some of them, such as the Hendricksons and the green drakes, may be as good above the dam as they are below it. These fantastic hatches are an indicator of the relative purity of the West Branch's water that feeds the reservoir. However, the East Branch's water, which flows into the Pepacton Reservoir, is even cleaner. Farm fields spread with manure allow nitrates to leach into the West Branch above the dam.

Management of Cannonsville Reservoir's water releases has always been a hotly contested issue. The reservoir's original release valves were unable to expel water in increments between 45 and 325 cubic feet per second (cfs). Minimum summer reservoir releases, from June 15 to August 15, were eventually set at 325 cfs to provide some basic protection to the trout fishery. But higher water volumes were often released to meet the court-mandated Delaware River flow target at Montague. These heavy summer water releases cooled not only the West Branch but also the Main Stem and created a wild trout zone that extended all the way to Callicoon, New York. But the fishing conditions weren't always ideal. The river basically relied on tributary water for its volume in the early spring, fall, and winter. Winters were often especially hard on the fishery. Water releases were usually curtailed to a pathetic trickle of 45 cfs, which allowed anchor ice to form, jeopardizing the wild brown trout's fall spawning redds.

A new valve was installed in 1997 at a cost of $3.4 million. Shortly thereafter, minimum summer releases were reduced to 160 cfs, but their duration was lengthened from June 1 to September 1. The new valve was controversial from its inception. Eventually, most Upper Delaware anglers supported the project, based on assurances from DEP officials of improved, trout-sustaining river flows. The DEP stated that too much water was being wasted with the old valve and its limited settings. A new valve would allow it to micromanage reservoir releases, ultimately ensuring that more water would be available within the reservoir to feed the fishery when necessary to maintain volume or mitigate thermal stress.

Most Upper Delaware anglers now believe that they were told a series of half-truths. It's true that New York City's DEP can now micromanage Cannonsville Reservoir releases to save water, but most of this "saved" water never sees the Upper Delaware's riverbed. It's often removed from the system underground, through the Delaware Aqueduct, or greedily hoarded behind the reservoir's high earthen dam. The former practice of maintaining constant releases of 325 or 160 cfs has been disregarded in favor of a new plan called Revision 7, which only attempts to maintain a 225-cfs flow at the West Branch's Hale Eddy gauge (to better understand the difference between flow and release, see chapter 8). The old days, when water released into the West Branch often topped 1,000 cfs, are long gone. And the once legendary wild rainbow Main Stem fishery has been steadily diminishing too.

The Cannonsville Reservoir has been mired in controversy since its inception, and it probably always will be. The world-class lake and tailwater fisheries created by the dam do little to ease the pain of the residents who gave everything they had for the betterment of New York City and the rest of the country. Some of the residents displaced by the reservoir left the Catskills forever. One of the reasons I feel obligated to protect the Upper Delaware River system is to give something back to those who stayed in the communities that are my adopted home. Of course, not all my reasons for advocating improved Cannonsville water releases are altruistic—after all, I did move here for the trout fishing. But the West Branch trout fishery also benefits the region economically, and it makes me feel good to know that my selfish efforts to improve the fishery also help my community of choice. So maybe the long-suffering residents of the Catskills can benefit in some small way by a project that was originally designed for the benefit of people who live elsewhere.

Pepacton Reservoir and the East Branch above the Dam

Pepacton Reservoir was built from 1947 to 1954. It is the largest of the four Delaware River system reservoirs—more than 30 percent larger than Cannonsville. Pepacton lies 1,280 feet above sea level, is 18.5 miles long and half a mile wide, covers 5,178 acres, and has a maximum water depth of 180 feet. It is surrounded by 51 miles of predominantly forested shoreline, encompassing 13,384 New York City–owned acres in New York's Delaware County. All this land is completely sheltered from future development to protect its water supply. Pepacton's earthen dam is 2,450 feet long and 204 feet high, and it retains 140.2 billion gallons of water when the reservoir is full. It drowned four Catskill communities—Arena, Pepacton, Shavertown, and Union Grove—along with their cemeteries, forcing the reinterment of 1,500 bodies from their original locations into Pepacton Cemetery (Galusha 1999).

This reservoir's construction created the same anger and mistrust for the city's DEP that the Cannonsville Reservoir did. But residents near the Pepacton Reservoir experienced these emotions first. Inhabitants of the now abandoned towns fought the reservoir project until they realized that there was no way to stop its momentum. By the time the construction of Cannonsville began, most of the local residents knew what to expect and realized there was no way to fight the DEP. They had seen it all before in the struggles of their friends and neighbors in the East Branch valley.

Pepacton is the largest of the Delaware's reservoirs—more than 30 percent larger than Cannonsville.

Approximately 20 miles of the East Branch still flow unfettered above the dam today. The river's water is especially clean because its banks are largely forested and few farms border the East Branch above the dam. Fishing is allowed on both the reservoir and the East Branch above it, and many consider Pepacton to be the best brown trout reservoir fishery within the Delaware system.

Pepacton's trout grow to such impressive proportions for the same reason that Cannonsville Reservoir's do—alewives. But Pepacton is seldom allowed to spill because of the high value placed on its clean drinking water. Most of Pepacton's water is shuttled underground, into Rondout Reservoir, whenever it comes close to spilling. The less desirable water in Cannonsville is permitted to spill almost every spring. Thus, alewives aren't nearly as important to the East Branch's tailwater fishery as they are to the West Branch's, because they are seldom spilled into the river.

The East Branch above the dam is a small river, averaging 20 to 25 feet wide. Mac Francis, in his wonderful book *Catskill Rivers: Birthplace of American Fly Fishing* (1996), says that the river's best fly fishing occurs from the reservoir upriver to Halcottsville, where anglers can expect to catch a lot of small stocked and wild brown trout up to about 12 inches. I have fished the river above the dam only once, near Margaretville, but I would agree with Mr. Francis, even though my experience occurred nearly 10 years after he wrote his book.

The Delaware Aqueduct

The creation of the four Delaware River system reservoirs (Cannonsville, Neversink, Pepacton, and Rondout) vastly improved New York City's water supply. But these large bodies of potable water would be of little value to the city without a way to transfer their water from the Catskills to the city's population. The Delaware Aqueduct was created for just that purpose. Construction of the Delaware Aqueduct began in 1937 and was completed in 1945. However, the entire water delivery system, which includes the West and East Delaware tunnels and the Neversink tunnel, wasn't completed until 1955 (Galusha 1999).

The Delaware Aqueduct remains one of the greatest engineering accomplishments of the modern world. It supplies more than 9 million New York City residents with nearly 80 percent of their water needs—more than 900 million gallons per day (Kennedy, Wegner, and Yaggi 2001). The aqueduct structure comprises 13.5- to 19.5-foot-diameter concrete-lined tunnels that run 85 miles from the Rondout Reservoir to the Hillview Reservoir in Yonkers, making it the longest uninterrupted tunnel in the world. The aqueduct is between 300 and 1,500 feet belowground, and it includes a section that lies 600 feet beneath the Hudson River near Chelsea, New York (Galusha 1999).

Water from the Cannonsville, Pepacton, and Neversink Reservoirs is gravity fed, without the aid of mechanical pumps, to the Rondout Reservoir through three separate tunnels. It then travels through the Delaware Aqueduct and ultimately arrives in the water faucets and fire hydrants of New York City.

The West Delaware tunnel, built from 1955 to 1964, connects Cannonsville Reservoir to Rondout. It is 44 miles long and can deliver a maximum yield of 500 million gallons of water per day through its 15- to 18-foot-diameter tunnel. The East Delaware tunnel, constructed from 1949 to 1955 to connect Pepacton Reservoir to Rondout, is 25 miles long and capable of delivering 700 million gallons of East Branch water per day through its 11-foot-diameter tunnel. The smallest of the three Catskill reservoir tunnels, the Neversink tunnel, is 6 miles long. It was constructed from 1949 to 1954 and can deliver 500 million gallons of water through its 10-foot-diameter concrete tunnel (Galusha 1999).

The once great construction achievement of the Delaware Aqueduct and tunnels has now fallen into a state of disrepair. The tunnels are crumbling, and 5 percent of all Catskill reservoir water now leaks through holes in the aqueduct (Kennedy et al. 2001). This leaking water is a terrible waste to both the rivers that surrender the water and to New York City, which relies on this water to sustain its population. The leaks are so severe that a 2001 report written by Robert Kennedy Jr. and his environmental advocacy group Riverkeeper describes their condition as "dire and critical." The New York City DEP concluded in 1996 and 1998 studies that one aqueduct leak loses 33 million to 37 million gallons of water per day. To help put these numbers in perspective, that leak loses more water per day than the entire city of Rochester, New York, consumes.

The DEP has known about these leaks for decades, yet it has done little to fix the problem. I often wonder what the Upper Delaware trout fishery would be like if just the leaking aqueduct water was used to maintain and preserve the trout fishery. The Delaware, its local human population, and its wildlife have given greatly of themselves to provide New York City with clean water. And because of this gift, New York City is blessed with one of the best water supplies of any major city in the world. The residents of the Upper Delaware basin were rewarded with one of the greatest wild trout fisheries in the world because of New York City's dams. But the crumbling aqueduct could turn all of the Upper Delaware's users from winners into losers.

CHAPTER 2

West Branch Tailwater

The West Branch tailwater is the most popular Upper Delaware fly-fishing destination, and rightly so. It has phenomenal insect life, a higher trout density than either the Main Stem or the East Branch, and the system's only no-kill section. The West Branch is also popular because its relatively uniform streambed is easy to wade, and it has a fair number of access areas. Plus, it receives most of the Delaware reservoir system's cold-water releases, creating the most reliable year-round fishing conditions.

The West Branch does have its problems, however. Increased angling pressure in recent years has turned some people off (reminding me of one of my favorite Yogi Berra-isms: "The place is so crowded that no one goes there

The Route 17 Bridge near Deposit, New York, is the beginning of the West Branch's no-kill section.

anymore"). Another drawback is Route 17, which follows the river for most of its course. The sound of cars zipping down the highway and the groan of tractor-trailer air brakes deter from the river's serenity, but it's amazing how little you notice the traffic when you're casting to pods of large, rising trout. In spite of the crowds and the highway noise, the West Branch remains a magnificent river—perhaps the best wild trout fishery east of the Rocky Mountains.

The West Branch tailwater begins northeast of Deposit, New York. It's a low-gradient river, falling 7.3 feet per mile along its course, and it's composed of 25 percent riffles and 75 percent pools. The river glides for approximately 17.5 miles, with an average width of 200 feet near Deposit and 242 feet near Hancock, New York, before joining the East Branch and forming the Main Stem (McBride 2002).

Although the West Branch originates entirely in New York State, the river becomes the border between New York and Pennsylvania 10.2 miles below Cannonsville Dam, just upriver from Pennsylvania's Upper Game Lands Parking Area. A reciprocal agreement between the states allows anglers to use either state's fishing license downriver from the boundary line.

The West Branch provides important trout spawning grounds for the entire Upper Delaware system. Extensive spawning occurs in the top half of the river, particularly in the gravel areas upriver from the Upper Game Lands

West Branch Floats, Distances, and Durations

Float	River Miles	Road Miles	Time*
Stilesville to Deposit sewage treatment plant	2.5	2.1	.75 hour
Deposit sewage treatment plant to Hale Eddy Bridge	4	5.4	1.5 hours
Hale Eddy Bridge to Balls Eddy	5.5	4.4	2.3 hours
Stilesville to Balls Eddy	11.4	11.9	4.5 hours
Deposit sewage treatment plant to Balls Eddy	9	9.8	3.75 hours
Balls Eddy to Hancock's 191 Bridge	4	3.3	1.5 hours
Hancock's 191 Bridge to Shehawken	.5	1	10 minutes
Shehawken to Junction Pool	1	3.3	15 minutes
Balls Eddy to Buckingham	10.8	10	4.5 hours
Shehawken to Buckingham	6.3	6	2.5 hours

Times are based on average float time during average water levels.

Parking Area to Stilesville. These spawning areas were identified in the New York State Department of Environmental Conservation (DEC) 1996 radio-telemetry study, which radio-tagged and monitored a cross section of the river's trout for several seasons (McBride 2002). The top of the West Branch, from the weir above Stilesville downriver to the Pennsylvania border, is closed to all forms of angling from October 16 to March 31 to protect the spawning wild trout.

The West Branch is predominantly a brown trout fishery, although it also contains a healthy population of rainbows, especially in its lower reaches, and a small population of wild brook trout. The West Branch hasn't been intentionally stocked with trout since 1994. But two of its largest tributaries, Oquaga and Shehawken Creeks, are currently stocked with brown trout. A few of these stocked fish occasionally make their way into the West Branch, perpetuating the rumor that the river is still receiving stocked fish. The only current West Branch "stocking" program occurs naturally via Cannonsville Reservoir. Cannonsville often spills in the spring, sweeping large reservoir browns over the breast of the dam with the water. These fish really shouldn't be called stocked, though, because some of the Cannonsville Reservoir brown trout are wild—spawned in the West Branch above the dam. These reservoir trout often fall prey to Upper West Branch spin fishermen using live or salted alewives—called saw bellies by the locals—as bait. A few of these "slammers"

Description

This short float for anglers with limited time includes the West Branch's coldest and most stable river section near Stilesville.

A good half-day float that allows a lot of fishing time in the West Branch's no-kill section.

This half-day float offers access to otherwise inaccessible wade-fishing reaches of the West Branch between Hale Eddy Bridge and the Pennsylvania Game Lands, and the mudflats and top of Balls Eddy.

This popular all-day trip provides an opportunity to fish all the water described in the first two float-trip options. Begin the trip either from Stilesville (provides more fishing opportunities in the upper part of the river), or from the Deposit sewage treatment plant (shorter trip with more time to fish downriver).

This short float allows access to most of the bottom part of the West Branch.

A short trip that provides access to the 191 Bridge Riffle and Pool and the braided water above and at the Shehawken boat launch.

This short trip permits anglers to fish the very end of the West Branch. Most boaters who complete this float are planning to fish the evening rise at Junction Pool.

A long, all-day trip that allows anglers to fish parts of two rivers in the same outing—the bottom of the West Branch and the Upper Main Stem.

This popular half- to full-day float provides fishing on the Upper Main Stem and is commonly used by Upper Main Stem fishing guides.

(a local term for large trout) have been caught by fly fishermen, such as the 33-inch, 15-pound monster that inhaled a White Zonker streamer in 1996; the 30-incher that sipped a size 16 Elk Hair Caddis dry fly in 2003; and a similar-sized fish caught on a Green Bead Head nymph in 2005.

I've listed 13 public-access areas for the West Branch, most of which are owned by the New York DEC or the Pennsylvania Fish and Boat Commission (PFBC), securing the public's right to use them indefinitely. I divide the West Branch into two sections for the purposes of this book, using the Hale Eddy Bridge as the dividing line. The effects of Cannonsville's cold-water releases tend to diminish below this point unless a substantial amount of water is released. The Upper (Stilesville to Hale Eddy) and Lower (Hale Eddy to Junction Pool) West Branch often look and behave like two different rivers due to these releases.

Fall is spawning time for the Upper Delaware's wild brown trout. Many of them ascend Shehawken Creek (above) from the West Branch.

West Branch Flows*

Water Level (cfs)	Wading	Drift Boats	Pontoon Boats and Canoes
<225	Excellent—nearly the entire river is wadable	Not floatable	Not advised
225–400	Excellent—nearly the entire river remains wadable	Not floatable below 400 cfs Not advised at 400 cfs (same reasons as for pontoon boats and canoes)	Not advised to poor—the river is floatable, but fish and fishermen will be centered in deeper water; boats would have to float through this water, disturbing those around them
400–600	Excellent to very good—most of the river is wadable	Not advised to poor—the river becomes easier to float as it approaches 600 cfs, but some dragging will be necessary; there are many exposed rocks	Fair to very good—easy to anchor; use the boat as transportation to more remote wading spots
600–800	Very good to good—over 50% of the river remains wadable	Poor to good—some dragging may still be necessary for inexperienced boaters	Very good to excellent—a better choice than a drift boat at this water level
800–1,000	Good to fair—50% of the river is wadable	Good to very good—fewer exposed rocks; no dragging	Excellent to good—fishing from the boat is required in some areas as wading possibilities diminish
1,000–1,500	Fair to poor—less than 50% of the river is wadable; wading becomes limited to shallow edges and the tails of some pools as flows approach 1,500 cfs	Very good to excellent—fewer waders creating obstacles	Good—most fishing will be from the boat
1,500–2,000	Poor to not advised—wading is limited	Excellent—drift become the best boats option at this and all higher flows	Fair—nearly all fishing will be from the boat.
2,000–2,500	Not advised and potentially dangerous	Very good	Poor—all fishing will be from the boat; anchoring in some riffles may be difficult
2,500–3,000	Not advised and potentially dangerous	Good—anchoring becomes difficult in some riffles	Poor to not advised—for experienced boaters only
3,000–4,500	Wading is dangerous	Fair—for experienced boaters only	Not advised—for expert boaters only
>4,500	Wading is dangerous	Poor to not advised—for expert boaters only	Not advised and potentially dangerous

Flows measured at the Hale Eddy gauging station.

Though most of the West Branch is easily waded, some anglers prefer to use drift boats to reach less accessible areas.

West Branch Fishing Regulations

River Section	Fishing Season	Harvesting Length	Daily Limit
Cannonsville Dam downriver to Route 17 overpass at Deposit	April 1–October 15	12 inches	2 trout
Route 17 overpass at Deposit downriver 2 miles (no-kill section)	April 1–October 15	Catch-and-release; artificial lures only	No harvest
Lower limit of no-kill section at Deposit downriver to NY-PA border, 1.7 miles below Hale Eddy Bridge	April 1–October 15	12 inches	2 trout
NY-PA border downriver to the mouth at Hancock, NY	8:00 a.m. on the first Saturday after April 11–October 15	12 inches	2 trout
	October 16–8:00 a.m. on the first Saturday after April 11 (PA's opening day of trout season)	Catch-and-release; artificial lures only	No harvest

Upper West Branch Tailwater:
Cannonsville Reservoir to Hale Eddy Bridge

The fishable portion of the Upper West Branch tailwater begins at the Stilesville parking area, less than a mile below the New York State Route 8 Bridge. Above the bridge, approximately half a mile of legal fishing water begins at a weir dam, but there are no parking areas to provide easy access to this area. The 1.4-mile stretch of river between the weir dam and the reservoir is private reservoir property owned by New York City. Trespassing above the weir dam has always been forbidden, but since the 9/11 terrorists attack, any threat to New York City's water supply—even a person with a fly rod—is taken very seriously.

The river around Stilesville is almost always cold, and it's one of the most reliable fishing sections in the system due to its fairly stable water temperature. Nearly all the water in this section comes from Cannonsville Reservoir. The constant, frigid water temperature does strange things to the timing of the insect hatches. I've seen green drakes emerging in early August and Hendricksons appearing outside the parameters listed in anyone's hatch chart. The cold water also affects the diversity of the river's hatches. The closer you get to the dam, the fewer insect species you'll find, but the species that live near the dam are more abundant.

The Upper West is blessed with several excellent spring and summer hatches, but its premier hatch is the summer sulphur. Sulphurs begin in June and can last as long as three months if enough cold water is being released from the dam. Water temperatures need to be in the upper 40s to low 50s for sulphurs to hatch. Many anglers have a difficult time believing that trout will be active in water this cold, but they are. Most books tell you that trout become active when water temperatures approach a trout's ideal of 55 to 65 degrees. Trout activity does increase in many sections of the Upper Delaware when water temperatures are moving toward that ideal, but this isn't always the case in the Upper West. Upper West Branch trout thrive in the cold water.

The Upper West Branch is smaller water than most other Upper Delaware River sections. Its pools are easily waded and are often preferred by anglers who appreciate the challenge of difficult trout but can no longer traverse the larger and more rugged sections downriver. Because of the lack of significant tributary water and the corresponding increase in river volume such creeks would provide, the Upper West is also one of the best sections to fish after a major rain. The Upper West can usually be fished within a day of a heavy rainstorm as long as the reservoir isn't spilling—long before other river sections return to their prestorm flows.

The lack of tributaries also enhances the amount of Cannonsville Reservoir debris released into the river. It's common for large chunks of algae and grass to be flushed out of the dam when reservoir releases are increased. The amount of debris is directly related to the holding capacity of the reservoir— the lower the reservoir level, the more debris there is. The lack of diluting tributary water, as well as insufficient distance from the reservoir for the material

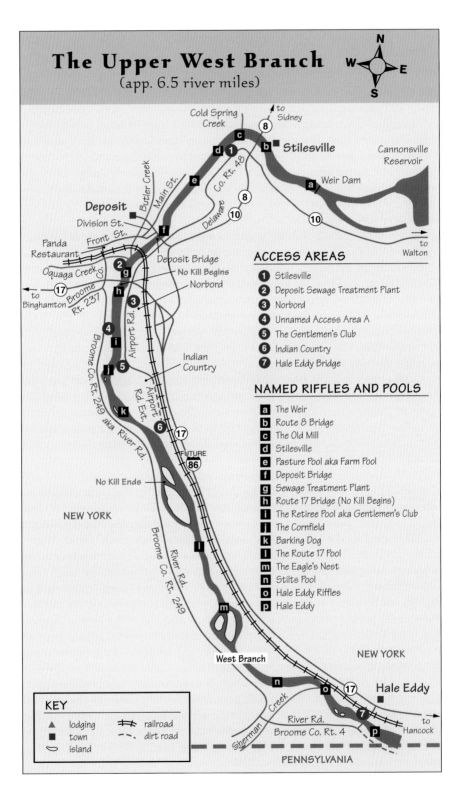

The Upper West Branch
(app. 6.5 river miles)

N
W E
S

to Sidney

Cold Spring Creek

c
d 1
8

b
Stilesville

a
Weir Dam

Cannonsville Reservoir

e

Co. Rt. 48

Butler Creek

Main St.

Deposit

Delaware

8

10

10

to Walton

Division St.

Front St.

f

Panda Restaurant

Oquaga Creek

2

g

Deposit Bridge

No Kill Begins

Norbord

h

17

Broome Rt. 237

3

to Binghamton

Airport Rd.

4

i

5

j

Airport Rd. Ext.

Indian Country

Broome Co. Rt. 249 aka River Rd.

k

6

17

FUTURE

86

No Kill Ends

NEW YORK

l

Broome Co. Rt. 249

River Rd.

m

West Branch

NEW YORK

n

o

17

Hale Eddy

Sherman Creek

River Rd.
Broome Co. Rt. 4

7

p

to Hancock

PENNSYLVANIA

ACCESS AREAS

1. Stilesville
2. Deposit Sewage Treatment Plant
3. Norbord
4. Unnamed Access Area A
5. The Gentlemen's Club
6. Indian Country
7. Hale Eddy Bridge

NAMED RIFFLES AND POOLS

a. The Weir
b. Route 8 Bridge
c. The Old Mill
d. Stilesville
e. Pasture Pool aka Farm Pool
f. Deposit Bridge
g. Sewage Treatment Plant
h. Route 17 Bridge (No Kill Begins)
i. The Retiree Pool aka Gentlemen's Club
j. The Cornfield
k. Barking Dog
l. The Route 17 Pool
m. The Eagle's Nest
n. Stilts Pool
o. Hale Eddy Riffles
p. Hale Eddy

KEY

▲ lodging
■ town
〰 island
┼┼ railroad
– –. dirt road

to filter out of the river, can make fishing the Upper West frustrating when the debris load is substantial. Occasionally, the debris load is so heavy that even dry flies are enveloped in a green slime on nearly every cast, and streamers and nymphs are certainly out of the question. It's usually better to fish lower in the river when the Upper West Branch is full of reservoir debris.

Reservoir releases also flush some things into the river that actually improve the fishing—alewives. These small baitfish, related to herring, average 5 to 6 inches long and live in the Delaware's reservoirs in massive numbers. They have bluish black backs, bright silver sides, and forked tails. Alewives are often expelled from the reservoir's release tubes in the fall, when the water level is especially low. This doesn't happen every year, however; the reservoir has to be below 40 percent for the alewives to be flushed into the river. In a year with significant drought, when Cannonsville is extensively drawn down to maintain the Montague target, alewives are usually flushed into the Upper West Branch. I've seen the riverbanks littered with alewives as far downriver as Stockport on the Upper Main Stem, but their highest concentration is in the Upper West Branch.

From early spring through midsummer, alewives spawn in the upper section of the reservoir's water column, where they can get swept over the dam when it is spilling. The fish are usually stunned after they are belched from the reservoir. Many die and float on the surface; others swim erratically as they try to regain their equilibrium. The dead and dying baitfish turn a pasty, bleached white and invoke some of the best streamer fishing I've ever seen. Large Upper West Branch brown trout gorge themselves on the hapless alewives until their stomachs are misshapen. This gluttonous feeding frenzy can continue for several days, but the memory of the alewives provokes aggressive strikes to white streamers long after the alewives are gone.

This brown was caught in an island's back channel. Small secondary back channels, opposite the river's main flow around an island, are good places to find unpressured fish.

I've listed seven public-access areas for the Upper West Branch. Access in this section is good, though the Upper West is often crowded during the famous spring and summer hatches. But you can often get away from many wading anglers by being willing to walk a little further then they do. The river's banks are easy to traverse and, generally, the further you roam from your initial entry to the river, the fewer wading anglers you will see.

Another way to avoid other anglers is to spend time in river areas that are bypassed by most people. The Upper West Branch is dotted with several islands. Most anglers only fish the river's main channels, the most obvious trout holding areas. The lesser island channels, not the main river flow channel, provide refuges for trout, especially during high water. It is advisable to search out these areas under normal to higher water conditions to find unpressured, feeding fish. You may find fewer fish. But you will probably have them all to yourself.

Stilesville

Stilesville doesn't have an "official" boat launch. The access is just a small parking lot with a grassy bank leading to the river. But you can launch drift boats from Stilesville by backing your boat trailer into the grass near the bank and pushing the boat onto the ground. Park your car as soon as the boat is off the trailer so you don't interfere with traffic; there is no way to be completely off of the road when unloading a boat at Stilesville. Parking is limited, so try to leave as much room as possible for other vehicles.

When you launch your boat, turn it so the bow faces down the grassy bank, toward the river. You don't want to launch a drift boat stern first at Stilesville, especially in higher flows, because that can submerge the boat. Attach the anchor, and release most of the anchor rope. Attaching the anchor at this time is critical, in case you lose hold of the rope while launching the boat. Push the boat to the edge of the grassy bank, grab the anchor rope, and gently nudge the boat until it begins to slide. Slowly release the anchor rope as the boat descends to the river. The boat will rest in the small eddy at the base of the bank.

Upriver

Upriver of the access, a series of small, eroding islands forces most of the river's flow toward its left bank, where you'll sometimes find rising fish. The Old Mill Pool, above the islands, holds more trout but is difficult to wade during moderate to high flows. Many of this pool's trout hold in its center or near the overhanging trees on the left bank. Drag-free casts, executed with little room to backcast, are required to catch these fish.

Downriver

A riffle, leading to the Pasture Pool, lies downriver from the shallow water adjacent to the access. The beginning of the riffle is also shallow, so you

An angler works his way downriver from the Stilesville access to the head of the Pasture Pool Riffle. The Pasture Pool is an excellent place to fish the West Branch's legendary little summer sulphur hatch.

should bypass it for the more productive water beside and below a small island and gravel bar. Many fish live in the Pasture Pool, especially in its center and in the pockets near the right shore. This pool's productivity is its only drawback. It's often crowded, especially during the summer sulphur hatch.

Getting There

From New York State Route 17 west, exit 84, to the Deposit Bridge:
1. Yield to the right, at the bottom of the exit ramp, onto Route 8/10 north.
2. Go straight until you see the green sign for the Deposit business district on the right side of the road. Turn left (just past the Wendy's restaurant and the ATV repair shop) toward the business district. The Deposit Bridge is straight ahead.

From New York State Route 17 east, exit 84, to the Deposit Bridge:
1. Turn left at the stop sign, at the bottom of the exit ramp, onto Route 8/10 north.
2. Follow step 2 above.

From the Deposit Bridge:
1. Turn right just before the Deposit Bridge (over the West Branch), onto Delaware County Route 48.
2. Travel 1.2 miles. The access area is on your left.

Parking Area GPS Coordinates

N42°04.4661'
W075°24.433'

Deposit Sewage Treatment Plant

The Deposit sewage treatment plant access is the primary boat launch for the Upper West Branch. Unfortunately, the boat launch was damaged during the 2006 flood, along with the treatment plant. Although it was unusable at the time of this writing, the launch is supposed to be repaired.

Upriver

Several small islands and converging riffles lie below a railroad bridge, immediately upriver from the boat launch. The riffled water slows in front of the access and forms the head of the flat, deep Sewage Treatment Plant Pool, which can be productive during a hatch or with streamers. If you wade above the railroad bridge riffle, you'll be in the tail of the Deposit Bridge Pool, which is good dry-fly water and worth the walk to reach it. The larger fish are usually in the middle of the pool or under the streamside trees on the right side of the river. Large fish also hold beneath the bridge, particularly on bright, sunny days.

Downriver

The Sewage Treatment Plant Pool continues downriver from the launch, before it braids around the Route 17 Bridge pylons, at the beginning of the no-kill section. All this water is worth fishing. Trout may be found on both sides of the river, but they often prefer to hold from the center to the left side during average to low flows. In high water, try casting streamers or wet flies into the pool's center and stripping them back toward shore.

Boat launch at the Deposit sewage treatment plant and the old railroad bridge.

Getting There

From the Deposit Bridge:

1. Go straight over the Deposit Bridge toward the Deposit business district.
2. Turn left at the blinking light onto Division Street (Division Street bends to the right at the West Branch Baptist Church and becomes Front Street).
3. Turn left immediately after the Panda Restaurant.
4. Go under the railroad overpass, and cross the Oquaga Creek Bridge.
5. Make the first left turn (there is a brown DEC access sign on a telephone pole on the right, signaling the turn), and travel down the paved road.
6. Turn left immediately before the chain fence of the Deposit sewage treatment plant.
7. The parking area is on the left. Continue down the dirt road to reach the access area and boat launch.

Parking Area GPS Coordinates

N42°03.467'
W075°25.415'

River GPS Coordinates

N42°03.442'
W075°25.352'

Norbord

The Norbord pull-offs, named for their close proximity to the Norbord Factory, are located on private property, and extra care should be taken to ensure that they remain open to the public. The three dirt and gravel parking areas on the right side of the road can each hold a couple of cars. Canoes and pontoon boats can be launched and retrieved at this access, but drift boats cannot.

Upriver

The middle and tail of the Treatment Plant Pool are upriver from the pull-offs. The pool is divided by an island below the Route 17 Bridge (the beginning of the no-kill section), and it's advisable to wade to the island to begin fishing from this access. Look for rising fish in the deep, slow-moving water in the island's right channel. The left channel is a long, riffled chute that contains excellent nymphing and dry-fly water.

Downriver

A huge gravel bar, formed during the 2006 flood, constricts the river to the right into a long, productive riffle beside and downriver from the access. The riffle feeds the head of the long Route 17 Bridge Pool. The pool contains large fish, especially from its center to its right bank, and it's a good place to fish a hatch. The pool eventually ends at an in-river gravel bar, which separates it from the Gentlemen's Club Pool.

Getting There

From the Deposit Bridge:
1. Turn left just before the Deposit Bridge.
2. Travel .6 mile east. The access areas are on your right.

Parking Area GPS Coordinates

N42°03.181'
W075°25.335'

Unnamed Access Area A

This access provides the same wading opportunities as the Norbord pull-offs, but from the wrong side of the river to fly-fish properly. The access is located on top of a hill and requires a walk down a fairly steep footpath to reach the river. The footpath meets the river slightly downriver of the Norbord pull-offs on the deeper, trout-holding side of the river. Deep water and dense forest cover make fly-casting and presentation difficult. Although it's not important now, this access could become vital if the privately owned Norbord pull-offs are closed to the public. Some anglers use this access during

Hiring a guide is a good way to shorten the Upper Delaware's learning curve.

higher flows to cast to trout they are unable to reach from the other side of the river. Boats can't be launched or retrieved at this access.

Getting There

From the Deposit Bridge:
1. Go straight over the Deposit Bridge toward the Deposit business district.
2. Turn left at the blinking light onto Division Street (Division Street bends to the right at the West Branch Baptist Church and becomes Front Street).
3. Turn left immediately after the Panda Restaurant.
4. Go under the railroad overpass, and cross the Oquaga Creek Bridge onto Broome County Route 237.
5. Travel .4 mile and turn left onto Broome County Route 249.
6. Travel .3 mile. The access area is on your left.

Parking Area GPS Coordinates

N42°03.050′
W075°25.382′

The Gentlemen's Club

There is a large dirt and gravel parking lot at this access. Although it's right beside the river, it's surrounded by rocks, and there is no ramp for launching drift boats. You can launch and retrieve canoes and pontoons here.

Upriver

The footpath meets the river near the tail of the Gentlemen's Club Pool and above the Cornfield Riffle. The Gentlemen's Pool is usually crowded because it's easy to wade and holds lots of trout. Most of the pool's trout hold from the middle of the river to the left bank.

Downriver

The short riffle, which begins beside the access, is usually too shallow in the upper half to hold many fish. But more trout begin to populate this section after it flattens into a brief pool above the Cornfield Riffle. The Cornfield Riffle begins around a small island before it bends to the left, into the head of the Cornfield Pool. The riffle holds some large fish, but it often holds many anglers as well. Both the Cornfield Riffle and Pool should be fished from the river's left side during low to normal flow conditions. Higher river flows often require anglers to cast from the river's right side to reach the fish, which tend to feed near the overhanging vegetation on the right shore. Anglers will have to cross the river to get to this side, which can be difficult during higher flows. Several well-trod paths along the edge of the cornfield, adjacent to the parking area, provide access to various locations along the Cornfield Pool.

Getting There

From the Norbord access:

1. Continue east (downriver) past the Norbord access.
2. Travel .6 mile to where the road bends sharply to the left.
3. The access area, marked with a brown DEC sign, is on your right, in the middle of the bend.

Parking Area GPS Coordinates

N42°02.713'
W075°25.157'

Indian Country

This access has a large dirt and gravel parking lot set back from the river, requiring anglers to walk through a long grassy field to reach the water. Boats cannot be launched or retrieved at this access.

Upriver

The anglers' footpath meets the river at the tail of the flat, slow-moving Barking Dog Pool. This pool provides good trout-holding water throughout its length, especially from the center to the right side. Be sure to examine the water closely before wading into the river—trout can be spooky because of the pool's flat surface. The pool is fairly long and requires a couple of minutes to walk to its head. Because it can be difficult to wade near the pool's head from the access side of the river during high flows, it's usually better to cross the river at the pool's tail if you want to fish this area. The head of the pool begins at the end of a riffle, which is formed by two island channels converging in a deep, braided run. The braided run is also a good spot to fish.

Downriver

The tail of the pool, at the end of the anglers' footpath, is divided by a series of islands that extend downriver to the top of the Route 17 Riffle. The islands' right channels are often shallow during average to low flows and usually hold only a few small trout. But in high water, larger fish sometimes move into this section to feed along the right bank, near the overhanging vegetation.

The islands' left channel is narrower and deeper and usually holds most of the trout in this section. The left channel forms two short riffles and mini-pools along the first island that sometimes hold fish. A portion of the river's right channel then flows between the first and second islands and rejoins the flow on the left side. The two channels reunite in a riffle, which dumps into a deep braided run at the top of a short pool. Although the fish like to hold near the left shore, adjacent to the large, overhanging tree on the bank, they feed throughout the pool.

The Route 17 Riffle begins below the tail of the pool. This riffle receives another small influx of water when the second island's right channel spills into it. The top of the Route 17 Riffle is usually shallow and holds only a few fish, but it gets deeper before it braids into the top of the Route 17 Pool.

The Route 17 Pool is a long, highly productive stretch of braided to slow-moving water. The fish often concentrate from the middle of the pool to the left side. The pool's distance from the access and the depth of its lower half limit further downriver wading.

Getting There

From the Gentlemen's Club Access:
1. Turn right (or continue east if you are on the road), leaving the access area.
2. Travel .3 mile to the dirt Airport Road Extension.
3. Travel .5 mile down the dirt road.
4. The access area is on your right, marked by several DEC signs.

Parking Area GPS Coordinates

N42°02.160'
W075°24.679'

Hale Eddy Bridge

Large rocks placed by the New York DEC prevented this access from being used as a formal drift boat launch before 2006. Some of the rocks have now been moved by the DEC, and a gravel boat launch has been created. I don't know whether the DEC is planning to make this access an official boat launch, but for now, you can launch and retrieve drift boats at Hale Eddy. Pontoon boaters and canoeists often use this access as a launch or takeout. The parking area has enough room for several cars.

Upriver

A series of riffles and small braided pools that form the Hale Eddy Riffles lies upriver from this access area. The riffles' uneven bottoms, composed of various-sized cobbles and swift currents, make wading difficult. During low to average flows, look for fish near the right bank and behind the many boulders scattered throughout the riffles. Fishing from a boat is the only option at higher flows. A streamer fished tight to the bank can be effective at this time. The tail of a flat, brief pool divides the riffles approximately 40 yards above the access, near a series of small islands. This pool and the riffles above it also hold fish, particularly on the river's right side. The riffles eventually flatten into a braided pool that ends above the bridge, in front of the access.

Downriver

The anglers' footpath meets the river just above the Hale Eddy Bridge. There is a deep slot of braided water above the bridge, which wraps around the bridge piers, before it begins to soften into the Hale Eddy Pool. Wading

The Hale Eddy Bridge provides access to one of the best fly-fishing riffles in the West Branch.

around the bridge is impossible due to the river's depth. The Hale Eddy Pool below the bridge is popular with anglers, who are often seen casting to its many trout, which usually rise between the pool's center and the right bank. The Hale Eddy Pool is fairly long, and anglers seldom wade below it from this access, but there's a lot of good water between this pool and the next public access at Pennsylvania's Upper Game Lands.

Getting There

From New York Route 17 east and west:

1. Exit at the Hale Eddy exit (there's no exit number, but it's marked by a green sign).
2. Go straight for .1 mile. The parking area is on your right, before the bridge.

Parking Area GPS Coordinates

N42°00.206'
W075°23.014'

River GPS Coordinates

N42°00.179'
W075°23.030'

Lower West Branch Tailwater: Hale Eddy Bridge to Junction Pool

The Lower West Branch, from the Hale Eddy Bridge to its union with the East Branch at Junction Pool, is almost twice the length of the Upper West Branch. Most of the time, the Lower West Branch offers some of the best fly-fishing opportunities in the entire Upper Delaware system. But this section's distance from the reservoir usually means warmer water temperatures than those found in the Upper West—sometimes much warmer. The effects of Cannonsville's releases begin to diminish near New York's Hale Eddy Bridge and continue to decline as the river flows downriver from the dam. It's possible for Lower West Branch temperatures to exceed 70 degrees without constant, adequate (400 cfs or more) reservoir releases throughout the summer. Occasionally, during summers with limited reservoir releases, the river can become so warm that anglers should not fish.

The river's width in this section also contributes to the warmer water temperatures. The Lower West Branch begins to look more like a smaller version of the Main Stem than the pastoral, spring creek–like Upper West above Hale Eddy. Its pools are wider, and its riffles are more rugged and better suited for nymphing. The river's width diminishes the cooling effects of the shade from trees and allows more of the sun's warming rays to reach the river.

Because of its temperature, the Lower West Branch loses most of the summer sulphur hatch that is so important to the Upper West Branch. The Lower West Branch is seldom cold enough for sulphurs unless a significant amount of reservoir water is being released. When an unusually high volume of water is released (600 cfs or greater), the Lower West gets a great blue-winged olive hatch that replaces the Upper West's sulphurs. The transition from cold-water sulphurs to blue-winged olives actually begins near the Hale Eddy Bridge. The Lower West Branch might not have the legendary Upper West Branch sulphur hatch, but it has many other excellent spring, summer, and fall hatches. Green drakes, golden stones, and *Isonychia* are just a few of the fantastic hatches that are heavier in the Lower West Branch than in the upper portion of the river.

The Lower West's summer hatches often occur earlier in the morning and later in the evening than they do in the Upper West. In fact, unless a good, steady water release is occurring, the Lower West fishes like most eastern trout streams during the hot summer months. Warm air temperatures raise the water temperature and delay hatches and spinner falls until evening; they can even occur early in the morning if it's especially warm. The Upper West's colder summer water temperatures often produce aquatic hatches that begin in the late morning and end in the early evening. In contrast, hatches often begin shortly before dark or continue to build as the sun sets on the warmer Lower West Branch.

The diversity of the trout population also varies between the Lower and Upper West Branches. The Lower West Branch has significantly more rain-

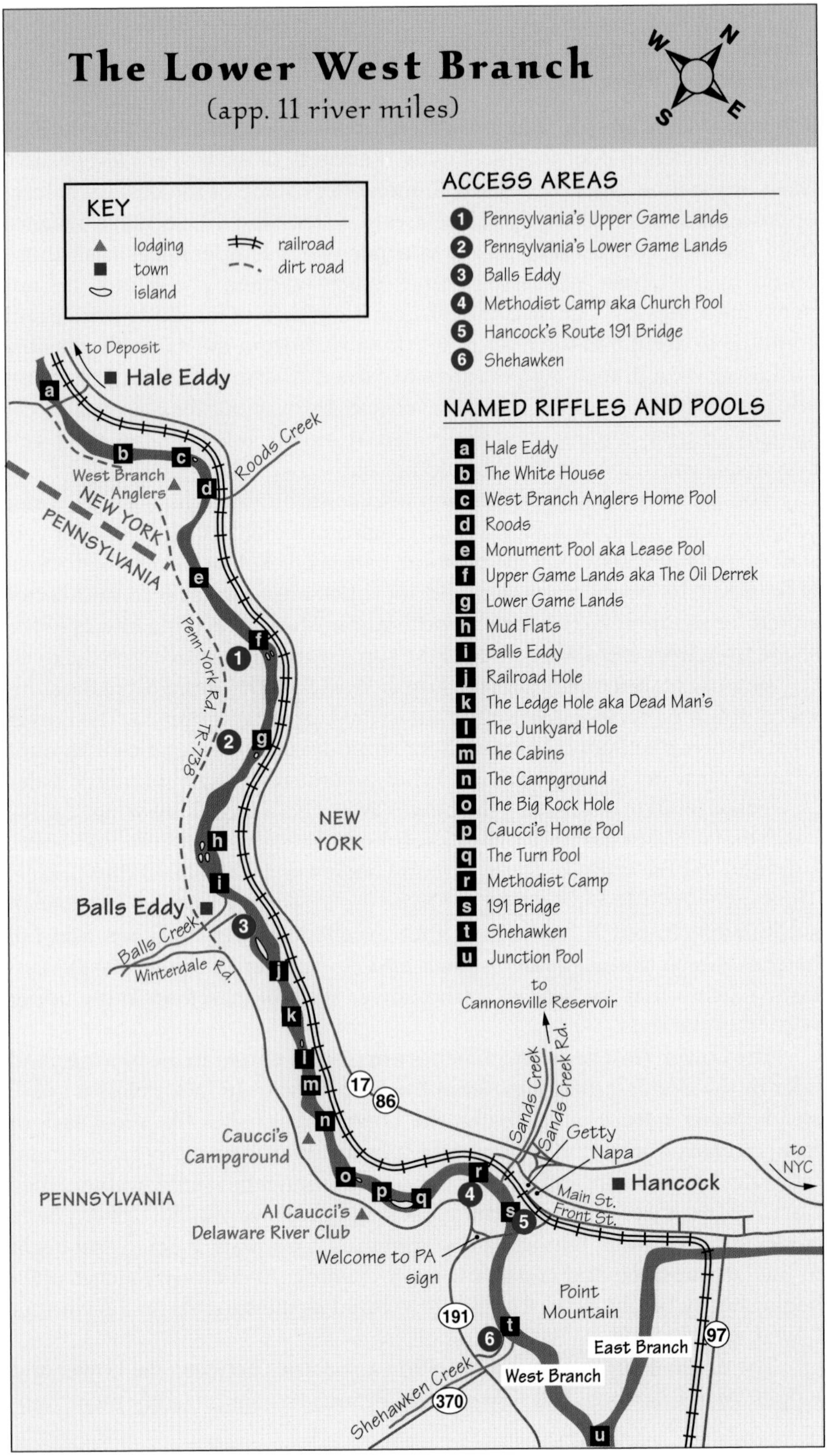
The Lower West Branch
(app. 11 river miles)
W N S E
KEY
lodging
town
island
railroad
dirt road
ACCESS AREAS
1 Pennsylvania's Upper Game Lands
2 Pennsylvania's Lower Game Lands
3 Balls Eddy
4 Methodist Camp aka Church Pool
5 Hancock's Route 191 Bridge
6 Shehawken
NAMED RIFFLES AND POOLS
a Hale Eddy
b The White House
c West Branch Anglers Home Pool
d Roods
e Monument Pool aka Lease Pool
f Upper Game Lands aka The Oil Derrek
g Lower Game Lands
h Mud Flats
i Balls Eddy
j Railroad Hole
k The Ledge Hole aka Dead Man's
l The Junkyard Hole
m The Cabins
n The Campground
o The Big Rock Hole
p Caucci's Home Pool
q The Turn Pool
r Methodist Camp
s 191 Bridge
t Shehawken
u Junction Pool
to Deposit
Hale Eddy
Roods Creek
West Branch Anglers
NEW YORK
PENNSYLVANIA
Penn-York Rd. TR-738
NEW YORK
Balls Eddy
Balls Creek
Winterdale Rd.
to Cannonsville Reservoir
Sands Creek
Sands Creek Rd.
17
86
Getty
Napa
Caucci's Campground
to NYC
Hancock
Main St.
Front St.
PENNSYLVANIA
Al Caucci's Delaware River Club
Welcome to PA sign
Point Mountain
191
East Branch
97
West Branch
Shehawken Creek
370

bows than the upper river. There are two possible reasons for this. First, Upper Delaware rainbows are primarily tributary spawning trout. In fact, I'm not aware of any documented cases of in-river rainbow trout spawning in the Upper Delaware watershed. The Lower West Branch has more tributaries to provide suitable rainbow spawning habitat. Second, Upper Delaware rainbows have developed a higher tolerance for warm water than most trout; they thrive in the Main Stem and Lower East Branch, both of which have water temperatures exceeding 70 degrees each year. These rainbows are descended from trout that were able to live in the Upper Delaware long before the dams and their cold-water flows. You may find an occasional pod of rainbows in the cool Upper West Branch, but most West Branch rainbows live in the lower, warmer end of the river.

Brown trout are still the predominant trout species in the Lower West Branch. It has a stable population of resident browns augmented with an influx of migratory browns that leave the Main Stem and Lower East Branch during periods of high thermal stress. Generally, Lower West Branch trout migrate more than those in the Upper West Branch because of water temperature fluctuations.

I've listed six public-access areas for the Lower West Branch. Four of them provide guaranteed public access through Pennsylvania state ownership; the New York State DEC doesn't own any land along the Lower West Branch. The other access areas, at the Methodist Camp and the 191 bridge, are on privately owned land.

It is often difficult to find solitude in the Lower West Branch due to the limited number of public-access areas and the high concentration of private property. This relative lack of public access creates crowded conditions near the river's few open areas. It's common to see full parking lots at the Upper and Lower Game Lands, Balls Eddy, and Shehawken when the Lower West is fishing well. But this section's predominantly gentle riverbed, and its status as a navigable public highway, allows anglers to walk great distances from the access points, as long as they remain within the high-water mark (see chapter 8). Sometimes you have to walk the Lower West Branch to avoid other wading fishermen.

Pennsylvania's Shehawken boat launch is the last place to take out a boat before reaching the Main Stem, but the West Branch continues past the Shehawken access for approximately three-quarters of a mile before it finally joins the East Branch at Junction Pool. The fishing below Shehawken can be very good, and I often like to fish my way downriver to the Main Stem.

The one time of year that the Lower West Branch isn't full of anglers, even though the fishing can be good, is the winter. The Lower West Branch is my primary winter fishing river. Its access areas are relatively easy to reach, in spite of possible snow cover, and the generally low wintertime flows create ideal fishing conditions.

Pennsylvania's Upper Game Lands

This access consists of an ample dirt and gravel parking area that requires a long walk though a grassy field to reach the river. The distance from the parking area to the river makes the launching or retrieval of any type of watercraft impossible. This access is located on public Pennsylvania hunting ground. Although it's not mandatory, it's a good idea to wear some type of fluorescent orange clothing when fishing from this and the Lower Game Lands access during Pennsylvania's hunting season.

Upriver

The anglers' footpath meets the river in the middle of the Upper Game Lands Pool. The Upper Game Lands Riffle lies upriver from the footpath. The deeper trout-holding water at the end of the riffle flows tight to the right bank and provides good structure for fishing nymphs and dry flies. The riffle's upper portion flows beside and around a series of small- to medium-sized islands. These islands are all surrounded by their own mini-riffles, each one holding fish. A long stretch of productive riffled and braided water lies upriver from the islands. These riffles form at the end of the Monument Pool (also called the Lease Pool).

Downriver

The Upper Game Lands Pool is great dry-fly water. It is shallow on the footpath side of the river but deepens toward the center and near the left bank, creating ideal wading conditions. Fish rise throughout the pool but tend to hold in the deeper water until evening, unless the river is cold and a hatch is

Islands at the top of the Upper Game Lands Pool create mini-riffles that hold fish.

Two anglers float through Lease Pool. This is also called Monument Pool by some anglers because the nearby stone marker, on River Road, delineates the border between New York and Pennsylvania.

occurring. The Upper Game Lands Pool is long and flat; it eventually shallows into the Lower Game Lands Riffle.

Getting There

For directions to Balls Eddy, see page 44. From the Balls Eddy access:
1. Turn right onto Penn-York Road TR-738 (a dirt road).
2. Travel for 1.8 miles. The access area is on your right.

Parking Area GPS Coordinates

N41°59.390'
W075°20.544'

Pennsylvania's Lower Game Lands

This access consists of an ample dirt and gravel parking area that requires a long walk through a grassy field and a Pennsylvania Fish and Game Commission food plot to reach the river. The distance from the parking area to the river makes the launching or retrieval of any type of watercraft impossible. This access is also on public Pennsylvania hunting ground.

Upriver

The top of the Lower Game Lands Pool is immediately upriver from the anglers' footpath. An island, surrounded by the Lower Game Lands Riffle, is at the head of the pool. The island's left channel contains most of the river's flow, but both sides of the island have good trout populations.

The island's right channel has a riffle at its head, which quickly braids into a deep mini-pool under and around a large rock on the right shore. The mini-pool is excellent dry-fly and streamer water, but it can be difficult for wade fishermen to navigate this side of the island during higher flows—the river gets deep quickly, close to the island. Vegetation growing on the island can also make casting difficult at times. The Lower Game Lands Riffle isn't long, but it's worth fishing.

Downriver

The middle and tail of the Lower Game Lands Pool are immediately downriver from the anglers' footpath. This water is flat and slow moving and often provides good dry-fly fishing. The pool deepens in the center and toward the left bank. Most of its trout feed in these deeper sections and in the tail of the pool. Below it, a series of islands and still water mark the top of the mudflats. Wading through this section is not recommended due to the pool's muddy bottom and depth.

Getting There

For directions to Balls Eddy, see page 44. From the Balls Eddy access:
1. Turn right onto Penn-York Road TR-738 (a dirt road), heading west.
2. Travel for 1.4 miles. The access area is on your right.

Parking Area GPS Coordinates

N41°59.011'
W075°20.589'

Balls Eddy

The Balls Eddy access is the first of two Pennsylvania-owned West Branch access areas (the other is Shehawken) that were built with boat launches. A long dirt road leading to the access area ends at an expansive parking lot equipped with a portable toilet. The access has a large boat trailer turnaround, making it easy to launch and retrieve boats. The boat launch is a concrete pad, so you don't need a four-wheel drive vehicle to get your boat in or out of the water.

The easiest way to find the Balls Eddy boat launch when floating the river at night is to look for the heavy riffle bending to the left and then to the right after you row through the mudflats. You'll recognize the end of the mudflats when, after floating through a long section of flat, still water freckled with islands, you reach a section of riffled water. Be careful when you float into the second riffle below the flats during high-flow periods; the river's momentum can suck you into the concrete wall on the left bank if you aren't careful. Back your boat into the slower water toward the right shore,

The wall above Balls Eddy is an important marker for boating anglers. It tells them that they're getting close to the boat launch.

at the head of the second riffle, to avoid the wall. The boat launch is located where the riffle slows into the pool. Stay to the right as you maneuver downriver, and you can't miss it.

Upriver

The long, deep Balls Eddy Riffle begins approximately 75 yards upriver of the Balls Eddy access. Balls Creek joins the West Branch about halfway up the riffle. The riffle's main current seam flows tight to the right bank and along a concrete retaining wall. This riffle, as well as the braided head of the Balls Eddy Pool, provides excellent fishing. Above the riffle, the river bends 90 degrees to the left into a small, short pool with another riffle at its head. The tail of the Mudflats Pool is above this upper riffle.

Downriver

The boat launch is near the head of the Balls Eddy Pool. The pool begins to flatten and eventually slows down, becoming glasslike at the boat launch. These middle and lower sections of the pool, downriver from the launch, provide good dry-fly action for trout of various sizes. Smaller fish tend to monopolize the pool's lower end and tail. A fairly long, productive riffle lies downriver from the Balls Eddy Pool. The trout in the upper half of the riffle hold on the left side. The lower half of the riffle has more trout, and they hold throughout. It's a good place to catch rainbows. The riffle quickly braids into a short pool that is also a good, and popular, place to find rising fish, especially near the rocks on the left side.

Balls Eddy is one of two Pennsylvania-owned boat launches along the West Branch—the other is Shehawken. (The boat launch is in the bottom right corner.)

Getting There

For directions to the Route 191 Bridge, see page 46. From the Route 191 Bridge:
1. Cross the Route 191 Bridge (over the West Branch).
2. You will see a large, blue "Welcome to Pennsylvania" sign on your right. Turn right at the sign onto Winterdale Road.
3. Travel 2.9 miles west (upriver) until you come to a stop sign.
4. Go straight at the stop sign onto Penn-York Road TR-738 (a dirt road).
5. Travel .1 mile. The access area, marked with a brown wooden sign, is on your right.

Parking Area GPS Coordinates

N41°58.076'
W075°20.103'

River GPS Coordinates

N41°58.183'
W075°20.035'

Methodist Camp

The Methodist Camp pull-off is a small grassy area that provides parking for one or two cars. It allows access to the Methodist Pool, also called the Church

Pool. Remove any trash you find, and don't stray from the footpath to ensure that this private access remains open to the public. If you arrive at this access and find it posted, then either the landowners have decided to close their property to the public or it has been sold (it has been for sale for several years). Boats cannot be launched or retrieved at this access.

Upriver

The upper half of Methodist Pool and the Methodist Riffle provide good fishing. Methodist Pool is deep and contains large, uneven rocks; this can make wading difficult, especially along the right bank. A brief pool and riffle lie upriver from Methodist Pool, and Turn Pool and Caucci's Island are above this water. Turn Pool flows beside a steep, rocky cliff that fishes best from the right side of the river. You'll need to cross the river to reach the fish that hold along the cliff. This can be difficult and should be attempted only in shallow riffle sections or the tails of the pools.

Downriver

Methodist Pool's tail, and its junction with Sands Creek, is downriver from the anglers' footpath. Fish rise throughout the tail, but they are generally smaller than the fish in the rest of the pool. The shallow Route 191 Riffle begins at the tail of Methodist Pool.

Getting There

For directions to the Route 191 Bridge, see the next page. From the Route 191 Bridge:
1. Cross the 191 Bridge and travel .3 mile until you see a large, blue "Welcome to Pennsylvania" sign on your right.
2. Turn right at the sign, onto Winterdale Road.
3. Travel .3 mile past Tinklepaugh's Propane and around a sharp curve in the road.
4. The unmarked access area is on your right.

Parking Area GPS Coordinates

N41°57.162'
W075°17.927'

Hancock's Route 191 Bridge

There are two access areas at the 191 Bridge—one on either side. The pull-off on the downriver side of the bridge has a medium-sized parking area and a short, steep footpath leading to the river. Boats cannot be launched or retrieved from this side of the bridge. The more popular access, the one with the boat launch, is on the upriver side. The boat launch is nothing more than a deeply rutted dirt road leading to the river. This launch can require four-wheel drive in the early spring, when it's muddy and sometimes ice covered.

It is relatively easy to find the 191 Bridge boat launch when floating after dark. If you stay in the deeper water on the river's left, from the top of the 191 Riffle, you will find the boat launch immediately before the bridge.

Upriver

The 191 Riffle begins approximately 100 yards above the 191 Bridge, at the tail of the Methodist Camp Pool. Small trout tend to dominate the riffle above the bridge.

Downriver

The 191 Riffle begins to braid under the bridge and flows into the deep 191 Bridge Pool. This pool holds a lot of smaller fish near the bridge, but larger fish are present in the deeper water downriver, near the pool's middle and left side. The pool gets deep about halfway down, making wading difficult. A productive section of riffles and short, braided pools lies between the 191 Bridge Pool and the next public access at Shehawken.

Getting There

From New York Route 17 west, Hancock exit 87:
1. Turn left at the stop sign at the bottom of the exit ramp.
2. Go straight to the next stop sign. Turn left.
3. Make a right turn onto an unmarked road after the Getty gas station and before the Napa automotive store.
4. The road curves to the left before reaching another stop sign.
5. Turn right at the stop sign and cross the railroad tracks onto Pennsylvania Route 191. The bridge is straight ahead.

From Route 17 east:
1. Turn left at the stop sign at the bottom of the exit ramp.
2. Follows directions 3 to 5 above.

Parking Area GPS Coordinates

N41°57.178'
W075°17.397'

River GPS Coordinates

N41°57.164'
W075°17.459'

Shehawken

The Shehawken access is named after Shehawken Creek, which joins the West Branch by the boat launch. A long dirt road leads to the access area, wraps around a former Orvis fly shop (currently a tree nursery and delicatessen), and dead-ends at an expansive parking area and the boat launch. This access has a portable toilet and a car and boat trailer turnaround, making it easy to launch and retrieve boats. The boat launch has a concrete pad, so you don't need four-wheel drive to get your boat in or out of the water.

It's easy to find the Shehawken boat launch after dark. Start looking for the launch after you pass under the 191 Bridge and float through the 191 Bridge Pool. Stay on the right side of the river. You will float through a riffle and braided pool before you come to the brief Shehawken Riffle, which bends to the left. The boat launch is immediately below it, on the right side.

Upriver

The entire Shehawken Riffle holds fish. The riffle braids and forms the top of the small Shehawken Pool in front of the boat launch. It's common to see fish rising a few feet from the boat launch at dark, especially during summer mayfly spinner falls. The Shehawken Riffle and Pool are good spots to fish in the winter because they're productive and easy to reach in spite of possible snow cover.

Downriver

Shehawken Creek flows into the West Branch to the right of the boat launch. Its gravelly mouth narrows the river channel, which helps form a short, deep chute that quickly riffles into the head of a brief, deep pool. This pool is really just a long braided run that holds a lot of trout, especially near the right side. The river bends to the right below the pool, forming a large back eddy on the left side and the head of another pool. This pool has a productive riffle at its head, which slowly braids into the top of a flat, glassy pool. There's another long riffle and deep chute on the left side of the river, below the pool's tail. This section eventually veers toward the left bank before flowing straight into another riffle, which joins with the East Branch to form the Main Stem's Junction Pool. Each of these bottom pools and riffles can be productive, especially in the summer, when large numbers of trout migrate out of the Main Stem and into the Lower West Branch.

Getting There

For directions to the Route 191 Bridge, see the previous page. From the Route 191 Bridge:

1. Cross the bridge, heading south into Pennsylvania.
2. Travel .9 mile and turn left at the brown Pennsylvania Fish and Boat Commission sign.
3. The dirt road dead-ends at the access.

Parking Area GPS Coordinates

    N41°56.451'
    W075°17.413'

River GPS Coordinates

    N41°56.533'
    W075°17.278'

CHAPTER 3

East Branch Tailwater

The East Branch is probably the most underrated of the three Upper Delaware branches. This is surprising, because at one time, the East Branch was the crowning gem of the system. Art Lee wrote some of the early *Fly Fisherman* articles publicizing the Upper Delaware's trout fishery, and most of them were about the East Branch. Pepacton was the first Delaware River reservoir to become fully operational, so for a brief period, its cold water was used to maintain the Montague target, just as Cannonsville's water on the West

Most Upper Delaware trout are wild, but brown trout are stocked in the East Branch and a few small tributaries. This fish's clipped adipose fin signifies that it was stocked before Leon Corl caught it.

Branch is used today (see chapter 8). The heavy volume of cold, reservoir-released water created a thriving East Branch trout fishery.

The early days after the creation of the East Branch tailwater must have been an exciting time for Catskill trout fishermen. Most of them had basically ignored the Upper Delaware branches before the dams were built—barely glancing at those rivers as they sped toward the legendary Beaverkill. The Beaverkill was, and still is, a great trout river. But it is a freestone river, vulnerable to the seasonal ebbs and flows of Mother Nature, and it often becomes low and warm in the summer.

It was during an especially warm, late-spring fishing trip to the Beaverkill that Walt Mercencavic first discovered the Upper Delaware's trout fishery. Walt and his father were driving along old New York State Route 17, near the town of East Branch, New York, when they noticed something strange about the Upper East Branch. The river was enveloped in a curtain of fog, and there were fish rising—lots of them. In the early days after the dam was built, few knew that cold water would be released, and Walt and his dad had no idea what was happening to the river. But the Beaverkill was fishing poorly that day, so the two explorers decided to try to catch a few of the rising fish. They assumed that the fish were trout, but they weren't sure until they began catching them: they were all trout. Walt and his dad quickly discovered that the reservoirs would change the East Branch, and ultimately the entire Upper Delaware watershed, forever.

Walt (a former Upper Delaware guide) still fondly reflects on his early pioneering days fishing the Upper East Branch. "If you think the river is good now, you should have seen it back then. My heart would pound all day long when I was on the river. You never knew what you would find around the next bend. There were no boats or other fishermen. We had it all to ourselves," he told me during a telephone conversation. He also mentioned that the Upper East was a great rainbow trout fishery at the time, which is an interesting footnote now that the Upper East is heavily dominated by brown trout.

The golden era of East Branch trout fishing didn't last long. Pepacton water releases were greatly curtailed when the Cannonsville Reservoir was completed. But the East Branch remains a great trout river today, in spite of the relatively stingy cold-water reservoir releases.

The East Branch flows for approximately 34 miles, from its humble beginnings within the Pepacton Reservoir tubes to its collision with the West Branch outside of Hancock, New York, and the formation of the Main Stem. The East Branch system, as a whole, is composed of 40 percent riffles and 60 percent pools. It falls 6.5 feet per mile along its course and is considered a low-gradient fishery (McBride 2002).

The East Branch is divided in half by the Beaverkill approximately 17 miles below the Pepacton Reservoir. The addition of the warm Beaverkill water (often 70 degrees or higher in the summer) and the distance from the Pepacton cold-water releases create two rivers that are vastly different. The Upper East, above the junction with the Beaverkill, is much more hospitable

Upper East Branch Floats, Distances, and Durations

Float	River Miles	Road Miles	Time*
Downsville Covered Bridge to Oxbow Campground	13	12.5	6.75 hours
Oxbow Campground to Beaver Del Campground	4.4	4.2	2.25 hours

Times are based on average float time during average water levels.

Lower East Branch Floats, Distances, and Durations

Float	River Miles	Road Miles	Time*
Beaver Del Campground to Cadosia	13	8.7	5.5 hours
Beaver Del Campground to Fishs Eddy	3.6	3.6	1.5 hours
Fishs Eddy to Cadosia	9.5	5.4	4 hours
Cadosia to Hancock Fireman's Park	2	1.5	.5 hour
Hancock Fireman's Park to Buckingham	5.8	8.3	2.4 hours

Times are based on average float time during average water levels.

for trout throughout the year. The water temperature rarely exceeds 70 degrees as far downriver as Harvard, New York. It has a weedy river bottom and looks very similar to a spring creek. The Lower East, below the junction with the Beaverkill, is far less dependable as a season-long trout fishery. Its temperature often exceeds 80 degrees during the summer months, which can be lethal to trout. The Lower East looks more like a freestone stream and is more similar in appearance to the Main Stem than to either the Upper East or the West Branch.

The two rivers also differ in their most prolific trout species. The Upper East is heavily dominated by brown trout, and the Lower East is a rainbow fishery. Although it maintains a stable population of wild and stocked brown trout, most anglers catch at least a few rainbows when they fish the Lower East. The East Branch as a whole is the only Upper Delaware branch that still receives stocked trout. Each year, 20.5 miles of the East Branch system, both in the upper and lower rivers, is stocked with approximately 3,000 brown trout from 8 to 15 inches long.

Description

A long, all-day float that provides access to most of the river. Boaters must have prior permission and pay a fee to exit the river at Oxbow Campground.

A short to half-day float trip that includes the bottom of the Upper East and top of the Lower East. Boaters must have prior permission and pay a fee to both the Oxbow and Beaver Del Campgrounds.

Description

This long, all-day float allows access to nearly the entire Lower East Branch and is the only trip available for drift boat users who wish to float above the Cadosia boat ramp. Anglers must have prior permission and pay a fee to the Beaver Del Campground to launch their boats.

A half- to all-day trip for canoes or pontoon boats only that provides access to some of the Lower East Branch's best water.

This half- to all-day trip for canoes or pontoon boats only allows access to the least fished and most beautiful part of the Lower East Branch.

An extremely short float that provides access to the end of the Lower East Branch.

Boaters usually launch from Hancock Fireman's Park (on the Lower East Branch) to float the Upper Main Stem only when West Branch flows are too low to float from the PA Fish and Boat Commission access at Shehawken (on the West Branch). The deep pool adjacent to the Fireman's Park access provides enough water to reach the Main Stem.

Upper and Lower East Branch Fishing Regulations

River Section	Fishing Season	Harvesting Length	Daily Limit
Pepacton Dam downriver to Shinhopple Bridge	April 1–October 15	12 inches	2 trout
Shinhopple Bridge downriver to the mouth at Hancock	April 1–October 15	12 inches	2 trout
	October 16–November 30	Catch-and-release only	Catch-and-release only
	December 1–March 31	Angling prohibited	Angling prohibited
All streams and their tributaries that flow into the East Branch between the villages of East Branch and Hancock	First Saturday after April 11–October 15	Any size	5 trout

Upper East Branch Flows*

Water Level (cfs)	Wading	Drift Boats	Pontoon Boats and Canoes
<175	Excellent—nearly the entire river is wadable	Not floatable	Not floatable
175–300	Excellent—nearly the entire river remains wadable	Not floatable	Not advised to poor—the river becomes floatable around 250 cfs, but fish and fishermen will be centered in deeper water; boats have to float through this water, disturbing those around them
300–500	Excellent to very good—most of the river remains wadable	Not advised to poor—the river becomes floatable around 400 cfs, but dragging may be necessary in shallow areas	Poor to good—easy to anchor; use the boat as transportation to more remote wading spots
500–700	Good to fair—50% or less of the river is wadable	Fair—fewer exposed rocks and minimal dragging	Good to very good—a better choice than a drift boat at the lower end of the scale
700–900	Fair to poor—less than 50% of the river is wadable	Good—no dragging required	Good—fishing from the boat becomes required in more areas as wading possibilities diminish
900–1,100	Poor to not advised—wading becomes limited to shallow edges near the shore and the tails of some pools at the lower end of the scale	Good to very good—nice level for boaters	Good to fair—nearly all fishing will be from the boat
1,100–1,400	Not advised	Very good—drift boats become the best option at this and all higher levels	Fair—all fishing will be from the boat
1,400–1,700	Not advised—wading can be dangerous	Good—for experienced boaters only	Poor to not advised—for expert boaters only
>1,700	Not advised—wading can be dangerous	Fair to not advised—for expert boaters only	Not advised

Flows measured at the Harvard gauging station.

Lower East Branch Flows*

Water Level (cfs)	Wading	Drift Boats	Pontoon Boats and Canoes
<750	Excellent—nearly the entire river is wadable	Not floatable—low water	Not advised to fair—low water; floating becomes an option at 600 cfs
750–1,250	Excellent to very good—most of the river remains wadable	Poor to fair—boats may require dragging at flows less than 1,000 cfs	Fair to very good—easy anchor; use the boat as to transportation to more remote wading spots
1,250–1,750	Very good to good—50% of the river remains wadable	Good—fewer exposed rocks	Very good to excellent—a better choice than a drift boat at this water level
1,750–2,250	Fair to poor—less than 50% of the river remains wadable	Very good—very few obstructions	Excellent to good—fewer wading opportunities
2,250–2,750	Poor to not advised—wading becomes limited to shallow edges near shore and the tails of some pools	Excellent—drift boats become the best option at this and all higher flows	Good to fair—fishing from the boat is necessary, as wading options are severely limited
2,750–3,250	Not advised—wading is strictly limited to areas near shore	Very good—no obstructions	Fair to poor—all fishing will be from the boat
3,250–3,750	Not advised—wading can be dangerous	Good—for experienced boaters only	Poor to not advised—only expert boaters should float at the lower end of the scale; drift boats should be used at higher levels
3,750–4,250	Not advised—wading can be dangerous	Fair—for expert boaters only	Not advised
>4,250	Not advised—wading can be dangerous	Fair to not advised—for expert boaters only	Not advised

Flows measured at the Fishs Eddy gauging station.

Upper East Branch Tailwater

The Upper East Branch is the smallest of the Upper Delaware branches and reminds me in many ways of central Pennsylvania limestone creeks. The river is only 80 feet wide at its source near Downsville, New York, but it expands to a maximum width of 135 feet above its junction with the Beaverkill and the end of its approximately 17-mile course (McBride 2002). The Upper East has more tributaries than the West Branch does; these feed the river and expand its size.

The small size of the river's channel makes it a poor choice for boating fishermen. On the West Branch and the Main Stem, most boaters can float behind wading anglers and avoid disturbing them. But you can't float the Upper East Branch during low to moderate flows without disrupting the fishing of waders. The river's channel just isn't wide enough. The only time that the Upper East should be considered a boating option is when the river is completely blown out with runoff and devoid of wading anglers. My good friend Joe Demalderis, a Delaware River guide, says, "You do a great injustice to both the river and other fishermen if you stuff a boat into the Upper East when it's wadable. You'll only be able to fish about 40 percent of the river, and you'll screw up the other 60 percent." I couldn't agree more.

The many Upper East Branch access areas negate the need for boats to reach the river's more remote sections. I've listed 17 possible access areas for the Upper East Branch—a combination of public footpaths, privately owned but publicly accessible footpaths, and private campgrounds that allow public

access for a fee. These numerous access areas make the Upper East the most wader-friendly river in the Upper Delaware system. And even though some sections are difficult to reach on foot, much of the river is accessible to anyone with enough desire and energy to walk into less-pressured areas.

This book includes several Upper East access areas that are open to public fishing only through landowner permission. Most of the New York State–owned Upper East Branch access areas are marked with small yellow DEC signs. If you are accessing the river from an area that doesn't have a yellow sign, you may be doing so at the pleasure of the property's rightful owner. The private access areas I've included have been open to

The wide pool above the Downsville Covered Bridge is atypical for the predominantly small and narrow Upper East Branch.

the public for years, but their status could change at any time. If you are asked to leave by a landowner, do so immediately.

Anglers need to know the enforceable laws, or lack thereof, regarding wading the river within its high-water mark. Because the Upper East Branch lies entirely in New York State, it may not be subject to the same public-access laws concerning the right to wade as the West Branch or the Main Stem. The Upper East Branch's public-access question has not been settled, and you will probably find varying opinions concerning the public's wading rights, depending on who you talk to at the DEC. I did when I tried to settle the issue for my own fishing purposes. Several landowners along the river don't like fishermen wading through their river sections, so if their riverbanks are posted or you are asked to leave, it's probably best not to force the issue of stream rights.

The Upper East has become popular with canoeists, who are drawn by the placid currents, abundant campgrounds, and beautiful scenery, especially during the summer months. Most Upper East canoeists are not fly fishermen, and they simply don't understand why it's bad form to float in front of anglers. I've had good luck by smiling and politely asking canoeists to float behind me, but I've also witnessed rock throwing and near fistfights between fly fishermen and canoeists. I would rather fish in peace than risk an altercation with a boater, so if the canoes are too thick on a summer weekend, I move to another Upper Delaware branch.

The Upper East's gentle river bottom is flat and nondescript throughout much of its course, which makes for safe canoeing and wading but poor trout cover. The river has few large rocks or other in-river structure to provide holding lies for trout. However, the Upper East's bottom is usually covered with weeds during the late spring and summer months, providing excellent cover for both trout and aquatic insects. Most of the river's weed beds were destroyed by the 2004, 2005, and 2006 floods, but hopefully the river will recover its former weedy character within the next few years.

The river is unique among the other Delaware branches because its comparatively narrow valley, which meanders predominately north to south, ensures that parts of the river are shaded by tree-covered mountains during the day. The increased shade keeps the Upper East Branch fairly cold, even though it receives significantly less reservoir water than the West Branch does.

The Upper East is predominantly wild brown trout water, but it is also stocked with approximately 2,000 hatchery brown trout measuring 8 to 15 inches each year. The river hosts a stable population of wild brook trout as well, which are especially prevalent near the mouths of the river's feeder creeks. The brookies average 8 to 10 inches long, but anglers occasionally catch much larger specimens. Rainbows are the minority trout species in the Upper East Branch, but their numbers appear to be growing.

I divide the Upper East into two sections: from the Pepacton Reservoir to Shinhopple, and from Shinhopple to Jaws, where the Beaverkill joins the East

Branch. The cooling effects of bottom-released water from the dam begin to diminish below Shinhopple.

Top of the Upper East Branch:
Pepacton Reservoir to Shinhopple

The fishable portion of the Upper East Branch begins at the Route 30 Bridge, slightly north of Downsville, New York. You can see the breast of Pepacton's dam upriver from the bridge. Fishing the .8 mile of water between the reservoir and the bridge is forbidden by the New York City DEP, as it is in the section above the Upper West Branch's weir dam. Al's Sports Store, owned by the son of former Upper East Branch fly-shop owner Al Carpenter, is located just beyond the bridge. It offers access and a boat ramp, but only for the shop's canoe rental clients. There is no public access at the bridge. The first public access is at the Downsville Covered Bridge, about a mile downriver.

The Upper East Branch from the reservoir to Shinhopple is small water and usually very cold because of Pepacton's water releases. Like on the Upper West Branch, the fewer insects that do hatch in the cold water flourish, making for prolific hatches of a handful of species such as sulphurs and blue-winged olives. This section has the same tailwater-induced summer sulphur hatch as the upper portion of the West Branch. Upper East Branch summer sulphurs usually begin hatching in late morning and continue through late afternoon or early evening, creating excellent dry-fly opportunities. The hatch has received far less publicity than the Upper West Branch's, so it's generally less crowded.

Pepacton Reservoir's breast and spillway. The Route 30 Bridge, in the foreground, is the beginning of the Upper East's legally fishable water.

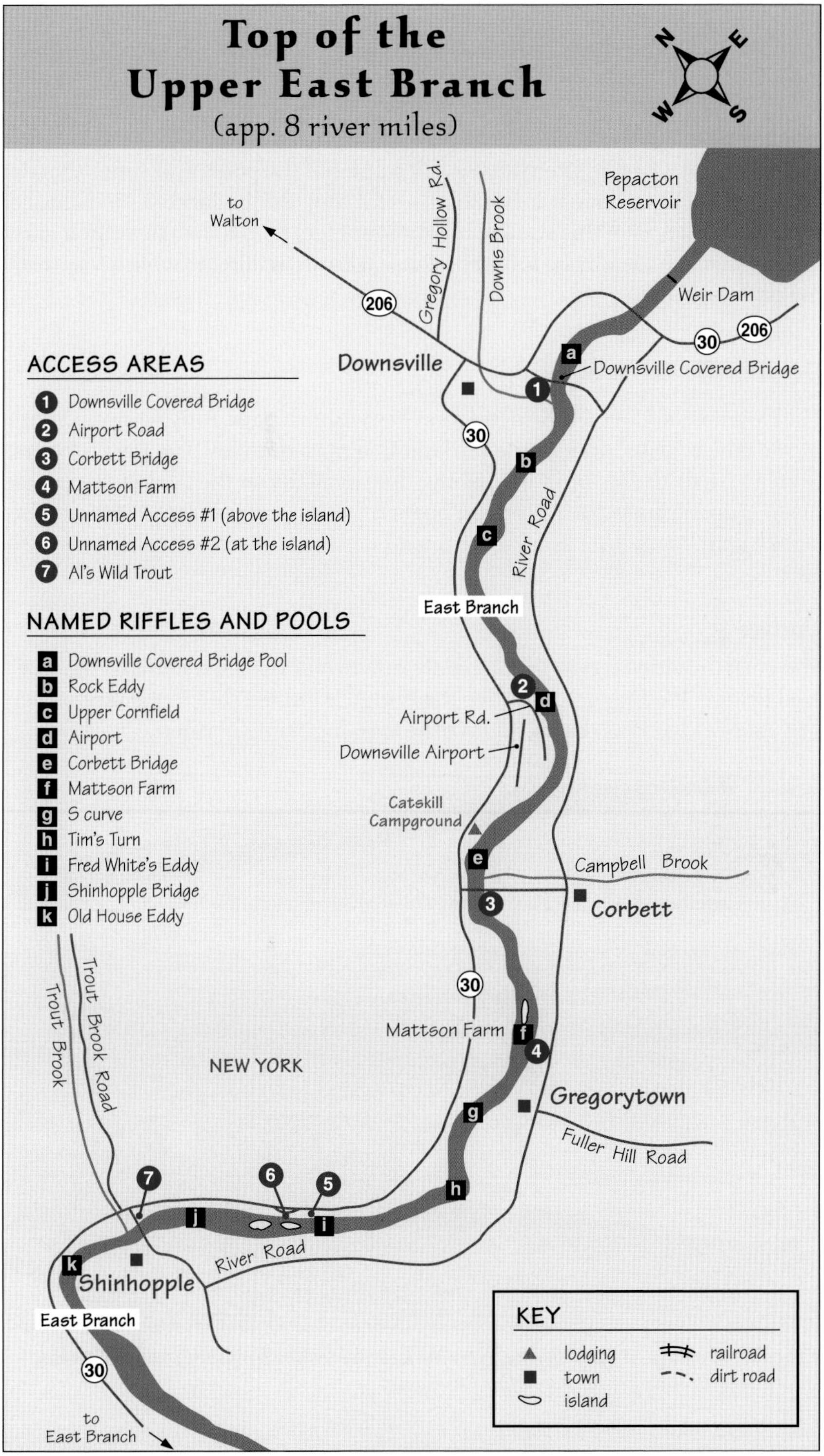
Top of the
Upper East Branch
(app. 8 river miles)
N
E
W
S
to
Walton
206
Gregory Hollow Rd.
Downs Brook
Pepacton
Reservoir
Weir Dam
30
206
Downsville
a
Downsville Covered Bridge
1
30
b
River Road
c
East Branch
ACCESS AREAS
1 Downsville Covered Bridge
2 Airport Road
3 Corbett Bridge
4 Mattson Farm
5 Unnamed Access #1 (above the island)
6 Unnamed Access #2 (at the island)
7 Al's Wild Trout
NAMED RIFFLES AND POOLS
a Downsville Covered Bridge Pool
b Rock Eddy
c Upper Cornfield
d Airport
e Corbett Bridge
f Mattson Farm
g S curve
h Tim's Turn
i Fred White's Eddy
j Shinhopple Bridge
k Old House Eddy
2
d
Airport Rd.
Downsville Airport
Catskill
Campground
e
Campbell Brook
3
Corbett
30
Mattson Farm
f
4
Trout Brook
Trout Brook Road
NEW YORK
Gregorytown
g
Fuller Hill Road
h
7
6
5
j
i
k
Shinhopple
River Road
East Branch
30
to
East Branch
KEY
lodging
town
island
railroad
dirt road

The top of the river also has good hatches of blue quills, march browns, quill Gordons, hebes, and various caddis species. It also has a green and brown drake hatch, but the drake hatches aren't as spectacular as those below Shinhopple.

Some parts in this stretch have few trout, but the pools and riffles that do hold trout tend to have a lot of them—and they can be large. I've included seven access areas in this stretch, but most anglers tend to fish near their cars. Open water can usually be found by those who are willing to walk away from the parking areas.

Downsville Covered Bridge

The Downsville Covered Bridge access lies within a park, fully equipped with picnic tables, grills, and ample parking in a macadam lot. The park's hours, from 6 A.M. to 10 P.M., limit the fishing time available at the bridge. It's possible to launch canoes and pontoon boats from this access. Some anglers also launch drift boats, but I don't recommend it because there is no official launch area.

Upriver

The park provides access immediately downriver from the Downsville Covered Bridge. Wading access above the bridge is limited due to the large, deep Covered Bridge Pool, but it's a favorite spot for bait fishermen.

The covered bridge at Downsville, New York, provides the first public access to the Upper East Branch below Pepacton Reservoir.

Downriver

A short distance downriver, the tail of the Covered Bridge Pool quickens into a nice riffle beside Downs Brook. The riffle braids into a flat, deep pool that holds some nice fish and is a good spot to fish a hatch.

Getting There

From New York Route 17 east, East Branch exit 90, to the Route 17 overpass on New York Route 30:
1. Yield to the left at the bottom of the exit ramp.
2. The overpass and Route 30 are straight ahead, just off the exit.

From Route 17 west, East Branch exit 90, to the Route 17 overpass on Route 30:
1. Turn left at the stop sign at the bottom of the exit ramp onto Harvard Road.
2. Go straight to the next stop sign.
3. Turn right onto Old Route 17.
4. Cross the Old Route 17 Bridge (over the Upper East Branch), and the overpass is straight ahead, just after the curve in the road.

From the Route 17 overpass on New York Route 30:
1. Stay on Route 30 north for 15 miles to the Downsville signal light.
2. Turn right onto Route 206 east, toward Margaretville.
3. Travel .3 mile and turn right onto Bridge Street.
4. The parking area is at the park on your right, before the bridge.

Parking Area GPS Coordinates

N42°04.602'
W074°59.490'

Airport Road

The Airport Road pull-off and footpath are privately owned but remain open to the public. The small dirt pull-off can hold a couple of cars and is located on the left side of Airport Road, where it bends 90 degrees to the right. Canoes and pontoon boat can be launched and retrieved from this access. Drift boats could also use the access, but I don't advise launching drift boats on private land that doesn't have a designated launching area.

Upriver

The anglers' footpath leads to a riffle at the head of a small pool. The riffle has a nice back eddy to the left and holds plenty of fish. Trout can be found throughout the riffle and pool. There are two smaller riffles and pools above the riffle at the end of the footpath. Both of them are worth spending time nymphing or studying to find rising fish. Another larger pool, with the crumbled remains of an old bridge on its banks, lies upriver and is good dry-fly water.

Downriver

Past the tail of the access pool, a stretch of braided water bends to the right into another long pool. This pool also has a deep back eddy on its left side that provides some excellent dry-fly water. This pool is fairly popular, and it's common to find anglers casting to rising fish in the back eddy.

Getting There

From the Route 17 overpass on Route 30:
1. Travel 12.8 miles on Route 30 north.
2. Turn right onto Airport Road.
3. The pull-off is straight ahead.

Parking Area GPS Coordinates

N42°03.340'
W075°00.605'

River GPS Coordinates

N42°03.343'
W075°00.580'

Corbett Bridge

The Corbett Bridge access doesn't have a parking area, and signs inform anglers not to park on the footpath side of the bridge. I usually park on the grass on the right side of the road, just beyond the Corbett Bridge, where there is room for several cars. Canoes and pontoon boats can be launched and retrieved from this access but must be carried a short distance to the river. Drift boats cannot be launched or retrieved here.

Upriver

The anglers' footpath follows Campbell Brook to its junction with the river, just above the bridge. The Corbett Bridge Pool is fairly deep, especially on the left side. It holds a lot of fish, but many of them are small. The Corbett Bridge Pool continues upriver to its riffled head. The entire pool holds fish and is a good place to fish dry flies during a hatch.

Downriver

The pool remains flat and slow below the bridge until its tail bends to the left and becomes a productive riffle. The riffle flows into the privately owned but now defunct Del Valley Campground. Several nice riffle-pool combinations follow, in downriver succession, below this point. There are no posted signs, and I have never been asked to leave when I've fished this section, but it couldn't hurt to ask permission before fishing the campground's water.

Getting There

From the Route 17 overpass on Route 30:
1. Travel 11.6 miles on Route 30 north.
2. Turn right onto the Corbett Bridge.
3. The footpath is on your left, immediately after you cross the bridge.

Parking Area GPS Coordinates

N42°02.761'
W075°01.589'

River GPS Coordinates

N42°02.786'
W075°01.620'

Mattson Farm

This access, located across the river from the Mattson Farm, has a parking area that is large enough to fit several cars. The footpath leading to the river is steep and slippery and should probably be avoided by anglers who are not sure-footed on inclines. This is one of only two access areas that provide public fishing on the opposite side of Route 30 (the other is Tomannex State Forest). Boats cannot be launched or retrieved at this access due to its distance from the river.

Upper Delaware trout sometimes feed in shallow water. This big brown, caught by Rich Tartaglia with a Truform dry fly, was feeding in 6 inches of water.

Upriver

The anglers' footpath leads to the middle of a large, deep pool below a large island. The pool holds a good number of trout and is a good place to fish a hatch. I usually cross the pool at the end of the footpath to fish upriver, but it's impossible to cross here during high river flows. The island's right river channel, at the pool's head, is narrow and usually shallow, so it's usually better to cross here during higher flows. Most of the river's flow travels to the left of the island in a deep riffle. This riffle and the water above it can all hold trout.

Downriver

A medium-sized riffle at the tail of the access pool flows into a deep, braided run near the left bank before slowing down and braiding into a flat pool. The upper part of the pool holds a fair number of trout and is good dry-fly water, but trout also rise in the bottleneck in the middle of the pool. The fish in this narrow section tend to gently sip dry flies, and they are easy to spook. Below the bottleneck, the tail of the pool shallows quickly and usually holds a few fish during cloudy weather or in the evening.

Getting There

From the Route 17 overpass on Route 30:
1. Travel 8.6 miles on Route 30 north to Shinhopple.
2. Turn right onto River Road.
3. Cross the Shinhopple Bridge.
4. Turn left, staying on River Road.
5. Veer to the left, past the sign for Peaceful Valley Campground.
6. Travel 2.5 miles. The parking area and footpath are on your left.

Parking Area GPS Coordinates

N42°01.966'
W075°01.963'

Unnamed Access #1 (above the Island)

This access consists of a dirt pull-off wedged between Route 30 and the river. It's located slightly upriver from the second unnamed access (at the island) described in the next section. Canoes and pontoon boats could be launched or retrieved at this access, but drift boats cannot.

Upriver

A long, moderately deep pool lies upriver from the anglers' footpath. The pool is deepest near the right side and can be a good place to fish a hatch. A nice riffle formed by two converging island channels feeds the top of the pool and is worth the walk. Few anglers seem to fish this far upriver from the access.

Downriver

The top of the island is described in the next section.

Getting There

From the Route 17 overpass on Route 30:
>   1. Travel 9.5 miles on Route 30 north.
>   2. The parking area and footpath are on your right.

Parking Area GPS Coordinates
>   N42°01.897'
>   W075°03.309'

Unnamed Access #2 (at the Island)

This access is in the middle of a short dirt road that is connected to Route 30 on both ends. A small dirt pull-off, capable of holding a couple of cars, lies beside the road. The footpath is adjacent to the pull-off. A large island dissects the river in front of the access. The island's channel closest to the access is often shallow and usually holds only small fish. I always cross the island to fish the better water in its far channel. Canoes and pontoon boats could be launched or retrieved at this access, but there isn't a ramp for drift boats.

Upriver

I usually walk the edge of the island, along the shallow channel beside the access, to reach the far channel beginning at the top of the island. Occasionally I find a few rising fish while I make my way to top of the island, but the channel is small and shallow, and trees growing on the island make casting difficult. The far channel is much deeper and usually holds larger fish.

Downriver

Two river channels converge below the island in a riffle that veers to the right. The riffle empties into a short, deep pool that also holds a few fish. Two more islands lie downriver from this point. Their right channels are deeper and hold more fish, but trout also hold in the left channels, especially during higher flows. The river eventually widens below the islands and forms the head of the Shinhopple Bridge Pool at Al's Wild Trout.

Getting There

From the Route 17 overpass on Route 30:
>   1. Travel 9.2 miles on Route 30 north.
>   2. The parking area and footpath are on your right.

Parking Area GPS Coordinates
>   N42°02.045'
>   W075°03.532'

Most of the Upper East Branch is ideally suited for wade fishermen, but some anglers still prefer to fish it from boats, such as this angler near Al's Wild Trout in Shinhopple, New York.

Al's Wild Trout

Al Carpenter owned Al's Wild Trout Fly Shop for many years. Sadly, Al passed away in 2004, and the shop is closed. Al's son now owns the property, and he still allows public access for fishing. The property is for sale, however, so this access may be lost. If you arrive and find posted signs, you should fish elsewhere. It may also be a good idea to call and ask permission (the phone number for Al's Sports Store is listed in the appendix), just as a courtesy.

Upriver

The Shinhopple Bridge Pool, ending at the bridge, has an excellent trout population that includes some big fish. But the water depth in the upper half and the tight vegetation covering the banks make it difficult to wade. The pool's middle and tail are shallower and easier to wade. Larger trout often feed under the bridge at dusk.

Downriver

Just below the bridge, the river narrows into a riffle before flowing into a braided pool. This riffle and braided pool are excellent water. The river riffles again below the braided pool and bends to the left, forming the head of the large, slow-moving Old House Eddy, which is lined with several houses on the left side. Wading Old House Eddy is problematic—the steep bank on the right side is difficult to traverse, and the pool itself is very deep.

Getting There

From the Route 17 overpass on Route 30:
1. Travel 8.6 miles on Route 30 north to Shinhopple.
2. Turn right onto River Road.
3. The parking area, designated by a sign, is on your left, beside the old fly shop.

Parking Area GPS Coordinates

N42°02.401'
W075°04.038'

Bottom of the Upper East Branch: Shinhopple to the Jaws

The New York State DEC's Upper Delaware radiotelemetry study declared that parts of this section, beginning 4 miles below Shinhopple, were unsuitable for trout "growth and survival" during most summer months (McBride 2002). The study revealed that water temperatures were often too warm to maintain a trout fishery. Despite this study, some of my favorite Upper East Branch pools are in this so-called marginal water.

Cold-water reservoir releases create summer fog that obscures anglers' silhouettes and movements, allowing them to wade very close to fish. But the fog also camouflages subtle riseforms. Listen for rising trout, and slowly inch your way into casting position.

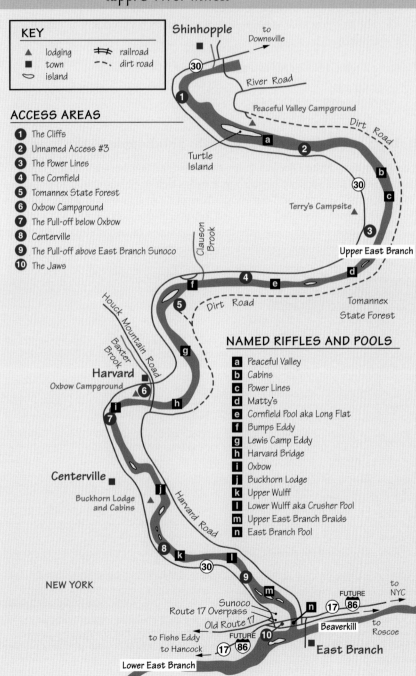

The Bottom of the Upper East Branch

(app. 9 river miles)

KEY

▲ lodging
■ town
⌒ island

╫ railroad
‐‐‑ dirt road

ACCESS AREAS

1 The Cliffs
2 Unnamed Access #3
3 The Power Lines
4 The Cornfield
5 Tomannex State Forest
6 Oxbow Campground
7 The Pull-off below Oxbow
8 Centerville
9 The Pull-off above East Branch Sunoco
10 The Jaws

NAMED RIFFLES AND POOLS

a Peaceful Valley
b Cabins
c Power Lines
d Matty's
e Cornfield Pool aka Long Flat
f Bumps Eddy
g Lewis Camp Eddy
h Harvard Bridge
i Oxbow
j Buckhorn Lodge
k Upper Wulff
l Lower Wulff aka Crusher Pool
m Upper East Branch Braids
n East Branch Pool

Shinhopple

to Downsville

River Road

Peaceful Valley Campground

Dirt Road

Turtle Island

Terry's Campsite

Upper East Branch

Clauson Brook

Tomannex State Forest

Dirt Road

Houck Mountain Road

Baxter Brook

Harvard

Oxbow Campground

Centerville

Buckhorn Lodge and Cabins

Harvard Road

NEW YORK

Sunoco
Route 17 Overpass
Old Route 17

to Fishs Eddy
to Hancock

Lower East Branch

FUTURE 86

to NYC

Beaverkill

to Roscoe

East Branch

Since 2002, this section has benefited greatly by the new Revision 7 flow plan, which requires that a 175-cfs flow be maintained year-round at the Harvard gauging station, approximately 3 miles above the Upper East's junction with the Beaverkill. The Upper East, which was severely dewatered and poorly maintained before 2002, has thrived since this plan was adopted, and this once marginal fishery has blossomed.

In spite of the new flow regulations, the cooling effects of Pepacton Reservoir releases are still largely diminished by the time they reach Shinhopple, New York. Drive along the Upper East Branch during the summer and you'll see what I mean. Above Shinhopple, the river is usually covered in fog on most summer evenings, caused by the cold reservoir water meeting the warm summer air. But the fog clears and becomes practically nonexistent by the time you get a mile or two downriver from Shinhopple, signaling that the river has warmed significantly. Fly anglers who want to fish the Upper East Branch in the summer should use Shinhopple as a dividing point. If you want to fish during the midday summer heat, head to the colder upriver section above Shinhopple. If you want to fish in the early morning or just before dark, fish below Shinhopple. However, I recommend that you avoid fishing the Upper East near or below Harvard entirely when the water temperature is over 70 degrees.

The Upper East Branch below Shinhopple has some terrific mayfly hatches. Its quill Gordon, green and brown drake, and Trico hatches may be the most prolific in the Upper Delaware system. I eagerly look forward to fishing each of these hatches at the beginning of every new fishing season—with the exception of the Trico. Upper East Branch Tricos are amazing to see. They often form funnel clouds on summer mornings, with thousands of the

Upper Delaware trout often rise very close to the shore.

mating mayflies twisting in the gentle breeze. But the river's trout don't seem to care. Sometimes I can't find a single fish eating the Tricos, even if the river is covered with them. And if the fish are eating them, it's usually only the smaller trout, although there are exceptions to this rule. So I don't spend too much time pursuing Upper East Branch Tricos. I would rather fish the hatch on the West Branch or the Main Stem, where I'll have a better chance of finding larger fish eating them.

Spring aquatic insect hatches often begin in this section of the Upper East Branch earlier than anywhere else in the Upper Delaware. Most years I find trout rising to Hendrickson hatches well before the bugs appear on the other branches. The progression of the Upper East's spring hatches is unusual. The Hendricksons often begin before the river's blue quill and quill Gordon hatches—a tendency that I have never witnessed anywhere else.

Many of the river's pools are long and slow moving in this section. The largest trout often rise in the pools' deepest slots near the banks. Quiet wading and long, gentle casts are necessary to catch these fish. The large wild brown trout that live here can be some of the most difficult to catch in the entire Upper Delaware system.

The Cliffs

The anglers' access at the Cliffs has a medium-sized dirt pull-off wedged between Route 30 and the guardrail. A footpath leads down a short, steep bank to the middle of a long, deep pool. The top of this pool is accessible by wading downriver from the Al's Wild Trout access at Shinhopple. Boats cannot be launched or retrieved at this access.

The deep pool at the bottom of the footpath and the steep, brush-covered bank on the access side of the river limit wading opportunities, but you could walk along the bank to fish downriver. The pool eventually riffles above the Peaceful Valley Campground.

Getting There
From the Route 17 overpass on Route 30:
1. Travel 8.1 miles on Route 30 north.
2. The parking area and footpath are on your right.

Parking Area GPS Coordinates
N42°02.223'
W075°04.448'

Unnamed Access #3

This access is a large dirt pull-off alongside Route 30, across the river from the Peaceful Valley Campground. It doesn't have a well-defined footpath, and anglers must bushwhack down a relatively steep bank to reach the river. Boats cannot be launched or retrieved at this access.

Upriver

The pull-off is located at the shallow end of a wide, slow-moving pool. If you wade upriver, the pool deepens and usually holds more fish. The pool can be crowded during the height of the fishing season. It's popular with the many fishermen who stay at the campground.

Downriver

A fairly long section of shallow, flat, and riffled water below the access area holds few fish. The riffles eventually bend to the right and dump into a short braided pool at the head of the Cabins Pool. The Cabins Pool is a beautiful piece of productive water, but its small size limits the fishing opportunities. It's often crowded with anglers from the cabins or the nearby campground.

Getting There

From the Route 17 overpass on Route 30:
1. Travel 7.1 miles on Route 30 north.
2. The parking area and footpath are on your right.

Parking Area GPS Coordinates

N42°01.480'
W075°03.971'

The Power Lines

Anglers must park in the grass alongside Route 30 to reach the anglers' footpath, which is marked with a small, yellow DEC sign. The footpath is the only public land at this access; the properties on either side of the path are posted. Canoes and pontoon boats can be launched or retrieved from this access, as long as you don't mind carrying them down the tree-lined footpath. Drift boats cannot be launched or retrieved here.

Upriver

The anglers' footpath leads to the upper half of the Power Lines Pool. The pool's center holds a lot of smaller fish and occasionally a brook trout. Larger fish, mostly brown trout, usually hold in the deeper water on the right side of the river, near the rocks and overhanging vegetation growing on the bank. The Power Lines Riffle flows into the head of this pool and holds fish throughout. Most of the larger fish tend to hold along the rocky seam near the right bank. If you wade above the head of the Power Lines Riffle, you'll find a long series of shallow riffles and pools until you reach the tail of the Cabins Pool.

Downriver

The middle and tail of the Power Lines Pool, immediately downriver of the footpath, constitute a long stretch of slow-moving, glasslike water. Trout feed in the middle of the pool, but most of the larger fish are under the overhanging vegetation on the left bank. You must wade slowly and be able to make long, drag-free casts to catch these fish. A medium-sized island divides the river into two riffles below the tail of the pool. Matty's Pool, which fishes similarly to the Power Lines Pool, lies below the island.

Getting There

From the Route 17 overpass on Route 30:
1. Travel 6.1 miles on Route 30 north.
2. The pull-off is on your right.

Parking Area GPS Coordinates

N42°00.735'
W075°04.178'

The Cornfield

There is no designated parking area at this access. Anglers usually park on the edge of Route 30 to reach the DEC footpath. The original access was located at the upriver end of the cornfield, but inconsiderate anglers trespassed through private property, including the farmer's field, and the access was closed. A new footpath, marked with a small, yellow DEC sign, leads through a patch of brush in the middle of the field. This new footpath could also be closed if anglers stray from it. Boats cannot be launched or retrieved at this access.

Upriver

The anglers' footpath meets the river in the bottom half of the Cornfield Pool. Some of the pool's trout hold in the center of the river, but most of the fish are near the right bank. The Cornfield Pool is long, flat, lovely dry-fly water that requires careful wading and long, drag-free casts. The Cornfield Riffle feeds the head of the pool, approximately 100 yards upriver. The riffle is shallow at its head and usually holds a few small fish. The lower half of the riffle, where it braids into the pool, holds a good number of fish near the right bank.

Downriver

The tail of the Cornfield Pool can be a good place to fish during a hatch or evening spinner fall. Bumps Eddy Riffle, below the tail of the Cornfield Pool, also fishes well during a hatch.

Getting There

From the Route 17 overpass on Route 30:
1. Travel 5.1 miles on Route 30 north.
2. The footpath is on your right.

Parking Area GPS Coordinates

N42°01.031'
W075°05.227'

Tomannex State Forest

This access area is part of a large forest preserve purchased several years ago by New York State. You must travel down a muddy, rutted, railroad bed—now a public dirt road—to reach the river. The dirt road parallels the river from the old Harvard Bridge to Shinhopple, New York, and travels through mostly public land. However, there are also several areas of posted private property along the road that should be avoided. The physical condition of the road makes the use of a high-clearance, four-wheel drive vehicle a good idea. The road is not aggressively maintained, and portions of it may be blocked by fallen branches or even entire trees. A couple of pull-offs along the road offer access to the river, including a parking area below the Bumps Eddy Island. But high cliffs and dense vegetation strictly limit much of the road's potential access opportunities. Boats cannot be launched or retrieved here.

Getting There
From Route 17 east:
1. Take the Route 17 east, East Branch exit 90.
2. Yield at the bottom of the exit ramp, and go straight.
3. Cross the Old Route 17 Bridge.
4. Turn left onto Harvard Road.
5. Travel 2.5 miles to the end of Harvard Road.
6. Veer to the right onto the old railroad bed (a dirt road).

A white-tailed deer crosses the Upper East early on a summer morning. Abundant wildlife, including bald eagles, foxes, minks, black bears, and rattlesnakes, all reside in the mountains and valleys that border the Upper Delaware system.

From Route 17 west:
1. Take the Route 17 west, East Branch exit 90.
2. Turn right at the stop sign at the bottom of the exit ramp onto Harvard Road.
3. Travel 2.4 miles to the end of Harvard Road.
4. Veer to the right onto the old railroad bed (a dirt road).

Railroad Bed (Dirt Road) GPS Coordinates

N42°01.265'
W075°07.080'

Oxbow Campground

The privately owned Oxbow Campground offers river access and a boat launch to its clients and to the general public for a small fee. Anglers should call ahead (607-363-7141) with any queries.

Getting There

From the Route 17 overpass on Route 30:
1. Travel 3 miles on Route 30 north.
2. Oxbow Campground is on your right.

Campground Entrance GPS Coordinates

N42°01.532'
W075°06.950'

Pull-off below Oxbow Campground

This access is a medium-sized dirt pull-off wedged between Route 30 and a guardrail. A footpath leads down a short, steep bank to the middle of Oxbow Pool. Boats cannot be launched or retrieved from this access.

Upriver

The head of Oxbow Pool, located a short distance upriver from the anglers' footpath, is composed of a short, heavy riffle that runs tight to the left bank. Oxbow Pool is deep and full of various-sized trout, which tend to feed from pool's center to the left bank. A long series of riffles and braided water connects the head of Oxbow Pool with the tail of Harvard Pool. This stretch of broken water also holds fish. The tail of Harvard Pool ends just upriver from the riffles, but the pool's depth and the base of the Harvard Bridge hinder further upriver wading.

Downriver

The middle and tail of Oxbow Pool, downriver from the anglers' footpath, remain deep along the right bank, where trout can usually be found. If you walk far enough, you'll eventually reach the productive riffles that flow around the island near the top of Buckhorn Lodge Pool.

Getting There

From the Route 17 overpass on Route 30:
1. Travel 2.6 miles on Route 30 north.
2. The parking area and footpath are on your right.

Parking Area GPS Coordinates

N42°01.492'
W075°07.388'

Centerville

The Centerville fishing access is another medium-sized dirt pull-off wedged between the road and the guardrail, a short distance below Buckhorn Lodge and Cabins (small, red riverside cabins). The anglers' footpath meets the river at the bottom of a gradual bank in the middle of a productive pool. Boats cannot be launched or retrieved at this access.

Upriver

A medium-sized pool is located at the bottom of the footpath. A productive riffle flows between two small grass islands and into the head of the pool. The tail of Buckhorn Lodge Pool ends at the top of the riffle, above another island. It's common for this pool to have several anglers fishing it, usually clients of Buckhorn Lodge and Cabins. The pool is on private property, and it's a good idea to request permission from Buckhorn Lodge before you fish it.

Downriver

The three Wulff Property Riffles and Pools—named after fly-fishing legends Lee and Joan Wulff, who used to own a significant portion of the left bank—lie downriver from the access. Each of the Wulff Property Pools maintains good trout populations.

Getting There

From the Route 17 overpass on Route 30:
1. Travel 1.3 miles on Route 30 north.
2. The parking area and footpath are on your right.

Parking Area GPS Coordinates

N42°00.531'
W075°08.208'

Pull-off above the East Branch Sunoco Station

There are no signs indicating this pull-off or its footpath. If you come to a large Department of Transportation pull-off on the right side of Route 30 north, you have gone just past the access. The pull-off consists of a grassy parking area and a grass road that ends abruptly at a high bank and footpath. The footpath leads to the middle of the Lower Wulff Pool, which is slow moving and glassy-smooth. Some large trout live in this water, but the middle and lower end of the pool are also heavily inhabited by carp, chubs, and a few smallmouth bass. Surface-feeding fish tend to cruise in the slow water and are often difficult to catch. There is no official boat launch at this access, although you could launch or retrieve canoes and pontoon boats if you don't mind dragging them up or down the bank.

Upriver

You can't wade far upriver from this access under average to high-water conditions. The pool is too deep to cross, and the access-side bank is too steep and brush covered to traverse.

Downriver

It is possible to wade downriver to the end of the Lower Wulff Pool from the access-side bank. You'll eventually reach the tail of the pool and the Upper East Branch Braids, a series of three slanted islands that separates the Lower Wulff Pool from the Upper East's final pool above the Route 17 overpass. The current seams between the islands and the small pools they feed usually hold a few trout, especially in the spring.

Getting There

From the Route 17 overpass on Route 30:
1. Travel .4 mile on Route 30 north.
2. The pull-off, a grassy area along Route 30, and the footpath are on your right.

Parking Area GPS Coordinates

N41°59.943'
W075°07.858'

The Jaws

The Jaws pull-off is a large dirt and gravel area that can hold several cars. The pull-off is on the left side of Old Route 17, immediately after the yield sign at the bottom of the ramp for new Route 17 east exit 90. This access provides an important entry point for fishing the junctions of the Beaverkill, Upper East Branch, and Lower East Branch—all within easy walking distance. You can launch or retrieve canoes and pontoon boats if you don't mind dragging them up or down the bank. Drift boats cannot be launched or retrieved here.

The Old Route 17 Bridge, near the aptly named village of East Branch, New York, signifies the end of the Upper East Branch.

Upriver

The anglers' footpath begins at the eastern end of the Jaws pull-off. The footpath leads to the end of the Upper East Branch, between the Old Route 17 Bridge and the new Route 17 overpass. The water upriver from the path is flat and deep in spots. Most anglers head downriver, below the bridges, to the beginning of the Lower East Branch and the Jaws Riffle (below the junction of the Upper East and the Beaverkill). Anglers can also wade under the bridges and head upriver to the left to fish the end of the Beaverkill. This part of the Beaverkill is usually warm in the summer, so I fish it only in the spring and fall.

Downriver

The Jaws Riffle begins downriver of the footpath and the Route 17 Bridges. Both the riffle and the pool are deepest in the center and near the right bank, which is where you'll find most of the fish. The pool is fairly long, and most anglers fish only as far as its tail. It has a good trout population, but its depth makes many of the fish difficult to reach without a boat.

Getting There

From Route 17 east, East Branch exit 90:
1. Yield at the bottom of the exit ramp, and go straight.
2. The pull-off—a dirt area before the Old Route 17 Bridge (over the Upper East Branch)—is on your left.

From Route 17 west, East Branch exit 90:
1. Turn left at the stop sign at the bottom of the exit ramp onto Harvard Road.
2. Go straight to the next stop sign.
3. Turn right onto Old Route 17.
4. Cross the Old Route 17 Bridge (over the Upper East Branch), and the pull-off—a dirt area after the Old Route 17 Bridge—is on your right.

Parking Area GPS Coordinates

N41°59.518'
W075°07.891'

Lower East Branch Tailwater

The approximately 17 miles of the Lower East Branch flow in stark contrast to its more trout-friendly conjoined twin, the Upper East Branch. The Lower East is 202 feet wide at its beginning at the Jaws, and it expands to 288 feet wide near Hancock, New York (McBride 2002). The Lower East's width and distance from Pepacton Reservoir, combined with the influx of tepid Beaverkill water, make it a summertime smallmouth bass fishery.

Most of the 14 access areas are confined to the top of the river. The bottom of the Lower East Branch—below the Fishs Eddy islands and downriver to Cadosia—is one of the least accessible areas in the entire Upper Delaware system. The only way to fish this section is to gain landowner permission or to float the river. But floating the Lower East Branch isn't easy either.

New York State doesn't own or maintain a single boat launch along the Lower East Branch. The only place to launch a drift boat is from the privately owned Beaver Del Campground. Beaver Del has allowed the public to launch boats from its property for a small fee for several years. But the public's ability to use this launch is tenuous at best. If the property is sold or the owners change their minds, there will be no boat launch at the top of the Lower East Branch.

Anglers floating downriver from the Beaver Del Campground in a drift boat can take out only at Cadosia. You could continue past the Cadosia boat launch and remove your boat at Fireman's Park in Hancock, but doing so only lengthens an already long float. There are no quick and easy drift boat floats on the Lower East Branch. If you want to float it, be prepared for a long day on the river. More portable watercraft, such as canoes and pontoon boats, are better options. These boats can be carried to the river from many of the public footpaths.

The Lower East is home to a significant population of wild rainbow trout, but it also holds an equal amount of both stocked and wild brown trout. A thousand 8- to 9-inch brown trout are planted in the river each year. Brook trout are rare in the Lower East. Many Lower East trout are forced to migrate long distances to survive. The best months to fish for them are April, May,

Canoes and kayaks are more versatile for floating the Lower East than are drift boats, due to the lack of accessible ramps.

and the first half of June in the spring, and then again at the end of September through mid-November in the fall. They usually move into the Upper East Branch, Main Stem, or West Branch when summer water temperatures soar over 80 degrees. But the Lower East's trout always return and are ready to feed when the river cools and the fall hatches begin.

In addition, the Lower East is a good smallmouth bass, American shad, and walleye fishery. It is also home to one of the last commercially operated eel weirs in the Delaware River system. Hancock, New York, native Ray Turner owns the weir, as well as the Delaware Delicacies smokehouse.

Most of the river's smallmouth bass average around 12 inches, but the river holds enough of them to make streamer fishing worthwhile. The shad usually reach the Lower East Branch by late May or early June and can provide excellent midday fly-fishing options at a time when the river otherwise fishes best in the morning or late evening. I know of a few anglers who have accidentally caught walleyes on black Woolly Buggers while fishing for trout. This fly pattern works well in the Lower East due to the river's large population of hellgrammites, the larval form of the dobsonfly.

The Lower East's hatches are on a par with those found on the other Upper Delaware branches. The river's premier spring hatches are its Hendricksons, green and brown drakes, grannom and apple caddis, *Isonychia*, and golden stoneflies. Its *Isonychia*, blue-winged olives, and hebes can also be very good in the fall.

The Lower East isn't always an easy place for wade fishermen. The river is large and drains the combined watershed of the Beaverkill and the Upper East Branch. It often runs high in the spring, during its most productive

Migrating Lower East Branch trout flee high summer water temperatures but always return to the river when it cools in the fall. Here, Ben Rinker and Ruthann Weamer fish in riffled water during a fall trip to the Lower East.

hatches. The Lower East, like the Upper East, isn't border water—the entire river is in New York State, so the public may not have the right to wade within the high-water mark along privately owned property. Any posted Lower East Branch riverfront property should be avoided.

Top of the Lower East Branch: The Jaws to Fishs Eddy

The top of the Lower East is a good place to fish during spring weekends when most of the system is packed with anglers. Many Upper Delaware fishermen see the entire Lower East Branch as an unreliable trout fishery and would rather pack into the West Branch, where they believe they'll have a better chance to catch fish. Trout populations are higher in other parts of the river system, but for me, the solitude, scenery, and excellent hatches are worth the trade-off.

The Lower East Branch as a whole may host the fewest anglers of all the Upper Delaware branches. But among the anglers who do fish the Lower East, most consider the top section their favorite. The primary reason for this stretch's popularity is that it holds more trout than the water downriver of Fishs Eddy. The New York DEC's radiotelemetry study found that underground springs create thermal refuges in the top of the river, allowing at least some trout to remain on a year-round basis (McBride 2002). Not all the river's trout stay in this section throughout the summer, but the ones that do stay can survive, as long as fishermen don't drag them out of their refuges during periods of elevated river temperatures.

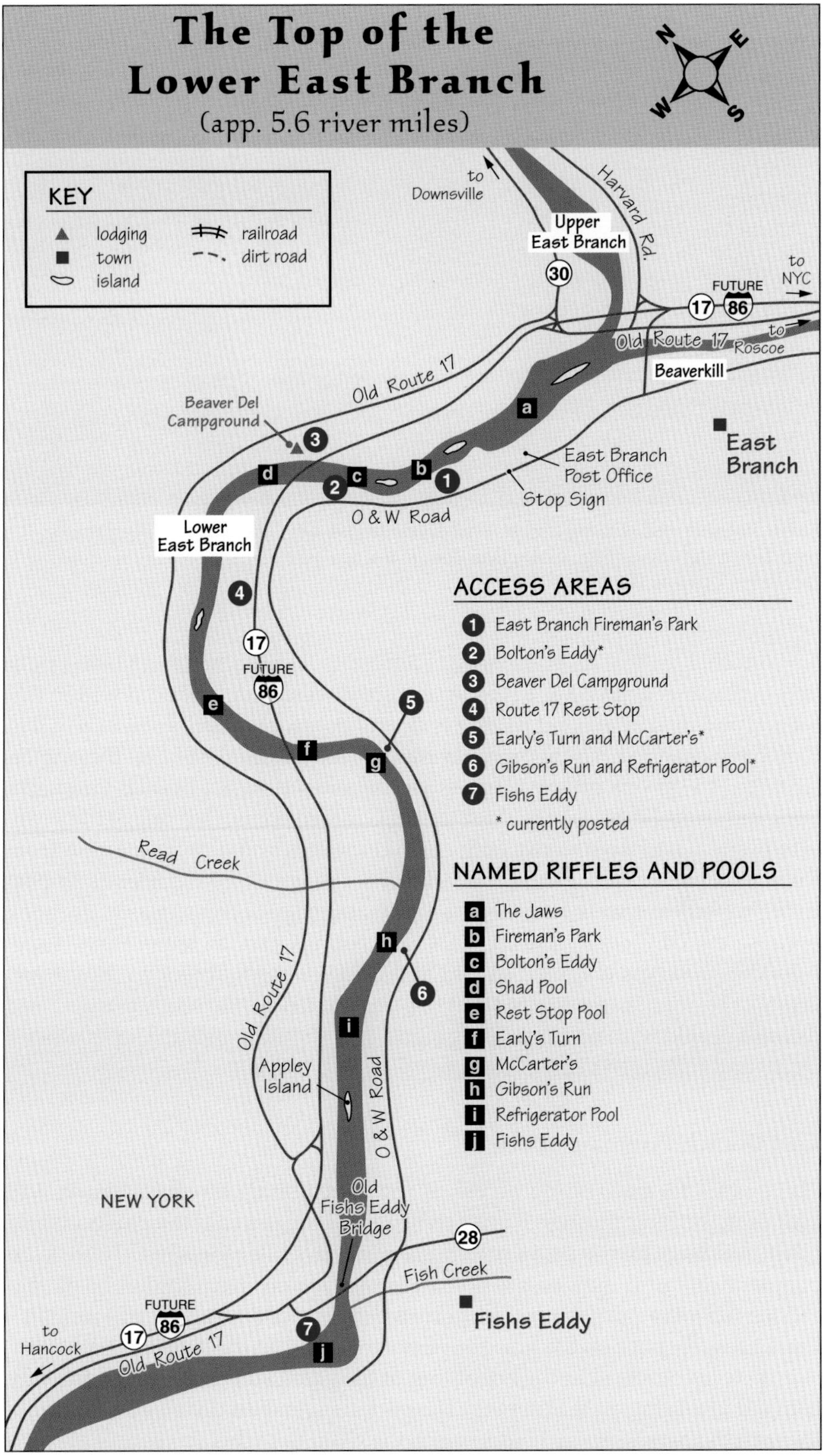

The Top of the Lower East Branch

(app. 5.6 river miles)

N E S W (compass)

KEY

▲ lodging
■ town
� island
╫ railroad
‐ ‐ dirt road

to Downsville

Harvard Rd.

Upper East Branch

30

to NYC

FUTURE 17 86

to Roscoe

Old Route 17

Beaverkill

Old Route 17

a

East Branch Post Office

East Branch

Beaver Del Campground

▲ 3

Stop Sign

d

2 c b 1

O & W Road

Lower East Branch

4

17 FUTURE 86

e

5

f

g

ACCESS AREAS

1 East Branch Fireman's Park
2 Bolton's Eddy*
3 Beaver Del Campground
4 Route 17 Rest Stop
5 Early's Turn and McCarter's*
6 Gibson's Run and Refrigerator Pool*
7 Fishs Eddy
  * currently posted

Read Creek

h

6

Old Route 17

i

Appley Island

O & W Road

NAMED RIFFLES AND POOLS

a The Jaws
b Fireman's Park
c Bolton's Eddy
d Shad Pool
e Rest Stop Pool
f Early's Turn
g McCarter's
h Gibson's Run
i Refrigerator Pool
j Fishs Eddy

NEW YORK

Old Fishs Eddy Bridge

28

Fish Creek

Fishs Eddy

FUTURE 17 86

to Hancock

Old Route 17

7

j

Early morning and evening are the best times to fish the Lower East during sunny weather in the late spring. Craig Bouslough and a friend fish the evening rise during a late-spring trip to the Lower East.

Another facet of its popularity is related to its long history of being publicly accessible. Until 2006, seven access areas were evenly spaced within this section and provided good fishing opportunities for wading anglers, but that may have changed. Three property owners have now posted all the angler-significant pull-offs on the O&W Road between the East Branch Fireman's Park and Fishs Eddy. An agent for the DEC informed me that one of the property owners had arguments with several anglers and a fishing guide from Roscoe, New York, inspiring the landowner to convince his friends to post their properties as well. I have elected to include these access areas in the book because the DEC agent told me that the postings may be temporary. Hopefully the problems will be resolved and the accesses will reopen. But if you arrive at one of the access areas that I've designated as "currently posted" and it is still posted with no trespassing signs, you should honor the landowner's rights and fish elsewhere.

East Branch Fireman's Park

There is no formal fishing access at the East Branch Fireman's Park, and accessing the river through it is a privilege. Be sure to avoid the pavilions and other buildings on the property, and remove any litter you find. There is no boat launch, but it may be possible to launch or retrieve pontoon boats and canoes from the park if you get permission first. Do not park in Fireman's Park. I usually park on the grass opposite the park, on the side of O&W Road. A private home sits near the beginning of the grass, so park far enough away to avoid intruding on the owners. The parking situation dictates a short walk through the park's grassy field to reach the river. Both this access and the next access, Bolton's Eddy, are predominantly low-water access points for waders. They are both deep, and wading is difficult to impossible at higher flows.

Upriver

An island divides the Lower East Branch in front of the park. The tail of the first Lower East Branch Pool at the Jaws ends at the top of this island. The channels on either side of the island both have good fish-holding water. But it can be difficult or impossible to reach the island during higher river flows due to the depth of the channel beside the park.

Downriver

The two island channels converge into a riffle and then a braided pool that hold trout throughout their length downriver from the park. But it can be difficult to impossible to reach this water during high flows, especially in late spring, because of the depth of the water and the dense vegetation growing on the bank.

Getting There

For directions for reaching the Jaws from New York Route 17 east and west, see pages 75 and 76.

From the Jaws access to the East Branch Village stop sign:
1. Turn left onto Old Route 17.
2. Make an immediate right turn, and cross the East Branch Bridge (over the Beaverkill).
3. Go to the stop sign and turn right onto O&W Road.
4. The East Branch Village stop sign is straight ahead, just past the post office.

From the East Branch Village stop sign to the access:
1. Go straight, continuing on O&W Road.
2. Travel .1 mile, and East Branch Fireman's Park is on your right.

Parking Area GPS Coordinates

N41°59.425'
W075°08.520'

Bolton's Eddy—Currently Posted

There is no formal parking area at this access. Park in one of the two single-car pull-offs on the river side of O&W Road. Two anglers' footpaths lead down a steep bank to the river. Boats cannot be launched or retrieved at this access.

Upriver

The footpath leads down a steep bank to a riffle beside an island at the head of Bolton's Eddy. The island constricts the right channel's flow and forces it toward the footpath. The riffle is too deep to cross where the footpath meets the river, but it can be crossed slightly upriver where it shallows. This is good nymphing water, and I like to blind-cast *Isonychia* dry-fly patterns here in the fall. The island's left channel is usually shallow and seldom holds fish. The tail of the braided pool below Fireman's Park Island lies above the island.

Downriver

The steep bank and deep water on the footpath side of the river make downriver wading difficult. In addition, overhanging trees and brush can create casting problems. I fish from this side occasionally when I want to nymph the rocky seam near the shore, but I usually prefer to cross the river to cast from the opposite shore. Downriver wading is also limited from this side of the river. Bolton's Eddy, below the footpath, limits downriver wading. The eddy has a good fish population, but it's very difficult to fish without a boat.

Getting There

From the East Branch Village stop sign:
1. Travel straight on O&W Road for .5 mile.
2. The pull-off and footpath are on your right.

Parking Area GPS Coordinates

N41°59.591'
W075°08.817'

Beaver Del Campground

The privately owned Beaver Del Bar, Restaurant, and Campground offers river access and a boat launch to its clients and to the general public for a fee. Anglers should call ahead (607-363-7443) with any queries.

Getting There

From New York Route 17 east, East Branch exit 90:
1. Yield to the left at the bottom of the exit ramp, and travel under the Route 17 overpass.
2. Turn left, heading toward Route 17 west, and stop at the stop sign.
3. Go straight on Old Route 17, past the on-ramp for Route 17 west.
4. Travel 1.3 miles.
5. Beaver Del is on your left.

From New York Route 17 west, East Branch exit 90:
1. Turn left at the stop sign at the bottom of the exit ramp onto Harvard Road.
2. Go straight to the next stop sign.
3. Turn right onto Old Route 17.
4. Cross the Old Route 17 Bridge and travel under the Route 17 overpass.
5. Follow steps 2–5 above.

Beaver Del Entrance GPS Coordinates
    N42°00.096'
    W075°09.122'

Route 17 Rest Stop

For access upriver from the rest stop, park at the rest stop and walk east through the field toward the rest stop entrance. A dirt road alongside the guardrail leads to the river. Follow the upriver directions once you reach the grass road. There is another grass field at the rest stop exit. You can also walk through this field to access the river above the Route 17 Bridge, downriver from the rest stop. Boats cannot be launched or retrieved at this access.

Upriver

The grass road at the rest stop entrance turns left before heading straight toward a telephone pole. An anglers' footpath begins beside the telephone pole and leads to the river. It meets the river across from a small peninsula at the tail of the Shad Pool. Shad Pool is excellent dry-fly water and, true to its name, is a good place to find shad in the spring. The pool is deepest in the middle and near the left bank, where most of the trout surface-feed.

Downriver

There is a long section of eroding gravel islands, riffles, and deep mini-pools downriver from Shad Pool. This section is shallow in the center but holds fish

The Route 17 rest stop provides varying water types, including gravelly slots, long tumbling riffles, and glassy-smooth pools.

along the banks all the way to the tail of the pool, where it forms a beautiful, long riffle. The riffle bends to the left and flows into a short braided pool before it riffles again and forms the head of Rest Stop Pool. Rest Stop Pool is deep and holds a good population of trout throughout. The tail of the pool, slightly above the Route 17 Bridge, is a good place to find large, cruising browns during a hatch or evening spinner fall.

Getting There

From New York Route 17 east:
1. Travel 1.7 miles past East Branch exit 90.
2. The rest stop is on your right.

From New York Route 17 west:
1. Exit at East Branch exit 90.
2. Yield to the left at the bottom of the exit ramp, and travel under the Route 17 overpass.
3. Turn left, heading toward Route 17 west, and stop at the stop sign.
4. Merge straight onto Old Route 17 and travel .1 mile. Veer left onto Route 17 east.
5. Travel 1.7 miles past East Branch exit 90.
6. The rest stop is on your right.

Parking Area GPS Coordinates

N41°59.673'
W075°09.632'

Early's Turn and McCarter's—Currently Posted

Anglers should park in the dirt pull-off on the right side of O&W Road (heading west toward Fishs Eddy). The pull-off can hold a couple of cars. An anglers' footpath begins beside the pull-off and leads down a steep, rocky bank to the river. Boats cannot be launched or retrieved at this access.

Upriver

If you look upriver from the anglers' footpath, you can see the Route 17 Bridge, the tail of Rest Stop Pool, and the long, tumbling Early's Turn and McCarter's (Run) Riffles. These riffles—with their excellent depth and good trout populations—provide fine water to nymph or blind-cast large, bushy dry flies. They are especially deep near the right bank, so you should concentrate your fishing from this area to the riffles' center. McCarter's Riffle bends sharply to the left in front of the footpath, forming the braided head of McCarter's Pool.

Downriver

It's difficult to wade downriver on the left side from this access. A large pile of riprap rocks protects O&W Road from the force and potential erosion of

McCarter's (Run) Riffle on this side. The rocks force anglers to wade very near the river at the end of the riffle and at the top of McCarter's Pool. Many of the trout in the riffle and pool hold near the rocks along the shore, and it's easy to spook them because you have to wade so close. It's not easy to present a fly accurately from the river's right side either. The riffle forms a deep eddy in front of the right bank and maintains significant depth in the upper half. To catch the fish rising across the river, you have to be able to present a drag-free fly accurately, over varying current seams, while wading in waist-deep water.

Getting There

From the East Branch Village stop sign:
1. Travel straight on O&W Road for 2 miles.
2. The pull-off and footpath are on your right.

Parking Area GPS Coordinates

N41°59.123'
W075°09.509'

Gibson's Run and Refrigerator Pool—Currently Posted

Anglers have to park in the large grass pull-off on the left side of O&W Road to fish from this access. The pull-off, which holds several cars, can be identified by a small red and white no-dumping sign. Two anglers' footpaths, beginning beside the pull-off, lead down a steep bank to the river. Boats cannot be launched or retrieved at this access.

Upriver

The anglers' footpath meets the river near the end of Gibson's Run Riffle. This riffle has a good trout population and can be fished effectively from either side of the river. Many of the riffle's trout hold in the center, but don't neglect the holding areas near the shore on the rocky right side. Read Creek flows into the river from the left shore at the top of the Gibson's Run Riffle. This creek provides an influx of cold tributary water to this section of the river, but it also tends to muddy the river quickly after a heavy rain.

Downriver

Gibson's Riffle slows and braids into the Gibson's Run Pool. You can fish the pool from either side of the river, but the right bank slopes gradually into the river, making it easier to wade than the steep, rocky left bank. The top of the Gibson's Run Pool has better fishing than its lower half. It holds trout in the spring and fall and includes all types of river habitat—slow pools, braided runs, tumbling riffles, and rock pocket water. A long stretch of shallow water and riffles lies below the Gibson's Run Pool until you reach the head of the Refrigerator Riffle and Pool. This pool and riffle are good trout-holding water and can be worth the effort it takes to reach them.

Getting There

From the East Branch Village stop sign:
   1. Travel straight on O&W Road for 2.8 miles.
   2. The pull-off and footpath are on your right.

Parking Area GPS Coordinates

   N41°58.685'
   W075°09.968'

Fishs Eddy

Fishs Eddy is one of the nicest New York State access areas on the Upper Delaware. The access starts at a gravel road, which is clearly marked with a brown DEC sign. The road ends at a spacious gravel parking area with room for several cars. The public anglers' footpath leads to the river through private ground that is clearly marked with no-trespassing signs (the owner of this posted land does not tolerate trespassers). This access has no formal boat launch, but some anglers launch and retrieve pontoon boats and canoes here.

Upriver

The anglers' footpath meets the river at a small sandy beach in the upper quarter of Fishs Eddy. Fishs Eddy is deep near the footpath and impossible to wade. The head of Fishs Eddy and Fish Creek flow into the pool a short distance above the footpath. The head of the eddy is shallower and can be waded during average to low flows. A medium-sized chute of heavy, riffled water

Look for rising fish from the Fishs Eddy Bridge on your way to the Fishs Eddy access.

The riffles above Fishs Eddy and the deep water surrounding the crumbled remains of the old bridge provide excellent fishing opportunities for those willing to walk.

flows into the head of the pool and holds good populations of fish. The chute flows downriver from the Fishs Eddy Bridge. The broken remains of the old Fishs Eddy Bridge lay crumbled in the center of the river, just upriver from the current bridge. The deep mini-pools and riffles that form on either side of the old bridge are also good places to fish.

Downriver

The lower three-quarters of Fishs Eddy glides below the anglers' footpath. Most of this water is deep, flat, and slow moving. The eddy holds a large population of fish that require accurate drag-free casts to bring them to net. The pool eventually ends at the riffles surrounding the first Partridge Island.

Getting There

From New York Route 17 east, Fishs Eddy exit 89:
1. Turn left at the bottom of the exit ramp.
2. Travel .2 mile, and turn right at the old Fishs Eddy Diner, toward Fishs Eddy-Rock Valley-Goulds.
3. Travel .1 mile. The access (down a gravel road) is on your right.

From New York Route 17 west, Fishs Eddy exit 89:
1. Turn left at the bottom of the exit ramp.
2. Travel .4 mile, and turn left at the old Fishs Eddy Diner, toward Fishs Eddy-Rock Valley-Goulds.
3. Travel .1 mile. The access (down a gravel road) is on your right.

Parking Area GPS Coordinates
    N41°57.980'
    W075°10.969'

River GPS Coordinates
    N41°57.861'
    W075°11.072'

Bottom of the Lower East Branch: Fishs Eddy to Junction Pool

There are seven access areas in this stretch, but none in the middle. Several parking areas, immediately below the Fishs Eddy Cemetery, provide access to the islands below the Fishs Eddy Pool, but that's where the public access ends until you reach Cadosia, just east of Hancock, New York. The section between the Alice's Way access and Cadosia has no public access at all and is one of the least fished sections in the entire Upper Delaware system. Pease Eddy Road in Hancock closely parallels the backside of the river for approximately 12 miles, but it doesn't provide river access because it's all private land.

Anglers who are willing to float the bottom of the Lower East Branch will find beautiful scenery and a relatively underused fishery—a rare combination in the Catskills. If you do float the bottom of the Lower East, you will eventually come to a V-shaped rock structure in the middle of the river a few miles before Hancock. This structure is the eel weir owned by Ray Turner mentioned earlier. Turner has to rebuild these weirs every year because they're often destroyed by floods or melting ice in the spring, so it's important to show his structure respect and not damage it in any way. If you're trying to navigate a boat around the weir, make sure that you don't float into the open end of the V, because you won't be able to get through the rocks and wooden steps at the closed end. The best path around the weir is on its left side. But pay attention when moving past the weir: trout like to hang out near the riffled water that squirts out the sides.

The trout that live in the bottom section of the Lower East Branch are highly migratory. The lack of groundwater infiltration, combined with the extreme distance from the Pepacton Reservoir, often produces lethally warm water temperatures for trout. Trout fishing should probably be avoided from the middle of June until the water temperatures return to trout-tolerable levels sometime in the fall. Most of the trout you catch in the bottom of the Lower East Branch will be wild. New York State is unable to space stocked trout throughout this section because of the lack of public access.

Below the Fishs Eddy Cemetery

This access has a medium-sized dirt pull-off at a break in the guardrail, with an anglers' footpath leading down a small, steep bank to the river. The pull-off is large enough for several cars. The footpath can be difficult to traverse

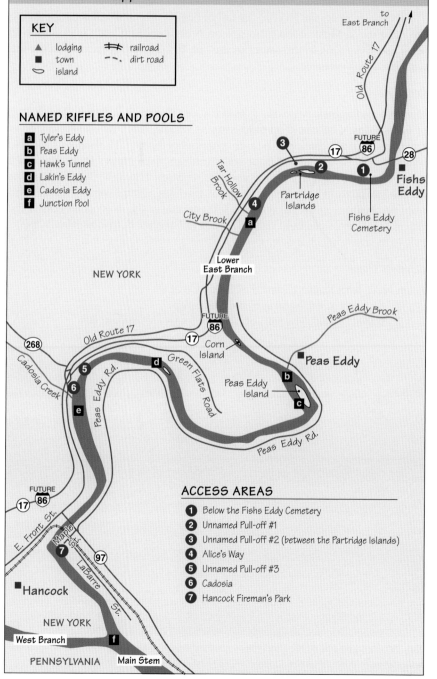

The Bottom of the Lower East Branch
(app. 11.4 river miles)

N E W S

to East Branch

KEY

▲ lodging   ╫ railroad
■ town   - - . dirt road
⌒ island

NAMED RIFFLES AND POOLS

a Tyler's Eddy
b Peas Eddy
c Hawk's Tunnel
d Lakin's Eddy
e Cadosia Eddy
f Junction Pool

Old Route 17

FUTURE 86
17
28

Fishs Eddy

3

Tar Hollow Brook

2

1

City Brook

4

a

Partridge Islands

Fishs Eddy Cemetery

NEW YORK

Lower East Branch

FUTURE 86
17
Corn Island

Peas Eddy Brook

268

Old Route 17

Cadosia Creek

Peas Eddy Rd.

5

6

e

d

Green Flats Road

Peas Eddy Island

b

c

■ Peas Eddy

Peas Eddy Rd.

FUTURE 86
17

E. Front St.

Maple St.

7

LaBarre St.

97

■ Hancock

NEW YORK

West Branch

f

PENNSYLVANIA   Main Stem

ACCESS AREAS

1 Below the Fishs Eddy Cemetery
2 Unnamed Pull-off #1
3 Unnamed Pull-off #2 (between the Partridge Islands)
4 Alice's Way
5 Unnamed Pull-off #3
6 Cadosia
7 Hancock Fireman's Park

from late spring until the end of summer owing to the dense vegetation. Boats cannot be launched or retrieved at this access.

Upriver

The footpath meets the river at the tail of Fishs Eddy. The tail is deepest near the right bank. Most of the trout rise on this side, but it's not uncommon to see a few fish rising in the center of the tail. Fishs Eddy upriver from the tail was discussed earlier.

Downriver

The first and largest Partridge Island divides the river in half below the tail of Fishs Eddy. The island's left channel is usually shallow and holds fewer fish than the right channel. The right channel begins with a shallow riffle and braided pool. The braided pool spills into another deeper riffle that has a short, deep pool below it that usually holds trout. The right channel remains deep near the right bank below the pool, through a couple of short riffles and mini-pools, until it merges with the left channel at the downriver end of the island. All these areas hold fish. The second, smaller Partridge Island begins below the merging channels.

Getting There

From New York Route 17 east, Fishs Eddy exit 89:
1. Turn left at the bottom of the exit ramp.
2. Travel .2 mile. The pull-off and footpath are on your left.

Ray Turner owns one of the last commercial eel weirs in the Delaware River system. Eels swim into the open end of the V and are collected in the wooden steps.

From New York Route 17 west, Fishs Eddy exit 89:
1. Turn right at the bottom of the exit ramp.
2. Travel .9 mile. The pull-off and footpath are on your left.

Parking Area GPS Coordinates
> N41°58.276'
> W075°11.480'

Unnamed Pull-off #1

This access consists of a medium-sized dirt pull-off at a break in the guardrail, with an anglers' footpath leading down a very steep bank to the river. The pull-off is large enough to fit several cars. This access is somewhat redundant because it meets the river between the access below the Fishs Eddy Cemetery and the one between the Partridge Islands. Boats cannot be launched or retrieved here.

Getting There
From New York Route 17 east, Fishs Eddy exit 89:
1. Turn left at the bottom of the exit ramp.
2. Travel .6 mile. The pull-off and footpath are on your left.

From New York Route 17 west, Fishs Eddy exit 89:
1. Turn right at the bottom of the exit ramp.
2. Travel 1.3 miles. The pull-off and footpath are on your left.

Parking Area GPS Coordinates
> N41°58.469'
> W075°11.738'

Unnamed Pull-off #2 (between the Partridge Islands)

This access is a medium-sized dirt pull-off at a break in the guardrail, with an anglers' footpath leading down a very steep bank to the river. The pull-off is large enough to fit several cars. Boats cannot be launched or retrieved here.

Upriver
The anglers' footpath meets the river at the riffle between the two Partridge Islands. This riffle flows into a deep, braided mini-pool that usually holds fish. The two river channels that surround the first Partridge Island, upriver from the footpath, were discussed earlier.

Downriver
The second Partridge Island also divides the river. The island's right channel has a riffle of varying depth at its head that flows into a short pool with a couple of large rocks. The pool holds trout, usually behind and on both sides of

The riffle below the first Partridge Island provides excellent angling opportunities for Andy Tumalo and a friend.

the rocks. The right channel then riffles again and merges with the left channel below the island. The island's left channel has a long, deep riffle at its head, which is excellent trout habitat. The riffle eventually slows into braided water near the end of the island and forms the head of a pool. The upper part of the pool is very deep and also has a good trout population. The shallower bottom half of the pool is inhabited by lots of chubs, but it holds trout as well.

Getting There

From New York Route 17 east, Fishs Eddy exit 89:
1. Turn left at the bottom of the exit ramp.
2. Travel .9 mile. The pull-off and footpath are on your left.

From New York Route 17 west, Fishs Eddy exit 89:
1. Turn right at the bottom of the exit ramp.
2. Travel 1.6 miles. The pull-off and footpath are on your left.

Parking Area GPS Coordinates

N41°58.524'
W075°12.123'

Alice's Way

This access has a large dirt and grass pull-off that can hold several cars and a grass path that leads to the river. A street sign (Alice's Way)—strangely out of place without an identifiable street nearby—stands in the center of the pull-off (Alice's Way is actually the dirt and grass road leading upriver through the trees). The access is located on private land, but the footpath to the river is not posted (although it could be closed to the public at any time). It is possible to launch or retrieve canoes and pontoon boats here, but I would ask permission first. Drift boats cannot be launched or retrieved here.

The footpath leads to Tyler's Eddy—a classic pool with a productive riffle at its head that braids into slower water before becoming flat and slow moving. The river immediately above the eddy is often shallow and sometimes unproductive, but it can hold a good population of rainbows in the spring, during average to high river flows. The eddy itself maintains a good trout population during the spring and fall, but its depth can make fishing without a boat difficult. Tar Hollow Brook flows into the eddy from the access side of the river in the pool's upper half.

Getting There

From New York Route 17 east, Fishs Eddy exit 89:
1. Turn left at the bottom of the exit ramp.
2. Travel 1.4 miles. The pull-off and footpath are on your left.

From New York Route 17 west, Fishs Eddy exit 89:
1. Turn right at the bottom of the exit ramp.
2. Travel 2.1 miles. The pull-off and footpath are on your left.

Parking Area GPS Coordinates

N41°58.457'
W075°12.633'

Tyler's Eddy is deep near its junction with Tar Hollow Brook, limiting wading opportunities to nearshore areas.

Unnamed Pull-off #3

This access has a small dirt pull-off, large enough for a couple of cars, and a footpath leading to the river. The footpath leads down a steep, brush-choked bank before it finally meets the river near the tail of a medium-sized pool. This pull-off basically provides same river access as the much more angler-friendly access at Cadosia Creek. Boats cannot be launched or retrieved here.

Getting There

From New York Route 17 east:
1. Take Hancock exit 87.
2. Turn left at the exit ramp stop sign.
3. Make an immediate right turn onto the unnamed road (after the Getty gas station and before the Napa automotive store).
4. The road curves to the left before reaching another stop sign.
5. Go straight to the Hancock signal light.
6. Go straight, traveling east out of Hancock, onto Route 286.
7. Travel 1.1 miles from the Route 97 Bridge and turn right, toward the New York Route 17 east on-ramp.
8. Turn right onto Green Flats Road, immediately before the Route 17 on-ramp.
9. Travel .2 mile. The pull-off is on your right.

The Cadosia boat launch is little more than a rutted dirt and gravel path leading to the river. Despite its poor physical condition, it is one of the only drift boat–accessible access areas in the Lower East. Here, Delaware River guide Tim Olyphant begins a trip.

From New York Route 17 west:
1. Take Hancock exit 87.
2. Turn left at the exit ramp stop sign.
3. Travel .1 mile and turn left, toward the New York Route 17 east on-ramp.
4. Follow steps 8 and 9 above.

Parking Area GPS Coordinates

N41°57.962'
W075°15.322'

Cadosia

This access area has a medium-sized parking area and a rutted dirt boat launch. Inexperienced drift boat operators often find the Cadosia boat launch difficult to use and probably should not try to launch or retrieve their boats without a four-wheel drive vehicle. The Cadosia boat launch, in spite of its poor physical state, remains an important access due to the lack of Lower East Branch drift boat launches.

The launch can be difficult to find when floating the river after dark. The river turns sharply to the left upriver from the launch and then becomes shallow and full of boulders. The boulders are hard to see after dark, and vegetation growing on the shore can obscure the entrance to the boat launch. I advise first-time Cadosia boat launch users to make sure they arrive well before dark until they become familiar enough with the area to find the launch and avoid the boulders.

Upriver

Trout love to hold in the riffled slots and mini-pools of the shallow, boulder-strewn Cadosia Riffle near the boat launch. These areas provide excellent structure for nymphing or prospecting with a dry fly. The tail of a medium-sized pool ends at the head of the Cadosia Riffle, just above the boat launch. The tail also has several boulders that are likely places to find rising fish. Most of the pool's trout are in the center, near the left shore, or in the riffle at its head.

Downriver

Cadosia Creek merges with the Lower East at the Cadosia Riffle, slightly downriver from the boat launch. The Cadosia Riffle flows into a deep, swift bottleneck on the river's left side. It eventually braids into a long bathtub-shaped pool that gets very deep a short distance from both banks. The pool flattens and remains deep on the left side throughout its length. The entire pool is good dry-fly water.

There are few obstructions to floating the Lower East, but the Cadosia Riffle's boulder field can be tricky.

Getting There

From New York Route 17 east:
1. Take Hancock exit 87.
2. Turn left at the exit ramp stop sign.
3. Make an immediate right turn onto the unnamed road (after the Getty gas station and before the Napa automotive store).
4. The road curves to the left before reaching another stop sign.
5. Go straight to the Hancock signal light.
6. Go straight, traveling east out of Hancock, onto Route 286.
7. Travel 1.1 miles from the Route 97 Bridge and turn right, toward the Route 17 east on-ramp.
8. Turn right at the break in the guardrail to reach the parking area.

From New York Route 17 west:
1. Take Hancock exit 87.
2. Turn left at the exit ramp stop sign.
3. Travel .1 mile and turn left, toward the Route 17 east on-ramp.
4. Turn right at the break in the guardrail to reach the parking area.

Parking Area GPS Coordinates

N41°57.839'
W075°15.706'

River GPS Coordinates

N41°57.808'
W075°15.723'

Hancock Fireman's Park

Fireman's Park in Hancock is a popular place to launch boats, usually for Upper Main Stem float trips, when low West Branch flows preclude anglers from using the Shehawken launch. This access is privately owned by the Hancock Fire Department, and it is occasionally closed for outdoor events or when the firemen are practicing. Never block or interfere in any way with the firemen's equipment or drive over a fire hose. Similar past incidents have nearly caused the closure of the access. Drive slowly through the access. It's adjacent to a ball field that is often used by young children.

The boat launch is an unimproved dirt and gravel road that leads to the river, at the left corner of the field. Anglers must park on the grass at the edge of the field to use this access. Four-wheel drive vehicles, though not necessary, are a good idea for launching or retrieving drift boats. The shore is sandy and full of loose gravel, which makes traction a problem at times.

Upriver

The top of the Fireman's Field Pool lies slightly upriver from the boat launch. These areas maintain a good trout population—both wild and stocked—in the spring and fall. The Fireman's Park access is occasionally used by the New York State DEC to stock trout. The riffle and the shallow glide flowing into the head of the pool also hold trout.

The boat launch at Hancock's Fireman's Park provides access to the Lower East Branch's final pool before it joins with the West Branch to form the Main Stem.

Downriver

The end of the Lower East Branch is basically one large pool and a shallow riffle below its tail. The Lower East's last pool is deep in the center and near the right shore, where rising trout can often be found in the spring and fall. The pool's depth makes wading difficult, especially during high-flow periods. You can only cross at the tail, where the West Branch flows in from the right to form the Main Stem.

Getting There

From Hancock's Route 97 Bridge:
1. Cross the Route 97 Bridge, heading south, and make an immediate right turn onto Maple Street.
2. Cross the railroad tracks and merge straight onto Park Street.
3. The parking area is straight ahead.

Parking Area GPS Coordinates

N41°57.028'
W075°16.893'

River GPS Coordinates

N41°57.021'
W075°16.893'

CHAPTER 4

Main Stem

The Main Stem's grand stature probably repels more new anglers than it attracts. Some sections are very big, such as the 2.3-mile section near Lordville, New York, which is 360 feet wide (McBride 2002). Few inexperienced anglers explore the Main Stem, especially its middle and lower sections below Pennsylvania's Buckingham access, without encouragement from someone else, such as a guide or a knowledgeable friend. In addition to its intimidating size, the river is bypassed because it hasn't been as highly publicized as the other branches, it's difficult to access, and it is subject to unreliable fishing conditions.

The Main Stem seldom receives the accolades that so many anglers and writers lavish on the West Branch or even the less popular East Branch. Parts

The view from the New York State Route 97 Bridge over Basket Brook. A total of 71.35 miles of Route 97, from Hancock to Port Jervis, has been designated the Upper Delaware Scenic Byway.

of the river host as few fishermen each year as the often neglected bottom half of the Lower East Branch. There are times when low-flow conditions in the Lower East and West Branches force boating anglers onto the Main Stem, but few people would prefer to be fishing the "big river." However, fishing the Main Stem isn't considered a last resort by everyone.

One of the things that surprised me most about the Upper Delaware fishery when I first moved nearby is the polarization of the river's anglers. Some anglers and even some fishing guides align themselves with just a single river branch. If one angler says that he had a lousy day on the Main Stem, another might quietly mutter, "What did you expect? He's a West Branch guy." The Main Stem in particular seems to inspire fierce loyalty from its most dedicated anglers, who tend to believe that there are two kinds of Upper Delaware fly fishers: those who fish the Main Stem and all the rest. I think this loyalty comes from a feeling of almost disdain for the East and West Branches and their popularity, as well as an unyielding dedication to the amazing and sometimes difficult to catch Main Stem rainbow trout. Anglers who frequently fish the Main Stem earn every fish they bring to their nets—perhaps even more so than West and East Branch fishermen. This is true not because the trout in those rivers are easier to catch but because the river conditions there are more stable, greatly aiding their ability to sustain larger trout populations. I must admit that I've been smitten by the Main Stem, even though I'm still a big fan of the West and East Braches. But I would rather fish the Main Stem than any other Upper Delaware branch.

The Main Stem's upper two-thirds, from Hancock to Long Eddy, New York, is considered low gradient, falling 4.8 feet per mile. It is composed of 15 to 20 percent riffles and 80 to 85 percent pools (McBride 2002). It drops a little quicker below Long Eddy, creating longer riffles and more of them. The river's entire 27-mile stretch from Hancock to Callicoon, New York, is probably the most unique river branch in the Upper Delaware system.

The river lies within a national park, yet its corridor possesses little public land—as much as 85 percent of the Main Stem corridor is privately owned property. There are only 13 public-access areas for the entire river, and three of them are privately owned campgrounds where anglers must pay a fee. The river is border water between New York and Pennsylvania, so the public can freely traverse its banks within the high-water mark. The problem for wading anglers is the lack of public-access points amidst all the private property—and their difficulties do not end when they get to the river. The Main Stem is seldom easy to wade because of the length and width of its numerous slow-moving pools. Many of them are too deep to be crossed anywhere other than at their heads or tails, even during the river's lowest flows. But wading anglers still fish the river, mostly because of its solitude, wild trout, and scenery. The physical nature of the Main Stem also makes it popular with boating anglers, especially those who use drift boats.

The wooded mountains that line the Main Stem's valley are beautiful—emerald green in the late spring and summer and brilliantly painted in the fall. The valley remains wild and sparsely populated, mostly with seasonal homes, in spite of being private property. The dominant reason that the river valley has remained largely undeveloped is that it's part of the National Park Service's National Wild and Scenic Rivers System.

Despite the Main Stem's federal protection, it is the most troubled branch in the Upper Delaware system because of its distance from both the Cannonsville and Pepacton Reservoirs and their cold bottom releases. River temperatures below Buckingham, and occasionally even above it, can exceed 80 degrees in the summer if insufficient releases are coming from Cannonsville. Pepacton is too far from the Main Stem to cool it.

The Main Stem has severely languished under the current flow-based management plan, called Revision 7, which has elevated the water temperature and reduced the number of fishable days since its enactment in 2002. The river's width doesn't allow the tree-lined banks to shade it, and the relentless summer sun often burns the edges of its rocky riffles a bone white during the summer months. Main Stem conditions were so poor during the summer of 2005 that the New York State DEC publicly abandoned the river, claiming that it didn't posses enough water in its thermal banks to protect the fishery (for information about thermal banks, see chapter 8). The river is one of the most mismanaged wild trout fisheries in the country, yet it survives.

The Main Stem survives as a trout fishery only because of the tenaciousness of its amazingly resilient wild trout. Like those living in the Lower East Branch, Main Stem trout are highly migratory. And the Main's Junction Pool

Evening spinner falls on the Main Stem can be prolific. They often provide anglers with the best opportunity of the day to catch fish.

holds hundreds of them during periods of high water temperatures. Many flee the warmer middle and lower sections of the Main to find refuge in and just below the cooler West Branch.

Historically, the river has been dominated by rainbow trout, but brown trout populations have greatly increased since 2002. Rainbows used to out-number brown trout five to one in the Main's upper section, but my records show that I actually caught more browns than rainbows in the Upper Main Stem during the 2005 and 2006 fishing seasons. Rainbows continue to domi-nate the Main's middle and lower sections. No one really knows why the browns are so plentiful in the upper river, but nearly all seasoned Main Stem fishermen agree that the composition of the upper river's trout population has changed. Brook trout are rare in the Main Stem, but anglers occasionally catch them. The largest Main Stem brook trout that I've seen was caught in 1999 by a spin fisherman. The fish lying dead at the bottom of a large, red cooler was every bit of 18 inches long.

Main Stem Floats, Distances, and Durations

Float	River Miles	Road Miles	Time*
Balls Eddy to Stockport	7.5	6.7	3 hours
Shehawken to Stockport	3	2.7	1.25 hours
Balls Eddy to Buckingham	10.8	10	4.5 hours
Shehawken to Buckingham	6.3	6	2.5 hours
Junction Pool (Bard Parker) to Buckingham	5.3	9.3	2 hours
Buckingham to Lordville Bridge	3.5	4.1	1 hour
Buckingham to Long Eddy	9.6	16.7	4 hours
Lordville Bridge to Long Eddy	6.1	12.6	2.5 hours
Long Eddy to Red Barn Campground	5.1	4	2 hours
Long Eddy to Tower Road	10.4	8.2	4.5 hours
Red Barn Campground to Tower Road	5	3.9	2 hours
Tower Road to the PA Access at Callicoon	2.3	1.3	1 hour

Times are based on average float time during average water levels.

The Main Stem can be a moody fishery. On some days, the trout decide to stay on the bottom of the river's long riffles and deep pools and never rise. Nymphing and streamer fishing can also be difficult. It's not easy to catch trout in riffles so big that it sometimes feels like you're fishing for a needle in a haystack. And Main Stem rainbows rarely eat streamers, although the river's brown trout will. But the relatively small number of browns, particularly in the middle and lower sections, ensures that streamer fishermen have to be patient and persistent.

The Main's difficult fishing conditions could leave an inexperienced angler with the impression that the river holds very few trout and that it isn't in the same league with the West or East Branch. But comparing the West or East Branch to the Main Stem is like comparing whiskey to a single-malt scotch. The Main is an acquired taste, born of success. I've fished the Main a few times when it appeared to be devoid of life—when my dries, nymphs, and streamers were completely disregarded by uninterested trout. But I've

Description

Boating anglers can shorten their Upper Main Stem trips by ending at Stockport. Since most boaters exit the river at Buckingham, those who exit at Stockport usually find more open water because other boats have pushed downriver.

A long, all-day float (from Balls Eddy) to a medium-length trip (from Shehawken) and the most common Upper Main Stem float trip—often preferred by Main Stem guides. Either float provides access to the entire Upper Main Stem.

A good half- to all-day float trip for canoes or pontoon boats that provides access to the entire Upper Main Stem. There is no drift boat ramp at Junction Pool.

A short float trip in the Middle Main Stem limited to canoe and pontoon boaters—the Lordville Bridge does not have a drift boat ramp.

A long, all-day float and the only option for drift boat anglers who want to float the Middle Main Stem. It's the most common float for Middle Main Stem guides.

A half- to all-day float trip in the Middle Main Stem for canoe and pontoon boaters. The Lordville Bridge does not have a drift boat ramp.

A short float trip that includes the upper half of the Lower Main Stem. Anglers must have prior permission and pay a seasonal fee to exit the river at Red Barn Campground.

The longest float in the Main Stem. It provides access to the entire Lower Main Stem section and is the most popular for Lower Main Stem guides.

A half-day float that provides access to the bottom half of the Lower Main Stem. Anglers must have prior permission and pay a seasonal fee to launch their boats from Red Barn Campground.

A short float with few areas of trout-holding water. The riffles surrounding the islands are good places to search for trout in the spring.

Streamer fishing in the Main Stem isn't as productive as it is in the Upper East or West Branch, but there are exceptions, such as this 20-inch Main Stem brown.

also seen days when amazingly heavy hatches were eagerly consumed by large pods of trout, days when the fish aggressively ate my stonefly nymphs, and days when I've caught some of my largest Upper Delaware trout on streamers. These days would make any angler believe that the Main is one of the best trout fisheries in the country.

The Main probably holds the smallest trout population of all the Upper Delaware branches, but it still holds plenty of trout. The vast difference between slow days on the Main Stem and days when the fishing is incredible is one of the reasons that the Main receives less angler attention than the other branches do. If you are lucky enough to hit the Main at its best during your first trip to the river, you'll probably be hooked for life. But if you've fished the Main several times and found only lousy, unproductive fishing, you probably won't give it another chance. And that's a mistake. There is a reason why the Main Stem's anglers are so adamant about the river's greatness: they have seen it for themselves.

Main Stem Flows*

Water Level (cfs)	Wading	Drift Boats	Pontoon Boats and Canoes
<1,000	Excellent—the Main is very low and as wadable as it gets; however, large pools limit wading.	Not advised to fair—the river is floatable until it drops below 600 cfs; those unfamiliar with the river will have extensive dragging at flows below 700 cfs	Excellent at flows above 500 cfs—easy to anchor; use the boat as transportation to more remote wading spots
1,000–2,000	Very good—50% of the river remains wadable	Fair to good—many exposed rocks; some dragging may be necessary at riffles, around islands, and at the tails of pools	Excellent—no dragging is necessary
2,000–3,000	Good—less than 50% of the river is wadable	Good to very good— fewer exposed rocks	Very good—nice level for pontoon boats and canoes
3,000–4,000	Fair—wading is limited to shallow areas near shore and the tails of some pools	Very good to excellent— the best all-around fishing level for drift boat anglers	Very good to good—most fishing is from the boat
4,000–5,000	Poor—wading is not advised if flows exceed 4,000 cfs	Excellent to very good— drift boats are the best option at this and all higher levels	Good to fair—anchoring becomes difficult in faster water
5,000–6,000	Not advised	Very good to good— anchoring in faster water becomes difficult at higher flows	Fair to poor—most of the fishing will be from the boat; for experienced boaters only
6,000–7,000	Not advised	Good—most of the fish will be holding near the shore and in the center and tails of pools	Poor—all fishing will be from the boat; using a drift boat is advised
7,000–8,000	Not advised	Good to fair—only experienced boaters should float at this and higher levels	Poor to not advised— anchoring can be dangerous and should not be attempted in faster water; for expert boaters only
>8,000	Not advised—wading is dangerous	Fair to not advised— for expert boaters only; anchoring in fast water can be dangerous	Not advised

Upper Main Stem flows calculated by adding the East Branch's Fishs Eddy gauge and the West Branch's Hale Eddy gauge. Lower Main Stem flows calculated using the Callicoon gauge.

Main Stem Fishing Regulations

River Section	Fishing Season	Harvesting Length	Daily Limit
From Junction Pool outside of Hancock, NY, south to Pennsylvania I-84	8:00 a.m. on the first Saturday after April 11–September 30	14 inches	1 trout
	October 1 to 8:00 a.m. on the first Saturday after April 11	Catch-and-release; artificial lures only	No harvest
All streams and tributaries that flow into the Delaware River in Delaware County downriver of Hancock, NY	NY Regulations: 8:00 a.m. on the first Saturday after April 11–September 30	Any size	5 trout
	PA Regulations: 8:00 a.m. on the first Saturday after April 15–September 4	7 inches	5 trout

Upper Main Stem: Junction Pool to Buckingham

The Upper Main is the shortest Main Stem section, with only 5.3 of the 27-mile trout zone from Hancock to Callicoon. It's also the river's most popular section, for three reasons. First, it's the most wader-friendly section. The Upper Main Stem has three public-access areas, which may seem limited until you consider the length of the section. The three access areas are spaced reasonably well at the beginning, middle, and end of the section. They allow wading anglers to reach most of the river within a reasonable walking distance. The Upper Main also has shorter pools that are easier for wading anglers to fish. Waders may not be able to reach all the trout in the Upper Main's pools, but they can reach even fewer fish in the larger and more isolated sections of the Middle and Lower Main Stem.

The second reason for the Upper Main's popularity is its relatively high trout population compared with the lower sections. The upper section is the closest to the Cannonsville Reservoir, and therefore the coldest. Trout from the Middle and Lower Main Stem often seek refuge in the Upper Main in late spring and summer due to its colder water temperatures. The Upper Main is susceptible to high temperatures when little water is released from Cannonsville in the summer, but the water gets even warmer by the time it reaches the Middle and Lower Main Stem.

Good float trips are the third reason for the Upper Main Stem's popularity. One of the Upper Delaware's most popular all-day float trips—and my favorite when I'm guiding—is from the Lower West Branch's Balls Eddy access to the Upper Main Stem's Buckingham boat launch. This long trip is popular because anglers can experience two rivers in one outing. It can be productive in the spring when either the Lower West Branch or the Main Stem is fishing particularly well. If the Lower West Branch is on fire, I'll spend most of the day fishing there and row quickly through the Upper Main at the

The Upper Main Stem
(app. 5.3 river miles)

N
W · E
S

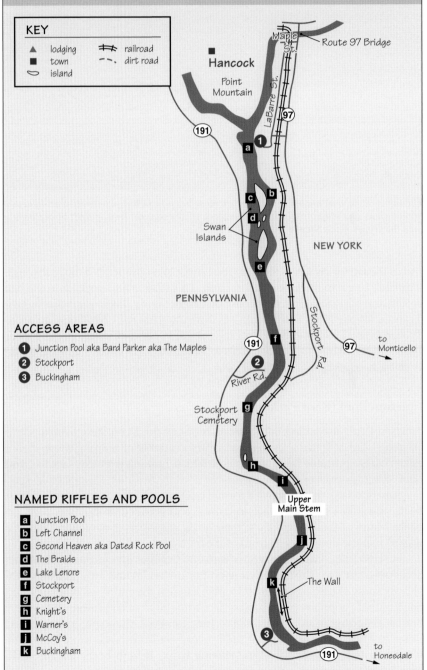

KEY

▲ lodging   ╪╪ railroad
■ town   ⌐⌐ dirt road
～ island

Maple St.
Route 97 Bridge

■ Hancock

Point Mountain

LaBarre St.

97

191

a ❶

c b

Swan Islands

d

NEW YORK

e

PENNSYLVANIA

Stockport Rd.

191 f ❷

97 to Monticello

River Rd.

Stockport Cemetery g

h

i

Upper Main Stem

j

The Wall

k

❸

to Honesdale

191

ACCESS AREAS

❶ Junction Pool aka Bard Parker aka The Maples
❷ Stockport
❸ Buckingham

NAMED RIFFLES AND POOLS

a Junction Pool
b Left Channel
c Second Heaven aka Dated Rock Pool
d The Braids
e Lake Lenore
f Stockport
g Cemetery
h Knight's
i Warner's
j McCoy's
k Buckingham

The upper section of the Main Stem is the most heavily fished, due to its well-spaced access areas and close proximity to Cannonsville Reservoir. Here, a drift boat floats into the Upper Main Stem's Knight's Riffle.

end of the trip. If fishing is slow on the Lower West Branch, I'll move through it quickly to get to the Upper Main Stem. This float is also popular in the late spring and early summer, especially on bright sunny days, when productive daytime Upper Main Stem fishing is difficult. This float trip helps alleviate that problem: I can spend most of the brightest part of the day in the Lower West and move into the Upper Main when the shadows start to form and the evening hatches or spinner falls begin.

Junction Pool (Bard Parker)

Junction Pool, also called Bard Parker, is one of the Main Stem's most popular access areas. It has a large parking area capable of holding more than a dozen cars, a portable toilet, and picnic tables, making it a nice place to bring nonfishing spouses or friends.

Junction Pool doesn't have a formal boat launch capable of handling drift boats, but it is a popular place to launch and retrieve canoes and pontoon boats. Many of these anglers use their boats not for river navigation but as a way to fish the deep pool in front of the access.

A scum line comprising white foam and bubbles is ever-present on Junction Pool's surface. The fish feeding on the surface in and around these bubbles are some of the most difficult trout to catch in the entire system. The scum line's path through the pool changes according to river conditions. If the West Branch is adding most of the water to Junction Pool, the scum line is pushed closer to the access area bank. If the Lower East Branch has more water, the scum line will be near the Pennsylvania bank. If both branches are fairly equal, the scum line will be in the center of the pool. The location of the scum line determines which side of the river provides the best dry-fly fishing opportunities. The scum line continues down the entire length of the pool and is important to both upriver and downriver fishing. Most anglers vie for a wadable spot near the scum line and stand, side by side, on both sides of the pool. These crowded conditions are compounded by all types of watercraft that attempt to float through this maze of people or to procure their own spots at the scum line.

Upriver

An anglers' path leads from the parking area and meets the river in the middle of Junction Pool. It continues along the right bank to the junction of the East and West Branches at the head of the pool.

Junction Pool is deep, full of trout, and an excellent place to fish a hatch. The pool is too deep to wade in front of the parking area, so most anglers walk up- or downriver. Junction Pool has a long stretch of productive braided water near its head, upriver from the parking area. The scum line begins just below this braided water, where the pool flattens. It's fairly wadable here, and you can cross the river at the beginning of the flat water and at several spots along the braided water during average to low-flow conditions. Trout often rise in this area, but the subtle nature of their rise forms, combined with sun glare on the river's braided surface, can make them difficult to detect. A riffle at the top of the braided water holds a lot of trout, especially in the deep slot at the end of the West Branch.

Downriver

Anglers trying to avoid the crowds at Junction Pool often wade downriver from the access to the tail, about 50 yards downstream. The tail is much easier to wade than the middle of the pool, and it also holds a lot of trout. The first of the two Swan Islands begins below the tail. Trout can be found on both sides of the island in the spring and fall, but they usually vacate the left channel during the summer months. The East and West Branch waters do not completely mix until they flow below the Stockport access area. The island's left channel is composed predominantly of East Branch water, which is significantly warmer in the summer than the West Branch water in the island's right channel. A large riffle and deep pool form at the top of the island's right channel—the Second Heaven Riffle and Pool. Second Heaven is a long stretch of water that's wadable at its head and downriver for about a quarter of the pool. The pool becomes deep in its lower three-quarters and is difficult to wade until you get near the tail.

Getting There

The direct route is quicker, but Bard Parker Road was barricaded at the time of this writing, inhibiting anglers from reaching the access. The road may reopen in the future, making the alternative route unnecessary.

The Second Heaven Pool is a popular destination for anglers accessing the Upper Main Stem at Junction Pool (aka Bard Parker). The middle and tail of the Second Heaven Pool are dotted with anglers and watercrafts.

Direct route from Hancock's Route 97 Bridge:
1. Cross the Route 97 Bridge (heading south) and travel for 1 mile.
2. Turn right onto Bard Parker Road.
3. Travel straight, over the railroad tracks, to the stop sign, and turn left.
4. Travel .2 mile and merge onto the gravel road. A small white sign on the road's right side indicates the gravel road to the Junction Pool access. The road dead-ends at the parking area.

Alternative route from Hancock's Route 97 Bridge:
1. Cross the Route 97 Bridge (heading south) and make an immediate right turn onto Maple Street.
2. Cross the railroad tracks, and make an immediate left turn onto LaBarre Street.
3. Travel .8 mile to the stop sign. Go straight.
4. Follow step 4 above.

Parking Area GPS Coordinates
N41°56.097'
W075°16.809'

River GPS Coordinates
N41°56.110'
W075°16.647'

Stockport

The township access at Stockport has no formal parking area. Anglers must park in a large dirt pull-off on the river side of Route 191. A mailbox belonging to an adjacent landowner is positioned near the middle of the pull-off, and inconsiderate anglers have blocked it more than once. They have also trespassed on the landowner's private property to reach the river, causing some bad blood.

The only public land, other than the pull-off, is the township road. The land surrounding the road is all posted. Anglers who want to wade from this access must park their vehicles at the Route 191 pull-off and walk down the township road to the river. Never cut through the landowner's yard or the forest: you'll be trespassing.

There is no formal boat launch at the Stockport access, and no drift boat turnaround. The launch ramp is a steep, rutted dirt road, which makes a four-wheel drive vehicle a good idea. The easiest way to launch or retrieve a boat at this access is to drive onto the riverbank, reverse along the river, pull forward up the road, and reverse again until your trailer wheels are in the river. Launching a boat this way may be impossible during high river flows, so I don't use this boat access when the river is running high.

Chris Pappas pleads for heavenly assistance while fishing the Braids, a group of small grassy islands between the first and second Swan Islands. This is a productive area for fishing nymphs and dries. The privately owned Shad Club is visible in the bottom right corner.

The Stockport launch is one of the most difficult to find after dark. Start looking for it after you pass through the long, flat Lake Lenore Pool into the head of the Stockport Riffle. Stay on the right after you enter the riffle. The riffle eventually bends to the right, and you'll see an in-river boulder on your right side, just before the launch.

Upriver

The Stockport boat launch meets the river in the lower half of the Stockport Riffle. Two medium-sized braided mini-pools (considered part of the Stockport Riffle), each with its own short riffle, are within a brief walk from the boat launch. These areas have good depth and hold trout throughout. Most of the fish tend to hold in the center of the river, near a series of large boulders. If you continue walking upriver from these mini-pools, you'll come to the tail of Lake Lenore. The tail is productive water and can be waded during average to low flows. If you continue upriver from the pool's tail, you'll reach the flat, pondlike center of Lake Lenore. Its cruising trout can be difficult to catch. Lake Lenore is deep on its left side and cannot be waded, but many of its trout feed on this side, and some of them are reachable from the shore.

Downriver

The lower half of the Stockport Riffle lies downriver from the boat launch. The riffle is deep and contains several large rocks, which create excellent trout habitat. The Stockport Riffle flows into the Stockport Pool approximately 100 yards below the boat launch. The pool is deepest near its left bank, and most of its surface-feeding trout can be found from the pool's middle to the left side. These fish can be difficult for wading anglers to reach due to the pool's depth. The remains of an old eel weir lie below the tail of the Stockport Riffle. The riffle that forms on the downriver side of the weir is an excellent place to nymph or to search for rising trout.

Getting There

From Pennsylvania's Route 191 Bridge (Hancock, New York):
1. Cross the Route 191 Bridge, heading south into Pennsylvania.
2. Travel 3.6 miles to the large pull-off on the left side of Route 191 south. If you reach the Stockport Cemetery on Route 191 south, you've gone too far.

Pull-off GPS Coordinates
N41°54.410'
W075°16.234'

River GPS Coordinates
N41°54.525'
W075°16.137'

Buckingham

The Buckingham access has ample parking, a portable toilet, a large drift boat turnaround, and a well-maintained concrete boat launch. It is the most heavily used boat access in the Upper Main Stem.

It's probably a good idea to fish downriver rather than upriver from the Buckingham boat launch any evening during the river's crowded season. Every boater who is exiting the river at Buckingham will do so upriver from where you are fishing, and anyone who is floating below the boat launch will be long gone well before the evening rise.

The Buckingham boat launch is one of the easiest Upper Delaware access areas to find from the river. You'll know that you're getting close to the launch when you see the large stone wall beneath the railroad tracks on the river's left side. The stone wall signifies the top of the Buckingham Riffle and Pool. The boat launch is approximately 200 yards downriver on the right bank, near the tail of the Buckingham Pool. You'll see a big hill, with a fluorescent orange post on top of it, immediately before you reach the boat launch. A gravel road sweeps down from the top of the hill to the drift boat turnaround and, ultimately, the boat ramp.

Upriver

The tail of the Buckingham Pool, directly in front of the boat launch, can be waded during average to low flows. The tail has a deep slot in the center, where most of the fish feed. The pool gets deeper and more difficult to wade the farther you travel upriver. Some of the pool's trout can be reached from the left bank (the same side as the boat launch), but the majority tend to hold in the pool's center and near the right bank. The Buckingham Riffle, lying at

The Pennsylvania Fish and Boat Commission access at Buckingham is the most heavily used Upper Main Stem boat launch.

the top of the pool, is deep enough to hold trout but shallow enough to wade in many spots.

Downriver

The Shangri-La (aka Paddlestop) Riffle holds a lot of trout and can be effectively fished from either side of the river. You can cross the riffle near its head during average to low-flow conditions. The Shangri-La Pool, which is fed by the riffle, is another good spot to find rising trout. The only problem with the pool is that it's deep and long, curtailing any further downriver wading.

Getting There

From Pennsylvania's Route 191 Bridge (Hancock, New York):
1. Cross the Route 191 Bridge, heading south into Pennsylvania.
2. Travel 7 miles.
3. Turn left onto the dirt road at the brown Pennsylvania Fish and Boat Commission access sign.
4. The parking area is straight ahead.

Parking Area GPS Coordinates

N41°52.029′
W075°15.969′

River GPS Coordinates

N41°52.028′
W075°15.828′

Middle Main Stem: Buckingham to Long Eddy

The Main Stem's middle section glides slowly for approximately 9.6 miles from Pennsylvania's Buckingham boat launch to New York's Long Eddy boat launch. It is one of the most beautiful sections of the entire Upper Delaware system. Two high waterfalls, pouring from the mountains above the river, plummet to the valley floor during spring runoff. There are few homes in the valley. The mountains that surround the Middle Main Stem are full of rattlesnakes, whitetail deer, black bears, turkeys, and ruffed grouse. The river feels wilder and more isolated because it bends and turns away from New York Route 97 and Pennsylvania Route 191—roads that closely parallel the Main Stem's upper section.

The Middle Main Stem has only three access areas, making it hard to fish without a boat. The most heavily used access by wade fishermen is the Bouchouxville footpath, but even Bouchouxville is seldom too crowded to find a spot to fish. Wading through this section is difficult because of its large, slow-moving pools, some of which are too long and wide to fish around them.

Springtime in the Middle Main Stem can provide some terrific fly-fishing opportunities, especially in its riffles and runs. The trout that live in these

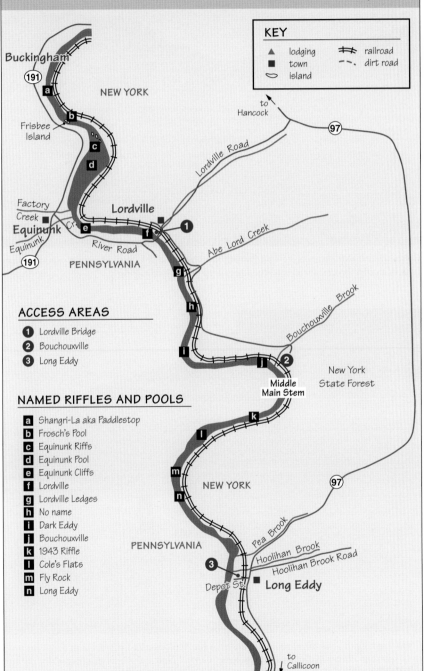

The Middle Main Stem
(app. 9.6 river miles)

KEY

▲ lodging   ╫ railroad
■ town   ⌐⌐ dirt road
⌒ island

Buckingham
(191)
a
NEW YORK
b
Frisbee
Island
c
d
to
Hancock
(97)
Lordville Road
Factory
Creek
Equinunk
Lordville
Cr.
e
f
1
191
Equinunk
River Road
Abe Lord Creek
PENNSYLVANIA
g
h
Bouchouxville Brook
i
j
2
New York
State Forest
Middle
Main Stem
k
l
m
n
NEW YORK
(97)
PENNSYLVANIA
Pea Brook
Hoolihan Brook
3
Hoolihan Brook Road
Depot St.
Long Eddy
to
Callicoon

ACCESS AREAS

1 Lordville Bridge
2 Bouchouxville
3 Long Eddy

NAMED RIFFLES AND POOLS

a Shangri-La aka Paddlestop
b Frosch's Pool
c Equinunk Riffs
d Equinunk Pool
e Equinunk Cliffs
f Lordville
g Lordville Ledges
h No name
i Dark Eddy
j Bouchouxville
k 1943 Riffle
l Cole's Flats
m Fly Rock
n Long Eddy

Boats are vital for accessing and fishing the Middle and Lower Main Stem due to the lack of public access areas and the long, deep pools and riffles.

Blind-casting drys is often more effective in the Middle and Lower Main Stem than it is in sections closer to the reservoirs. Ron "Curly" Huber is blind-casting a dry fly in a riffle above Dark Eddy.

areas are less selective and leader-shy than their upriver relatives. Blind-casting dry-fly patterns can be effective in the Middle Main Stem's riffles, because the trout here see fewer fly patterns than those found in other river sections. However, the many trout that live in the Middle Main Stem's pools are not as easy to catch. Most trout-fishing opportunities are over by the end of June because the river gets too warm, but good fishing usually returns in the fall as the river cools. The Middle Main Stem's summer water temperatures are better suited to smallmouth bass, but it still maintains some of its trout population throughout the year. Trout that do not migrate upriver find thermal refuge in this section's many large underground springs.

The Middle Main Stem's aquatic insect hatches are some of the heaviest in the entire Upper Delaware system and include some predominantly warm-water species such as the whitefly. The whiteflies are an amazingly prolific hatch, but they tend to emerge in river sections that are too warm to hold trout. In years when a lot of water is being released from Cannonsville or when natural weather patterns create a colder than average summer, the Middle Main Stem's trout may remain in their springtime holding areas. Under these conditions, the whitefly hatch provides one of the best summer fly-fishing opportunities in the system.

Lordville Bridge

This access has a small parking area beneath the Lordville Bridge and an anglers' footpath to the river. Large rocks block the access, but anglers who don't mind carrying their canoes and pontoon boats over these rocks can launch or retrieve their watercraft.

Upriver

The anglers' footpath meets the river underneath the Lordville Bridge. The river is deep under the bridge, and wading is impossible. Wading anglers should bypass this section to fish the Lordville Riffle above the bridge. The riffle is long and deep but wadable in some sections, especially near its head. Trout hold throughout the riffle.

Downriver

The deep Lordville Bridge Pool continues downriver, under the bridge, and past the access area. The pool's depth makes it difficult to wade, but sometimes you can find reachable rising fish near the left bank beneath the overhanging trees.

Getting There

From Hancock's Route 97 Bridge:
1. Cross the Route 97 Bridge, heading south out of Hancock, and travel 4.8 miles.
2. Turn right onto Lordville Road.
3. Travel 3 miles and turn left into Lordville.

The view beneath the Lordville Bridge shows the Lordville Pool, which is too deep to wade, and the more wader-friendly Lordville Riffle.

4. Veer to the right and cross the railroad tracks (toward the bridge).
5. The access is down the dirt road to the right, adjacent to the Lordville Bridge.

Parking Area and River GPS Coordinates

N41°52.110'
W075°12.832'

Bouchouxville

The Bouchouxville (pronounced Bushy-ville) access is a large New York State Forest parking area with an anglers' footpath leading to the river. The footpath is located on private property, and the landowner has placed a large green metal box containing a sign-in sheet at the trailhead. The landowner requests that all anglers using the footpath sign in, recording their name, address, and time they enter or exit the river. The landowner also requests that no boats of any kind be launched or retrieved from this access.

Upriver

The anglers' footpath leads up and over the railroad tracks before meeting the river beside Bouchouxville Brook. A deep braided pool and medium-sized riffle lie upriver from the footpath. These areas are the most common destinations for anglers. The tail of Dark Eddy flows into the top of this section, but its depth and distance from the access limit further upriver wading.

Downriver

A wall of gravel, formed by the mouth of Bouchouxville Brook, narrows the river's channel into a deep, swift-flowing chute called the Bouchouxville Riffle downriver from the anglers' footpath. The chute quickly braids into the deep Bouchouxville Pool. Some of the pool's trout hold in the middle, but many of them prefer to feed near the right bank. You can cross the river near the top of the riffle, below Dark Eddy's tail, to reach the fish on the right bank, but crossing should be attempted only during low-flow periods. The Bouchouxville Pool flattens out below its braided head and becomes pondlike. This part of the pool is home to a lot of chubs, but large browns also cruise through it occasionally.

Getting There

From Hancock's Route 97 Bridge:
1. Cross the Route 97 Bridge, heading south out of Hancock, and travel 4.8 miles.
2. Turn right onto Lordville Road.
3. Travel 3 miles and turn left into Lordville.

Railroad tracks closely parallel the river at Bouchouxville, but roads do not. Anglers must access this area through a privately owned footpath.

4. Do not cross the railroad tracks or the Lordville Bridge.
5. Continue straight onto Bouchouxville Road for 2.8 miles.
6. Cross Bouchouxville Brook and turn right into the DEC State Forest parking lot.
7. Access is straight ahead, down the anglers' footpath, which follows Bouchouxville Brook to the river.

Parking Area GPS Coordinates
N41°52.523'
W075°10.799'

Long Eddy

The launch is a simple, unimproved dirt road leading to the river. Currently, there is no officially designated parking area near the Long Eddy boat launch. Anglers must park somewhere along the railroad tracks, on Route 97, or in the streets of Long Eddy. Wading options are limited near the Long Eddy fishing access, because Long Eddy is too deep to easily wade in either direction.

The Long Eddy boat launch can be difficult to find after dark. Begin to look for the launch in the Long Eddy Pool, which is aptly named, because you'll be wondering whether the flat water will ever end. Eventually, you'll come to a very large in-river rock that looks like a miniature island near the right bank. The river bends to the right below the rock, and you'll begin to see lights from the riverside houses in the village of Long Eddy on the left side of the river. Stay on the river's left side. The boat launch is on your left, approximately 100 yards above the pool's tail.

Getting There
From Hancock's Route 97 Bridge:
1. Cross the Route 97 Bridge, heading south out of Hancock, and travel 14.4 miles.
2. Turn right onto Depot Street (in Long Eddy, New York).
3. Cross the railroad tracks, and the boat launch is straight ahead.

Boat Ramp and River GPS Coordinates
N41°50.933'
W075°08.081'

Lower Main Stem: Long Eddy to Tower Road

The Lower Main Stem is the longest of the three Main Stem sections—it includes 10.4 miles of the 27-mile-long Main Stem trout zone. The section's length requires an all-day float trip if you want to see it all. I've included six access areas for this section, not counting the New York State DEC and Pennsylvania Fish and Boat Commission accesses in Callicoon, almost 2 miles

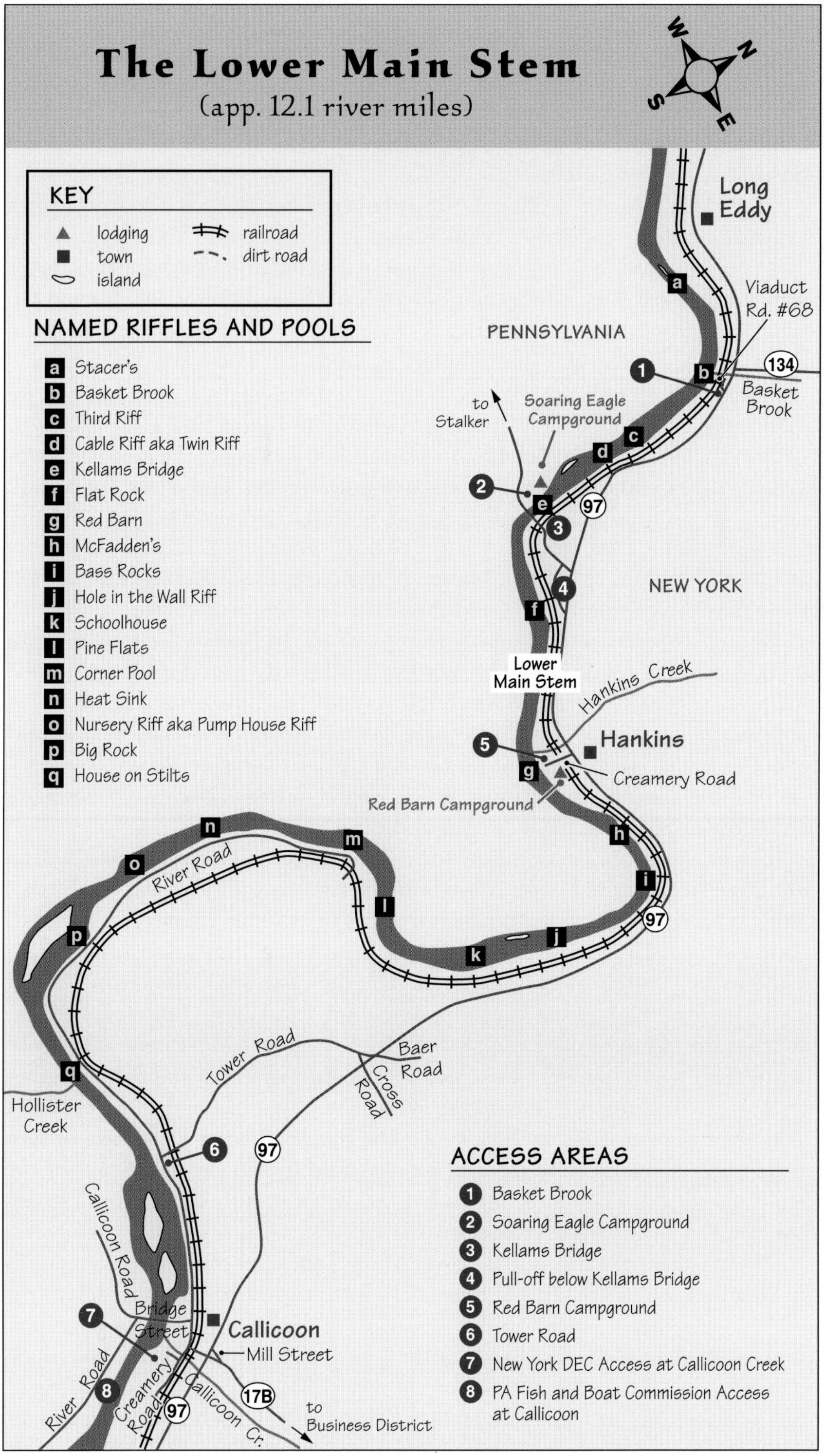

The Lower Main Stem
(app. 12.1 river miles)
W
N
S
E
KEY
lodging
town
island
railroad
dirt road
NAMED RIFFLES AND POOLS
a Stacer's
b Basket Brook
c Third Riff
d Cable Riff aka Twin Riff
e Kellams Bridge
f Flat Rock
g Red Barn
h McFadden's
i Bass Rocks
j Hole in the Wall Riff
k Schoolhouse
l Pine Flats
m Corner Pool
n Heat Sink
o Nursery Riff aka Pump House Riff
p Big Rock
q House on Stilts
Long Eddy
Viaduct Rd. #68
134
Basket Brook
PENNSYLVANIA
to Stalker
Soaring Eagle Campground
97
NEW YORK
Lower Main Stem
Hankins Creek
Hankins
Creamery Road
Red Barn Campground
River Road
Tower Road
Baer Road
Cross Road
Hollister Creek
Callicoon Road
Bridge Street
Callicoon
Mill Street
17B
to Business District
River Road
Creamery Road
Callicoon Cr.
ACCESS AREAS
1 Basket Brook
2 Soaring Eagle Campground
3 Kellams Bridge
4 Pull-off below Kellams Bridge
5 Red Barn Campground
6 Tower Road
7 New York DEC Access at Callicoon Creek
8 PA Fish and Boat Commission Access at Callicoon

downriver from Tower Road. Four of these access areas are within walking distance of Kellams Bridge. Access from the bridge to Tower Road is limited unless you want to pay a seasonal fee at the Red Barn Campground. The lack of access makes this one of the Upper Delaware's most underfished river sections, especially by waders.

The Main's lower section is undiscovered territory for many Upper Delaware anglers, and that's what makes it so attractive. You never know what you may find in it. A group of anglers that included Bud Sherry, Carter Stark, and myself was sitting on a Lower Main Stem bank in 2005 when we found something very interesting. A large mayfly came floating down the middle of the river, and it immediately grabbed our attention. The bug was much larger than any mayfly we had ever seen—easily a size 6. All of us rushed into the river to collect the specimen, but it was Bud who netted it. The mayfly looked like a genetic mistake. It had a body like a golden stonefly, the wings of an *Isonychia*, the legs of a grasshopper, and a two-toned tail. None of us could identify the bug, so we showed it to several respected fly-fishing entomologists, and they didn't know what it was either. The insect was later identified by a professional entomologist as a *Heptagenia culacantha*—a mayfly considered rare and threatened in New York State.

Strange insects aren't the only thing you might find in the Lower Main Stem. Rumors of a very large brown trout, allegedly found dead by a DEC officer, circulated in the late 1990s. But this wasn't just any brown trout. It was supposedly a potential New York State record brown trout—one you would expect to find in the Great Lakes, not the Upper Delaware River. The story was nothing more than a rumor, but it was believable, because there have been some exceptional trout caught in this section.

Upper Delaware River guide Tony Ritter had his own encounter with a very large trout in the Lower Main Stem. Tony was guiding near the Basket Riffle on June 6, 2004, when he anchored his boat so his clients could cast to a few rising fish. One of them hooked a very big trout, and after a few moments he brought it to Tony's net. The fish was a 23.5-inch-long brook trout. The trout had a blue tag in its dorsal fin, but Wayne Elliot of the DEC said that the fish had not been stocked by his agency. Most people surmise that the fish was a hatchery escapee, but it was an exceptional fish nonetheless. I've also had my own encounter with a very big trout in the Lower Main. I was fishing near dusk in 2001 when the biggest Upper Delaware brown trout I've ever seen rose in front of me. I would like to say that I caught the fish, but I didn't. I can still remember the fish's mouth closing on a green drake; it was large enough to eat my fist.

These stories of exceptional Lower Main Stem trout might leave you with the idea that the river is full of these fish. It isn't. And before you plan a trip to this river section, you should know its drawbacks as well as its potential. The Lower Main is the most inconsistent part of the river; it is the moodiest section of a system characterized by moody, difficult rivers. If you've never been skunked on an Upper Delaware fishing trip, then head to the Lower

Main several times this year. You'll probably go fishless on at least one of those outings. The Lower Main holds even fewer trout than the Upper and Middle Main Stem. Its fishing season is wildly unpredictable and usually limited to the spring and fall because the river is too warm (exceeding 80 degrees) in the summer. The Lower Main is too far from the reservoirs to receive any cooling effects with the way the reservoirs are typically managed today. And although the Lower Main may see the fewest fly fishermen each year, it probably hosts more canoeists than any other Upper Delaware River section. Canoeists like its warmer water for swimming.

Basket Brook

This access has a dirt pull-off that can hold several cars. An anglers' footpath begins at the top of a small hill beside the pull-off and leads downhill to Basket Brook. It then follows the brook to its junction with the Main Stem. Boats cannot be launched or retrieved here.

The tail of a large pool limits upriver wading from the Basket Brook access, so most anglers wade downriver to fish the Basket Brook Riffle. This deep, boulder-strewn riffle has excellent cover for trout. You can fish the upper half of the riffle from either bank, and you can usually cross at its head during low to average flows. However, only strong, experienced waders should attempt to cross the river here.

The head of the Basket Brook Riffle can be difficult for wading anglers to cross, and the pool above it is too deep to wade.

The riffle eventually slows into the head of the Basket Brook Pool. The braided water is the pool's best section to find rising trout. Some of this water can be fished from the left bank, but it's steep and brush covered, forcing wading anglers to the river's edge and complicating casting. The braided head of the pool flattens into a long section of slow-moving water inhabited predominantly by smallmouth bass and chubs, but a few browns also live in this section.

Getting There

From Hancock's Route 97 Bridge:
1. Cross the Route 97 Bridge, heading south out of Hancock, and travel 16 miles.
2. Turn right onto Viaduct Road #68.
3. Travel .3 mile, and the pull-off is on your left.

Parking Area GPS Coordinates

N41°50.644'
W075°06.761'

Soaring Eagle Campground

The privately owned Soaring Eagle Campground offers river access only to its customers. Anglers should call ahead (570-224-4666) with any queries.

Getting There

From Hancock's Route 97 Bridge:
1. Cross the Route 97 Bridge, heading south out of Hancock, and travel 17.1 miles.
2. Turn right (onto an unmarked paved road) toward Kellams and Stalker, Pennsylvania (a green sign on the right side of Route 97 indicates the turn).
3. Travel .3 mile, and cross the railroad tracks and Kellams Bridge (into Pennsylvania).
4. Travel .1 mile, and the campground entrance is on your right.

Campground Entrance GPS Coordinates

N41°49.477'
W075°07.083'

Kellams Bridge

The Kellams Bridge access has a large dirt parking area that can hold several cars. The parking area is on the right side of the road (if you're traveling from New York Route 97) before you reach the railroad tracks. You have to walk across the tracks and travel a few yards downriver to reach the footpath,

Riffles and glare combine to obscure the subtle rises of Upper Delaware trout above Kellams Bridge.

which begins at the top of a steep mud and rock bank. A rope has been tied between the trees lining the path to aid anglers walking up and down it. Boats cannot be launched or retrieved at this access.

Upriver

The footpath meets the river slightly downriver from Kellams Bridge. A long series of rocky riffles, small braided pools, and pocket water ends at the bridge—at the head of Kellams Bridge Pool. The roiling river above the bridge is an excellent area to nymph or fish dry flies, but wading it can be difficult. Large boulders near the right bank and swift-flowing currents combine to make footing tenuous at several spots.

Downriver

The braided head of Kellams Bridge Pool begins to slow into flat water in front of the anglers' footpath. The pool is deep and holds a lot of trout, but much of it cannot be waded effectively. The pool's head, near the bridge, is one area that can be waded. Trout are usually found in the current seams in the middle of the pool. A sloping riverbed on the footpath side of the river provides good footing to reach these fish. The middle of Kellams Bridge Pool is too deep to wade, limiting further downriver wading.

Getting There

From Hancock's Route 97 Bridge:

1. Cross the Route 97 Bridge, heading south out of Hancock, and travel 17.1 miles.
2. Turn right (onto an unmarked paved road) toward Kellams and Stalker, Pennsylvania (a green sign on the right side of Route 97 indicates the turn).
3. Travel .3 mile. The parking area, marked with a brown DEC sign, is on your right.

Parking Area GPS Coordinates

N41°49.433'
W075°06.753'

Pull-off below Kellams Bridge

This access has a small dirt pull-off that holds two or three cars. An anglers' footpath begins across the road from the pull-off, leads across the railroad tracks, and descends down a steep bank to the river. Boats cannot be launched or retrieved at this access.

Upriver

The footpath meets the river slightly downriver from the beginning of a deep chute below the Kellams Bridge Pool tail. Both sides of the chute provide excellent nymphing opportunities, but its current is swift, even in the slower areas on either side of the chute. Some areas of the Kellams Bridge Pool tail can also be waded, but most of the trout hold in the deep slot near the river's left bank. The tail's depth makes many of these fish difficult to impossible to reach on foot.

Downriver

The chute slows and forms the braided head of a pool. This pool has a good population of trout and is also an excellent place to find schools of shad in the spring. The pool's bottom section becomes wide and flat, and it often holds more chubs than trout.

Getting There

From Hancock's Route 97 Bridge:

1. Cross the Route 97 Bridge, heading south out of Hancock, and travel 17.1 miles.
2. Turn right (onto an unmarked paved road) toward Kellams and Stalker, Pennsylvania (a green sign on the right side of Route 97 indicates the turn).
3. Turn left at the first unnamed dirt road.
4. Travel .4 mile. The pull-off is on your left.

Parking Area GPS Coordinates
N41°49.178'
W075°06.053'

Red Barn Campground

The Red Barn Campground offers river access and boat launch facilities to the general public for a seasonal fee. Red Barn stopped offering daily rates for use of its boat launch in 2006.

Getting There
From Hancock's Route 97 Bridge:
1. Cross the Route 97 Bridge, heading south out of Hancock, and travel 18.3 miles.
2. Turn right onto Creamery Road (in Hankins, New York).
3. The campground entrance is straight ahead.

Campground Entrance GPS Coordinates
N41°48.841'
W075°05.188'

Tower Road

Tower Road parking area and boat launch are not at the same place. The parking area is a rutted dirt pull-off capable of holding several cars, located slightly downriver from the boat launch (toward Callicoon, New York, on the left side of River Road). The boat launch is an unimproved, rutted dirt road that connects River Road to the river.

The Tower Road access offers little fishable water for wading anglers—much of the river is too deep. The best section for wading is near the two islands, 200 yards downriver from the boat ramp.

The Tower Road boat launch can be difficult to find after dark. Look for it after you float through a heavy riffle with a brown house on stilts on the left bank. The riffle flows into the aptly named House on Stilts Pool. Stay on the left side of the river after you enter the pool. The river eventually bends to the left and becomes very flat and slow moving. You will be able to see the lights of Callicoon straight down the river. The access is a small dirt road that seems to appear out of nowhere through the grass on the left bank.

Getting There
From Hancock's Route 97 Bridge:
1. Cross the Route 97 Bridge, heading south out of Hancock, and travel 20.8 miles.
2. Turn right onto Tower Road (just past the Holy Cross Church).
3. Travel 1.4 miles to the stop sign. The boat ramp is straight ahead.

4. Turn left onto River Road, and the dirt parking area is just past the creek, on your left.

Parking Area GPS Coordinates

N41°46.330'
W075°04.446'

River GPS Coordinates

N41°46.324'
W075°04.477'

New York Department of Environmental Conservation Access at Callicoon Creek

This access has a spacious dirt and gravel parking lot capable of holding many vehicles. Rocks line the parking area, preventing anglers from using it as a drift boat launch; however, pontoon boats or canoes can be launched or retrieved from this access. The large, deep pool in front of the access limits upriver and downriver wading opportunities.

The bridge at Callicoon marks the end of the Upper Delaware's "official" trout zone, but anglers catch many trout below Callicoon, especially in the spring.

Getting There

From Hancock's Route 97 Bridge:

1. Cross the Route 97 Bridge, heading south out of Hancock, and travel 22.8 miles to the Callicoon traffic light.
2. Turn left onto Mill Street, and travel to the stop sign.
3. Turn right, toward the Callicoon business district, and travel to the stop sign.
4. Turn left onto Creamery Road. Cross the Callicoon Creek Bridge, and the entrance to the access area is on your immediate right.

Parking Area GPS Coordinates

N41°45.793'
W075°03.533'

Pennsylvania Fish and Boat Commission Access at Callicoon

This access has a large dirt and gravel parking area capable of holding many vehicles. The boat ramp is a simple, unimproved dirt and gravel road leading down a short bank to the river. All types of watercraft, including drift boats, can be launched or retrieved here. Upriver wading opportunities are limited due to the large pool that lies between this access and the New York DEC access at Callicoon Creek. A single island lies downriver from the boat ramp, and the riffles surrounding the island provide the best wading opportunities.

Getting There

From Hancock's Route 97 Bridge:

1. Cross the Route 97 Bridge, heading south out of Hancock, and travel 22.8 miles to the Callicoon traffic light.
2. Turn left onto Mill Street, and travel to the stop sign.
3. Turn right, toward the Callicoon business district, and travel to the stop sign.
4. Veer right onto Sullivan County Route 133.
5. Travel .3 mile and turn left.
6. Cross the Callicoon Bridge (over the Main Stem).
7. Turn left at the end of the bridge onto River Road.
8. Travel .5 mile, and the parking area, marked with a brown PFBC sign, is on your left.

Parking Area GPS Coordinates

N41°45.400'
W075°03.471'

River GPS Coordinates

N41°45.396'
W075°03.440'

CHAPTER 5

The Fish and How to Catch Them

The Fish

Brown Trout

Although not native to the Upper Delaware, brown trout are the most plentiful trout species. They live in all the river's branches, but they dominate the Upper East Branch and the West Branch. Average fish are about 15 inches long and usually weigh between $1/2$ to $1^1/2$ pounds. These statistics are misleading, however. Upper Delaware brown trout are predominantly in-river

The trout living in the Upper Main Stem's pondlike Lake Lenore Pool are some of the most difficult to catch in the entire river system. Upper Delaware guide Wally Falkoff was able to fool this beautiful Lake Lenore brown.

spawners, so the prime, gravelly spawning areas of the Upper West and Upper East Branches can sometime hold large population of small yearling trout. These same river sections can also hold brown trout that have been flushed out of the reservoirs and are well over 2 feet long and weigh close to 10 pounds, or they may hold older river-born fish that also exceed 20 inches in length. Brown trout are famously selective feeders, and that trait, combined with the Upper Delaware's vast aquatic food supply, makes Upper Delaware browns some of the most difficult to catch in all of North America.

Rainbow Trout

The story of the rainbow trout's introduction to the Upper Delaware is legendary, and it has been retold countless times. A train was traveling along the Lower Delaware River near Callicoon, New York, in the 1880s with a shipment of McCloud River strain rainbows (from California) that were destined to be stocked in the Upper Delaware's West Branch or somewhere in Pennsylvania (the exact destination depends on who's telling the story). A wreck delayed the train just outside of Callicoon, and the trout would have perished in the warming train cars if not for Dan Cahill, the kindly brakeman. He and his crew heroically carried the trout in buckets, for over a mile, to release them into Callicoon Creek. The fish thrived in the creek, and it wasn't long before

Upper Delaware rainbows seldom eat streamers. Mark "Striperman" Celebuski caught this one on a dry fly.

they began to colonize the rest of the Upper Delaware system, creating the brood stock for all the wild rainbows that live in the river today.

I've heard the story many times, but the problem is that it may not be true. Ed Van Put, the Upper Delaware's foremost fly-fishing historian, could find no concrete historical records to prove that Cahill's rainbow stocking ever took place. So, if the Cahill legend isn't true, how did the rainbows get into the Upper Delaware? Rainbow trout are native to the Pacific Coast, so they didn't exist in the system until someone stocked them. The solution to the mystery surrounding the rainbow trout's origin in the Upper Delaware system probably cannot be found in any single source.

Van Put has found historical records documenting planned McCloud River strain rainbow trout stockings in the East and West Branches in 1881 and in Callicoon Creek in 1885. Theodore Gordon wrote in the early twentieth century that rainbow trout were also stocked into the Beaverkill, the Upper Delaware's largest tributary (McDonald 1995). There is no reason that all these stockings couldn't have combined to create the unique genetics of the rainbows that dominate the rivers today—and Delaware River rainbows are genetically unique. According to Van Put, a Cornell University study found that the Delaware's rainbows are genetically distinct from rainbow trout found anywhere else in the world.

How the rainbows made their way to the river really doesn't matter. What does matter is that they remain in the river, wild and self-sustaining, and provide some of the best trout fishing opportunities in the eastern United States. Rainbows tend to dominate most of the Main Stem, and they are also prominent in the Lower East Branch. The West Branch and Upper East Branch maintain the smallest populations of rainbows.

Upper Delaware rainbows average about 15 inches long and usually weigh between $1/2$ to $1^1/2$ pounds. Rainbows longer than 19 inches are rare. They usually fail to reach 20 inches because they have a shorter life span than brown trout do. Delaware River rainbows reach sexual maturity at age 3 years, and very few of them live past age 4. Van Put's research shows that only 1 in 100 Upper Delaware rainbows will ever reach the age of 5, but that one fish will be over 20 inches long.

Rainbows tend to dominate river sections with less than ideal habitat. In fact, Upper Delaware rainbows tend to monopolize the rivers' warmest sections. They seem to have evolved the capacity to survive in water temperatures that would be lethal to most trout.

Rainbow trout were my least favorite trout species before I began fishing the Upper Delaware system. I was never impressed by the skinny, sickly looking stocked rainbows that I caught elsewhere. But comparing Upper Delaware rainbows to any other eastern rainbow is like comparing a thoroughbred racehorse to an old nag. Sure, they're both horses, but only one of them has what it takes to star in the Kentucky Derby. And only a special breed of rainbow has been able to survive in the Upper Delaware system.

Brook Trout

Brook trout are the one trout species (they are actually a member of the char family) that is native to the Upper Delaware River. The entire Upper Delaware system, including the expansive Main Stem, was once considered prime brook trout habitat (Karas 1997). The rivers were narrower, faster, and probably not as deep before Europeans settled in the region. These immigrants brought industry to the Upper Delaware valleys: lumberyards and acid factories that cut the bordering forestland, allowing erosion to eat away at the riverbanks and widening their channels. The modern Upper Delaware system is a much warmer, slower, and silt-laden version of the river that once teemed with brook trout.

The destruction of the brook trout's habitat wasn't the only factor in its decline in the Upper Delaware system. Introduced fish species such as brown and rainbow trout and smallmouth bass were able to outcompete brook trout for the best of the remaining river habitat. These fish have the ability to grow larger more quickly than the brook trout can, and they have a greater tolerance for warm water. They forced the rivers' remaining brook trout populations into the small, icy-cold, more acidic tributaries where brook trout thrive.

But the brookies did not completely abandon their former river homes. They are still present today in the Upper Delaware branches in small, isolated pockets, especially near tributary mouths. Most of these fish average only 5 to 6 inches, but much larger specimens are possible. Upper Delaware brook trout are relatively rare, but there are a few river sections where an angler has a greater chance of catching one. The Upper East Branch, in particular, probably has the system's highest concentration of brook trout, but brookies can be found in the Main Stem, Lower East Branch, and West Branch as well.

I've fished through several Upper Delaware trout seasons without catching a single brook trout, and anglers visiting the river should never expect to catch one. But the fishing trips that did produce a brook trout for me seem a little more blessed than those that didn't. I've caught a lot of Upper Delaware brown and rainbow trout, and I remember very few of them. But I think I remember every brook trout I've caught in the river. They're native and rare, and that's what makes them memorable.

American Shad

The Lenni-Lenape Indians that lived in the forested land along the Upper Delaware system used to rely heavily on migrating shad for sustenance, and so did the white settlers who came after them. Both the Indians and the white settlers built V-shaped rock structures in the river to corral the shad (structures very similar to Ray Turner's modern Lower East Branch eel weir mentioned in chapter 3). The shad were driven into these traps and poisoned, netted, or speared and then collected for food (Van Put 1996). Shad are still considered excellent table fare by many anglers today. They are prized not only for their bony flesh but also for their roe (eggs), which is often sautéed in butter. A lot of people consider the roe a delicacy, but to me, it will always look and smell like bait.

An average Delaware River shad is about 15 inches long. The females are much larger than the males, which are usually called bucks. Shad begin their Delaware River spawning migration from the ocean in late April or early May; they usually don't reach the Upper Delaware and its branches until late May or early June. But if the Main Stem is especially low and warm in the spring, few shad complete their upriver journey to the Upper Delaware. Instead, they stop in the lower river sections and spawn there. Many of the shad that do reach the Upper Delaware continue past the beginning of the Main Stem, spreading into the river's branches and sometimes even into the Beaverkill and Willowemoc.

Shad do not feed when they first enter the river, before spawning. But they may strike a streamer or small, brightly colored flies and lures (called darts) out of aggression. Shad feed after spawning, and nearly all my fly-caught Upper Delaware River shad have been taken on dry-fly patterns. Shad seem particularly fond of the little sulphur duns and spinners that are often on the river's surface in mid-June. Many of the shad die after they spawn, and it's common to see the dying fish swimming erratically on the surface of the river's many deep pools.

The Delaware River Shad Fishermen's Association maintains a telephone hotline (610-954-0577 or 610-954-0578) to provide information to anglers who are seeking shad. Most of the Upper Delaware's fly shops also offer information on the shad migration and some of them even sell flies and offer guided fly-fishing trips for shad.

Stripers

Stripers were largely absent in the Delaware River above Callicoon, New York, until recent years. Legislation that greatly curtailed the overharvesting of stripers in the ocean has led to an increase in their populations throughout the northeastern United States. It has also helped them become reestablished in their native ranges, and stripers have returned to the Upper Delaware. Stripers, like American shad and brook trout, are native to the Upper Delaware system. In fact, it appears that the stripers may actually follow the schools of migrating shad all the way from the ocean to the Upper Delaware—kind of like chasing a traveling buffet.

Stripers are usually found in the Upper Delaware's Main Stem, but they have also been seen in the West Branch, the Lower East Branch, and even the Beaverkill. Average fish are between 20 and 30 inches long and weigh from 5 to 10 pounds. Pods of "schoolie" stripers, fish less than 20 inches long, are also common. The Main Stem's Junction Pool is famous for maintaining a fairly significant striper population in the summer. Very few Upper Delaware fly anglers target these fish, but I know two who have: former Upper

Delaware guide Danny Peterson and Mark Celebuski. Both these anglers have intentionally caught stripers with large streamers. Many other Upper Delaware anglers have also had tussles with stripers, although most of those encounters were unintentional. Stripers have a fondness for rainbow trout. Every year, several anglers have their fly-caught trout attacked by stripers as they are bringing them to the net.

The striper's fondness for Upper Delaware trout has inspired some anglers to seek legislative changes to reduce the legal creel size for stripers. These people believe that the striper populations need to be curtailed to protect the trout fishery. I want to protect the Upper Delaware's wild trout population as much as anyone, but I don't believe we need to wipe out the stripers to do it. Stripers are native to the system and belong in the river. The Upper Delaware has many more pressing threats to its trout fishery, and stripers just aren't that high on my list. If we fight to ensure adequate water releases from the reservoirs, the river will hold more than enough trout for us to share with the stripers.

Smallmouth Bass

Many anglers incorrectly assume that smallmouth bass, also called black bass, are native to the Upper Delaware River system. The smallmouth's native range was originally found largely in the midwestern United States and areas just east of the Great Lakes. Portions of western Pennsylvania and western and northern New York (outside of the Adirondacks) also fall within the

Summer water temperatures in river sections far from the reservoirs are often better suited for bass than trout. Monte Burke, the author of **Sowbelly: The Obsessive Quest for the World Record Largemouth Bass,** *caught this smallmouth bass in the Lower East.*

native range of smallmouths. Smallmouth bass from the Ohio River were stocked in the Upper Delaware system in 1870 by the Erie Railroad Company, creating the foundation for the fish populations that live in the river today (Francis 1996).

The stocked bass thrived until the completion of the Delaware reservoirs and the commencement of their cold-water releases—water that is too cold for optimal smallmouth bass survival. The creation of the reservoirs pushed the ideal smallmouth habitat downriver, to areas below Callicoon. Most anglers consider the Delaware River section from Narrowsburg to Barryville, New York, to be the best section for pursuing smallmouths today. However, smallmouths do maintain small populations in all of the Upper Delaware's branches. I've caught bass in all three Main Stem sections and in the Lower East Branch. The Upper East and West Branches probably maintain the smallest bass populations, largely because they are closest to the reservoirs and maintain the coldest conditions. The Upper Delaware's largest tributary, the Beaverkill, also has a stable population of smallmouths, especially downriver from Cooks Falls, New York.

Most Upper Delaware smallmouths are small, averaging only about 11 inches. But occasionally, much larger specimens are caught. In 2002 I caught an 18-inch smallmouth on a streamer in the Main Stem near Hankins, New York. Specimens up to 26 inches long and weighing nearly 10 pounds have been caught in the Delaware River.

Walleyes

The midwestern United States and most of Canada lie within the native range of walleyes; the Upper Delaware does not. Walleyes were stocked into the Upper Delaware system in 1925, just like smallmouth bass in the 1800s (Van Put 1996). They tend to populate the river's cold, deep pools and average 17 or 18 inches long and about 2 to 4 pounds.

Walleyes aren't usually targeted by Upper Delaware fly anglers, but I know a few who have caught them. My friend Mark Celebuski once caught a very nice walleye on a black Woolly Bugger streamer in the Main Stem's Junction Pool. Most fly-rod-caught walleyes that I know of have been caught in the same way that Mark caught his—by accident, while stripping streamers on a deep-sinking fly line for trout.

Walleyes are eagerly sought by a small group of die-hard Upper Delaware spin fishermen, many of whom fish the river at night from small johnboats. It's common to see them launching their boats on the Main Stem when most fly fishermen are exiting the river. One of these anglers used to fish Lake Lenore, the deep Upper Main Stem pool in front of the former Wild Rainbow Lodge (now a private residence), which I used to manage. I would watch him from the lodge's deck on many a summer evening. On one particular occasion he was doing very well, pulling fish after fish from the pool's depths and then unceremoniously tossing them back into the river. I knew that this man often ate his walleyes—they are delicious—so I was curious as to why he was letting them all go. I walked to the river's edge and called out, asking him how the fishing was going. "Terrible," he grumpily replied. "I can't keep these damn rainbow trout from eating my jigs."

Equipment

Rods

The best all-around rods for the Upper Delaware are medium- to fast-action 5- or 6-weights. Although the most common rod by far is a 9-foot 5-weight, I like to use a 9½-foot 6-weight. The extra length helps keep the average caster's backcast off the water when wading deep (which is often necessary), and the extra line weight helps in the wind, which is common in the spring. A 6-weight is also easier to cast a little farther than a 5-weight, and casting distance is often important on the big water.

Sean Connery's character in the movie *The Untouchables* warned a hit man not to "bring a knife to a gun fight." This also applies to fly rods. Light-line graphite and bamboo rods (1- to 3-weights) have their place in fly fishing, but they are not suited for most of the situations you'll encounter on the Upper Delaware. Even if you wanted to cast only dry flies, most anglers can't make the necessary cast of at least 40 feet with a 3- or even a 4-weight rod.

Reels

Some Upper Delaware anglers still use click and pawl reels, but I recommend reels with large arbors and disc drags. Large-arbor reels crank in line much faster than a standard arbor does. The ability to reel in line quickly can make all the difference when you're trying to land a blistering-fast trout on the expansive pools of the Upper Delaware, where a fish could run all the way to the ocean if it wanted to. Upper Delaware trout have the creative tendency of ripping off fly line while they head downriver on their initial run. But they often turn and run straight at you on their second run. If you're unable to put line back on the reel fast enough to keep pressure on the fish, it will usually throw the hook. Large-arbor reels greatly aid anglers who are quickly reeling to maintain pressure on a trout.

I've also found a disc drag to be a tremendous aid for landing Upper Delaware trout. Many click and pawl drags just aren't tight enough. They allow a trout to run farther than it could with a disk drag. Click and pawls also tend to give line with small jerks as the clicker moves between pawls. This slight hesitation can break the wispy tippets that are often necessary on the Upper Delaware's flat pools.

A modern disc drag has one final advantage over click and pawl reels: the ability to adjust drag settings. The drag system on a modern disc reel can be micromanaged to provide just enough resistance to tire a fish without breaking it off; many click and pawl reels cannot. Most click and pawl reels have fixed drag systems, and the ones that are adjustable usually don't adjust very well. I often set the drag on my disc drag reels very light for a trout's first run. I can then slowly turn the drag tighter as the fish tires. I believe that this ability allows me to fight fish better and bring them to my net quicker than I could with a click and pawl reel.

Whatever type of reel you decide to use on the Upper Delaware, you need to be sure that it's equipped with the appropriate fly line and backing. You need to have at least 100 yards of 25-pound Dacron backing on your reel. On many eastern trout streams you'll never see the backing, but on the Upper Delaware you will. Make sure that the backing is in good shape and not tangled on the reel. If you don't, you'll eventually hook an Upper Delaware trout that will make you wish you did.

Waders and Boats

Because of the cold-water releases on the Upper East and West Branches, wet wading there is not wise. In many areas throughout the system you have to wade deep, so hip boots aren't adequate. The best wader system for the Upper Delaware is a good pair of breathable chest waders with an underlayer of polar fleece. The fleece can be removed if you're fishing farther away from the reservoirs in the warmer sections. But if you're wading near the dams, you won't be doing it very long without the fleece. Evenings in the Catskills can be chilly, even in the summer months. A day that begins with sunburn and sweat can end with shivering if you don't have the extra insulation of fleece. I don't advise using neoprene waders because they are so uncomfortable—too hot in the summer and often too tight fitting with a layer of winter clothes.

I also prefer stocking-foot over boot-foot waders. Boot-foot waders are easier to put on and take off, and I know several older gentlemen who swear by them. But they are also less comfortable and provide less ankle support than stocking-foot waders do. That comfort and support are important when you spend all day on the water wading through rocky riffles or walking substantial distances from access areas. Stocking-foot waders also give anglers more options for the boots they can wear over them.

Felt-bottomed boots are another Upper Delaware standard. They provide good traction, and the felt can be replaced once it wears out. Rubber-bottomed boots have become popular recently. I'm not talking about the old rubberized bottoms on hip boots. These new boots have specially formulated rubber bottoms designed for river use. I've tried several pairs of these boots but never found one I like. I just don't think the rubber bottom provides as much traction as the felt.

I've found that the best bottom for my Upper Delaware wading boots is a felt and stud combination. These boots are excellent for wading rocky river sections, especially those areas common on the Lower Main Stem. They do have one drawback: you should never wear stud-bottomed boots in a drift boat. Besides abrading the boat's fiberglass hull, they also make your footing in the boat treacherous—it's like wearing a pair of ice skates.

Other Equipment

It's often the little things that make the difference between a comfortable, productive Upper Delaware River fishing trip and one that's disappointing. One of the most important items for fishing the Upper Delaware is a small flashlight. Much of the river's best fishing, especially during the summer months, occurs right before and after dark. A good light is vital not only for changing flies but also for finding your way back to the car without breaking any of your equipment or yourself. I always keep several lights tucked into the pockets of my fishing vest in case I lose one of them or its batteries die. I've also drowned several lights by wading too deep into the river, which brings us to the next vital piece of equipment—the fly-fishing vest.

There are almost as many options for vests as there are for rods and reels. Most anglers are individualistic by nature, but the one vest type that I strongly suggest for Upper Delaware anglers is a "shorty" model. These vests are one-third shorter than the standard fly-fishing vest. As I mentioned earlier, many of the Upper Delaware's pools are deep, requiring anglers to wade up to and past their waists. Sooner or later, the sight of rising fish will cause you to wade deeper than you wanted to. Your vest will submerge, and you may ruin some of the important items inside it. A shorty vest keeps your fly boxes, lights, and other gear high and dry while you're wading deep.

In addition, you should choose a vest that has enough pockets to fit everything you want to carry, but more importantly, find one that distributes its weight evenly around your neck. If you want to get away from the crowds on the Upper Delaware, you're going to have to do a lot of walking. A comfortable vest makes the travel much more enjoyable. I would also suggest choosing a vest with a large, zippered back pocket. This pocket is a great place to keep your rain jacket. Summer storms can appear very quickly in the Catskill Mountains, and carrying a rain jacket allows you to either fish through the rain or stay dry until it ends. Anglers who don't keep their rain jackets in their vests tend to leave them in the car.

There are many other items that you might want to bring to the Upper Delaware. Nippers, fly floatants or sinkants, knot-tying tools, sunscreen, various fly boxes, magnifiers for attaching flies to tippets, thermometers, wading staffs, and nets are all important. Individual fishing style, wading ability, and fly-fishing skill level determine which of these items are important to you.

Dry-Fly Fishing

Ten Tips for Success

1. Floating fly lines. Because of the casting distances required, the best floating fly lines for Upper Delaware River dry-fly fishing are weight forward. This extra weight near the line's head helps anglers generate greater line speed for distance casts. Weight-forward lines are especially good for distance casting because their thin running line helps them shoot better than a double-taper line does.

2. Dry-fly leaders and tippets. Use the longest leader-tippet combination that you can effectively cast and turn over. That combination may be only 9 feet for a new angler, but it's better to be able to cast a shorter leader than to struggle all day with a longer one. I never fish dry-fly leader and tippet combinations shorter than 12 feet. You usually don't need the leader and tippet to be that long in the spring, because the fish are hungry and less wary. But I do it anyway, for one important reason. During the basketball days of my youth, one adage was pounded into my head: you play like you practice. Shorter leaders may be as effective as longer leaders in the spring, but they won't be in the summer and fall when the rivers are low and clear. Most anglers would be better, more accurate casters if they became familiar with one leader-tippet length and did not deviate.

I feel the same way about tippet material. Ninety percent of my dry-fly fishing is done with 6X fluorocarbon tippet. Why? Because fishing 6X tippet almost exclusively has made me very familiar with its breaking point. I know exactly how much force it can withstand on a hook set and how much pressure I can put on a fish before I'll break it off. Many anglers use every size between 4X and 7X tippet on every fishing outing. Each time they go up or down a tippet size, they have to work through a transition period to readjust to the increase or decrease in tippet strength. This is one of the reasons that so many anglers break off fish—they simply aren't accustomed to the tolerances of their tackle. Rarely will an Upper Delaware trout refuse a fly because it's attached to 6X tippet.

The only time I use heavier tippets on the Delaware is during periods of high river flows or when I'm fishing from a boat. I don't like chasing a running trout or tiring it unnecessarily, and a 5X or even 4X tippet provides the added strength necessary to land a large fish in heavy water. I seldom use 7X tippet for the large, hard-fighting trout of the Upper Delaware. In the hands of most anglers, 7X just won't hold an Upper Delaware trout.

3. Casting skill and distance. If you can't cast at least 40 feet, you won't be able to reach many of the Upper Delaware's rising trout, especially during periods of moderate to high flows. Drift boats and superior wading skills can sometimes reduce the distance you need to cast, but not always. The cruising nature of many Upper Delaware trout enhances the importance of casting long and accurately. The fish don't always continue feeding in their original positions after they begin rising, and chasing them around a pool is seldom effective. You must be able to put your fly in front of the fish at varied distances.

I learned to double haul when I began fishing the Upper Delaware—I never had to on the small limestone creeks I fished. But the double haul is one of the most important elements of Upper Delaware dry-fly fishing, because it's very difficult to attain adequate casting distance without it. Every year I guide several clients who just don't have the casting skills to be effective. By the end of the trip, their casting has usually improved, but that won't bring back the many fish they were unable to catch at the beginning of the trip. The

Long, accurate, drag-free casts are vital for fishing the Upper Delaware's flat pools.

farther and more accurately you can cast, the more trout you'll catch in the Upper Delaware. It's as simple as that. Learn how to double haul and practice distance casting before you get to the river.

4. The reach cast. Controlling drag by mending the fly line may be the most important skill for catching Upper Delaware trout with a dry fly (drag occurs when a fly moves unnaturally on the water because the line is being pulled by the current). There are many ways to mend fly line both on and off the water—too many to discuss here. But the most important mending technique for Upper Delaware River dry-fly fishing is the reach cast.

Making a reach cast is fairly simple once you understand its objective. The reach cast places the fly ahead of the leader and tippet, controlling drag and ensuring that the trout will see the fly first, not the line or tippet. That's important if you want to catch the many trout rising in the Upper Delaware's flat-water pools.

The reach cast is made at the end of a forward cast, right before the line is laid on the water. Sweep your rod tip upriver while your fly line, still in the air, straightens in front of you. Then lay the cast on the water. Your fly, leader, and line will be at a 45-degree downriver angle from your rod if you've executed the cast successfully. It takes a little practice to master, but it's worth the effort. Expect a lot of frustration and fishless days on the Upper Delaware if you can't perform a reach cast.

5. Observation and patience. The sight of large trout eating flies off the surface quickens an anglers' pulse. It also makes some of us to charge into the

It's always best to study the water, looking for insects and rising fish, before wading into the Upper Delaware's flat pools.

river and start casting as quickly as possible. This probably causes anglers to scare more fish than they catch. Upper Delaware trout are known to rise subtly in water that's barely deep enough to keep their backs wet. Anglers who charge at obvious rising fish often miss the quiet rises near the riverbanks.

I never tie a fly to my leader at the car. I seldom even string my rod until I reach the river. I find that it calms me and gives me more time to observe what is really happening if I wait until I'm standing near the water to ready my tackle. The extra time encourages patience and ensures that by the time my gear is ready for fishing, my eyes and head are also ready.

6. Casting downriver to rising fish. Nearly all my initial dry-fly fishing experiences in small Pennsylvania limestone creeks involved casting upriver to rising trout. But this technique doesn't work well in the Upper Delaware system—most of the time. The biggest exception to this rule occurs when you fish riffles. Riffles break the river's surface and help disguise leaders and tippets in the chop. I have caught a lot of trout by blind-casting dry flies upriver in the Upper Delaware's riffles, but very few while casting upriver in the pools.

Upper Delaware pools are too flat and slow moving for upriver casts, and their trout are too wily to be fooled by such an obvious act. All successful Upper Delaware dry-fly anglers spend most of their time casting downriver to rising fish. The proper casting position is simple. You should always stand across and slightly upriver from a rising trout. This casting position, combined with the reach cast, ensures that your casts will reach the fish, fly first, with as little drag as possible.

Upper Delaware trout often cruise when they surface feed. Sometimes, after you've already cast your fly on the water, the target fish rises again, but downriver from where you expected it to be holding. You have to be able to extend your fly's drift to catch a fish that eats this way. And you need to be able to feed line to extend your cast. Feeding line is easy to do: move your rod side to side while letting loose line from the reel shake out of the rod's guides. The extra line extends the drift and allows the fly to reach the fish without drag. The amount of force you use to let out the line is critical. If you move your rod too aggressively, you'll pull the line and drag your fly. If you move the rod too gently, the line won't come out of the rod fast enough. You need to practice to get a feel for how much force is needed to feed line. If your fly covers the target fish but it isn't taken, be sure to let it drift below the target fish before you recast. Impatient anglers often pluck the refused fly from the water immediately, while it's still near the fish, to cast again. But if you do that in front of an Upper Delaware trout, it will probably stop rising.

7. The rule of three. Dry-fly fishing on the Upper Delaware can be frustrating. It's hard to remain focused when the river seems to be boiling with rising trout or when fish finally begin to rise just as darkness approaches, after you've been standing on the riverbank for two hours waiting for something to happen. I've watched many Upper Delaware anglers aggressively move into casting positions and flog rising trout with long, incessant series of casts. They pound a trout until it moves to another feeing lie or returns to safety, away from the river's surface.

To counteract this problem, I have developed the rule of three: Once I find a rising fish and slowly move into the proper casting position, I cast only three times for each time the fish rises. If the fish hasn't eaten my fly by the third cast, I stop casting and watch and wait until the fish rises again. I might change flies, if I feel I had a good drag-free cast over the fish, or I might not. But I won't cast until the fish rises again. You probably won't have time to cast to every rising fish you see if you use my rule-of-three casting method, especially if it's getting dark. But you'll have a much better chance of hooking a few rising fish instead of just watching a lot of them.

8. Avoid the midday heat. Fly fishing the Upper Delaware with dry flies can be brutally difficult during bright, hot summer afternoons. In fact, it's usually a waste of time. Many anglers fish all day under these conditions and are too hungry or tired by the time they should be most focused on fishing. If you want to be a successful Upper Delaware dry-fly fisherman, start by fishing at the most productive times. Get to the river at dawn or arrive an hour before sunset during the summer. You'll often find fish feeding heavily on the surface at these times. This rule is directly related to river temperature and volume. Upper Delaware trout may aggressively feed in the middle of the day with a bright sun if the river temperatures are cold or the rivers are running high. This usually occurs in the early spring or during periods of significant reservoir water releases.

9. Fly patterns. Use flies that are equal in size or smaller than the naturals. This rule is self-explanatory. I usually begin fishing a hatch by matching my fly pattern to the size of the natural. If I'm not catching any fish, I'll drop down one fly size before I change patterns. An exception to this rule occurs

Upper Delaware trout surface-feed in bright sunlight in the spring, when the river is off-color, and when cold water is being released from the reservoirs. Bill Herrick caught this brown trout on a sunny day in the West Branch.

during some of the Upper Delaware's blizzard hatches, such as the green drake. Then, I'll often use a much larger fly, up to two sizes larger than the natural, if the water is blanketed with insects, particularly during spinner falls or nighttime hatches. The larger fly stands out amidst the many naturals, making it easier for me to see and more attractive to the fish.

10. Moving on. If nothing is rising during a hatch in the pool you're fishing, then move. Fish are probably rising somewhere. Most Upper Delaware anglers eventually develop a few favorite access areas or pools. It's a natural phenomenon born of success and individual water-type preferences. But don't let your comfort level with a few river sections stop you from exploring other areas when your favorite water isn't producing.

Anglers often post fishing reports on the Internet after their trips to the Upper Delaware. Sometimes, two anglers who fished very close to each other post very different reports. For instance, one of them had a lot of bugs but saw few fish eating them. The other had only a few bugs but found several rising fish. How could two anglers in close proximity experience such divergent fishing conditions? One of them must be lying, right? Not necessarily. The Upper Delaware is famous for producing isolated pockets of good fishing. If you're in a spot with little happening, move. You might find hatches and rising fish nearby. I've floated the Upper Delaware many times when one pool had no fish targets but the next pool downriver held several rising fish. You need to be willing to hunt the trout of the Upper Delaware system to catch them.

Dry-Fly Patterns

Some of the following dry-fly patterns use CDC feathers or snowshoe rabbit's foot hair. Gel or paste dry-fly treatments, such as Gink, should never be used on these flies because they mat the CDC and snowshoe fibers and cause the flies to sink. I recommend a dry powder desiccant, such as Frog's Fanny.

Antron and Hackle Wing Spinners

Spinner imitations may account for more dry-fly-caught Upper Delaware trout than any other pattern. The high visibility and buoyancy of the Antron spinner's wings make it an ideal choice for evening spinner falls; the hackle wings provide a more subtle, less bulky look for daytime fishing.

Antron spinner.

> Hook: Daiichi 1170 (for most mayflies) or 1280
>   (for drakes and other longer-bodied flies)
> Thread: 8/0 Uni-Thread
> Tail: divided Micro Fibetts
> Wing: Antron or hackle
> Body: beaver dubbing

Catskill Style and Wulffs

Catskill- and Wulff-style dry flies are as much a part of the fabric of the Upper Delaware River system as the water, trout, and mountains. Both these dry-fly styles are often used for blind casting through Upper Delaware riffles during the day and for their high visibility when fishing near and after dark.

Catskill-style Dette Coffin
Fly (tied by Mary Dette).

> Hook: Daiichi 1170
> Thread: 8/0 Uni-Thread
> Tail: clump of hackle fibers (Catskill style) or
>   calf tail (Wulff style); the Dette Coffin Fly
>   uses three divided peccary fibers.
> Wing: hen hackle tips or feather fibers (Catskill style)
>   or calf tail (Wulff style)
> Hackle: same size as the hook; color varies according
>   to the mayfly species
> Body: beaver dubbing

CDC Caddis.

CDC Caddis

Caddis dry-fly imitations may be less glamorous than most dainty mayfly patterns, but they are vital for catching Upper Delaware trout. The CDC Caddis has a great, flush-riding profile for fishing daytime caddis hatches on flat, glassy pools.

Hook: Daiichi 1170
Thread: 8/0 Uni-Thread
Wing: CDC
Legs: CDC
Body: beaver dubbing

CDC, Snowshoe, and Deer-Hair Emergers

CDC Burke Emerger.

Many Upper Delaware anglers' favorite dry-fly patterns are CDC, snowshoe, and deer-hair emergers. These versatile patterns can be tied to match any mayfly hatch. One of my favorite CDC emergers is a minor variation of the standard pattern I tie for the *Isonychia* hatch. It incorporates a trailing shuck of mink guard hairs instead of the traditional Antron shuck and a more substantial CDC wing tied at a 90-degree angle to the hook shank. I call this pattern the Burke Iso, after the well-known writer and my good friend Monte Burke. Monte prefers this pattern above all others for imitating the Upper Delaware's legendary *Isonychia* hatch.

Deer-hair and snowshoe emergers are tied nearly the same as CDC emergers. The only difference is the wing material—the CDC wing is replaced with either deer hair or snowshoe rabbit's foot hair.

Hook: Daiichi 1130
Thread: 8/0 Uni-Thread
Shuck: Antron or mink guard hairs
Wing: 4 to 6 CDC feathers, elk or deer hair, or a clump of snowshoe
         rabbit's foot fur
Body: beaver dubbing

Deer hair and CDC Comparaduns and Sparkle Duns

Comparadun.

The Comparadun, invented by Upper Delaware legend Al Caucci, is one of the most effective and best-selling dry-fly patterns ever created. The popularity of CDC has also inspired tiers to replace the Comparadun's traditional deer-hair wing with one made from CDC. Both styles work very well on the Upper Delaware. The famed western fly tier Mike Lawson added a trailing shuck to the Comparadun to create his Sparkle Dun. It's quite probable that more Upper Delaware trout are caught on Comparaduns and Sparkle Duns than any other dun-imitating dry-fly pattern.

Hook: Daiichi 1170 (for most mayflies) or 1280 (for drakes and other longer-bodied flies)
Thread: 8/0 Uni-Thread
Tail: divided Micro Fibetts (Comparaduns) or Antron (Sparkle Duns)
Wing: deer hair (standard Comparaduns and Sparkle Duns) or CDC (CDC Comparaduns)
Body: beaver dubbing

Elk Hair Caddis and X Caddis

The highly visible Elk Hair Caddis, invented by Pennsylvania's Al Troth, is one of the most heavily fished caddis patterns on the Upper Delaware. The Elk Hair Caddis's palmered hackle body and elk-hair wing make the pattern very buoyant and an excellent choice for fishing the Upper Delaware's many long, productive riffles. The X Caddis is an Elk Hair Caddis with a trailing shuck and shortened wing and without the palmered hackle. It's better suited for fishing flat water or when trout are eating emerging caddisflies.

Elk Hair Caddis.

Hook: Daiichi 1170
Thread: 8/0 Uni-Thread
Wing: elk hair
Ribbing: fine gold or copper wire
Palmered hackle (Elk Hair Caddis only): same size as the hook, colored to match the body
Body: beaver dubbing
Shuck (X Caddis only): Antron or Z-Lon

Parachutes

Parachutes are probably the second most commonly used Upper Delaware dry-fly pattern. Their low profile makes them an excellent choice for fishing mayfly hatches on slow-water pools. I tie them with and without trailing shucks.

Hook: Daiichi 1170 (for most mayflies) or 1280 (for drakes and other longer-bodied flies)
Thread: 8/0 Uni-Thread
Tail or shuck: Divided Micro Fibetts or Antron
Parachute post: Antron
Hackle: one size larger than the hook, colored to match the body
Body: beaver dubbing

Parachute.

Stimulator.

Stimulators

Randall Kaufmann's Stimulator is an extremely effective pattern for blind-casting in the many Upper Delaware riffles when the giant and golden stoneflies are hatching.

Hook:　Daiichi 1270
Thread:　8/0 Uni-Thread
Tail:　elk hair
Palmered hackle: colored to match the natural, or use brown for the abdomen and grizzly for the thorax
Ribbing:　fine gold wire
Abdomen: yellow dubbing or yarn for Golden Stone; orange dubbing or yarn for Giant Stone
Wing:　elk hair
Thorax:　yellow dubbing or yarn for Golden Stone; orange dubbing or yarn for Giant Stone

Weamer's Truform Emerger.

Truform Flies and Comparachutes

I developed my Truform and Comparachute series of dry flies specifically for the Upper Delaware system. These two patterns have caught more trout for me than any other dry fly since 2001. Truform flies and Comparachutes are tied almost identically, except that Comparachutes utilize a deer-hair wing, similar to a Comparadun, instead of the CDC wing on the Truform flies. I find that deer hair is a little more buoyant for fishing riffles, and it also allows the use of paste and gel dry-fly floatants, which some anglers prefer over powder floatants.

Hook:　Daiichi 1230 (for 2XL flies from size 8 to 14) or Montana Fly Company Weamer's Truform Mayfly Hook (for 1XL flies from size 14 to 18)
Thread:　8/0 Uni-Thread
Tail:　divided Micro Fibetts or Antron for a shuck
Truform wing: 3 to 6 (depending on the quality of the CDC and the size of the fly) CDC feathers
Comparachute wing: deer hair
Parachute post: Antron to match the body color
Hackle:　approximately one size larger than the hook—it should extend almost to the hook's point.
Body:　beaver dubbing or Montana Fly Company Wabbit dubbing

The Usual

The Usual.

The Usual incorporates snowshoe rabbit's foot fur for both the wing and the tail. This dry-fly style was created by the legendary fly tier Fran Betters for use on the rivers near his Adirondack Mountains home. It is also a very effective pattern for the great trout rivers of the Catskill Mountains.

Hook:	Daiichi 1170
Thread:	8/0 Uni-Thread
Tail:	clump of snowshoe rabbit's foot fur
Wing:	clump of snowshoe rabbit's foot fur
Body:	beaver dubbing

Nymph and Wet-Fly Fishing

Ten Tips for Success

1. Leaders and tippets. I prefer my wet-fly and nymph leaders to be 12 feet—the same as my dry-fly leaders. This length is versatile for fishing river sections of varying depths. I don't have to add or remove tippet to change the length of my leader to fish effectively. All I have to do is slide the indicator up or down the leader (for nymphs) or add or remove weight (for wet flies) to get the flies to the proper depth. I usually use 5X tippet for nymph and wet-fly fishing, but I'll drop down to 6X if the river is low and clear. I prefer 5X not for its fish-hooking or fish-holding power but because I tend to lose fewer flies to the river bottom with it.

2. Weight and depth. Nymph and wet-fly patterns won't be effective if they aren't fished near a trout's feeding zone. Use weight—split shot attached to the leader, or lead wire wrapped on the fly's body (beadheads can also be applied to add weight)—to get your nymph and wet-fly patterns deep enough for the trout to see them. You'll know you're fishing deep enough when your flies are ticking the river bottom and you're occasionally losing them.

3. Bright flies on cloudy days, muted flies on bright days. It's popular to incorporate beads or other bright, flashy synthetic materials into nymph and wet-fly patterns. It's widely believed that the flash makes the fly look alive and encourages a trout to eat it. I also use flashy materials in my subsurface fly patterns, but I fish them only on cloudy days. The bright sun reflecting off a synthetic material makes a flashy fly glow. Too much flash, especially on sunny days during low-flow periods, actually scares the fish instead of attracting them. Tie duplicate nymph and wet-fly patterns with muted natural materials for fishing on bright sunny days, and you'll catch more fish.

4. Dissimilar flies. I always fish nymphs or wet flies with a tandem (a two-fly combination), and I always begin fishing with two dissimilar flies: a large fly with a small one; a bright, flashy fly with a dark, muted pattern; a beadhead with a traditionally tied fly. I like to give trout options until I know what they want to eat. Then I'll concentrate on the most effective pattern. Charlie Meck, a tandem fishing expert who is largely responsible for bringing the western tandem fishing method to eastern anglers, taught me this technique for rigging tandem flies. Tie the first large, bright pattern to the tippet at the end of the leader. Then attach another piece of tippet material (6 inches for shallow water, and up to 12 inches for deeper water) to the bend of the first fly's hook. There are many ways to attach the second piece of tippet, but Charlie suggests (and I agree) that a clinch knot is the best method. Tie a loose clinch knot, slide it over the lead hook's point, and then pull the knot tight.

5. Casting tandem flies. Casting a tandem fly is not the same as casting a single fly. Fly fishermen spend a lot of time, and sometimes a lot of money, to learn to cast with tight, crisp loops. A tight loop cuts through the wind, improves accuracy, and adds distance to the cast. But you really don't want a tight loop when you're fishing a tandem fly. The problem is that the trailing fly always falls below the lead fly as they travel together through the air. The trailing fly invariably catches the leader or the line and tangles. You need to learn to open your loops to effectively cast a tandem fly.

It's relatively easy to learn to cast with open loops. You need to focus on how deep your rod tip is dipping on your forward cast and backcast. The fly line always follows the tip of the fly rod. Pressing your thumb down into the cork handle during a forward cast drops the rod tip and opens your loops. Actually, pressing your thumb into the cork causes your wrist to bend forward slightly. But I've found that it's better to ask anglers to press their thumbs rather than bend their wrists, because many of them already use too much wrist in their casts.

6. Wet-fly swing and nymph dead-drift techniques. Most anglers are aware of the negative aspects of a dragging dry fly—trout usually won't eat one. But few spend much time trying to control drag on the subsurface patterns. Nymphs and wet flies differ in their use of drag. Most of the time, you want to fish nymphs on a dead drift—a drift without drag. But wet flies are often intentionally fished with drag to make them appear alive. The difference between the two patterns is based on what you're trying to imitate. Nymphs are used to imitate the larval stage of aquatic insects. They are fished without drag because many of the real insects either flow with the river currents or crawl along the riverbed.

Wet flies are typically used to mimic emerging mayflies or caddisflies, but they can also be used to imitate some swimming nymph species such as the *Isonychia.* Wet flies are fished with a slightly downriver cast. As soon as the line hits the water, it should be mended (gently flip the small section of fly line near the leader upriver to complete a mend). Mend it upriver again when the line begins to straighten. After the second mend, the flies should be ticking as they bounce along the river bottom. If they aren't, mend the line again. If they still don't tick, add more weight before the next cast. Once the flies are ticking the river bottom, the river's flow causes the fly line to belly

New York City chef Tom Valenti caught this nice brown with a beadhead Pheasant Tail Nymph.

and drag the wet flies from the river bottom toward the surface. Most trout take the flies as they are swinging toward the surface. Allow the flies to dangle at the end of the cast—they look like emergers trying to break free of the surface film. Retrieve the wet flies with a twisting motion in your line hand to mimic swimming nymphs. Recast after you have retrieved the flies.

Nymphs are usually fished with a slight upriver cast and an immediate upriver mend to get them to sink as quickly as possible. The flies need to reach the river bottom to be effective. Start watching the indicator as soon as it hits the water. If it doesn't occasionally hesitate, the flies aren't on the bottom. Add more weight or perform more mends to get the flies deeper. Mend the line to keep the indicator floating at the same speed as the river. If a bubble or leaf is near the indicator, try to match its speed with the indicator. One of the most common failures of neophyte nymph fishermen is that they don't lift their rod tips each time the indicator pauses. Some of my clients have told me that they didn't lift their rod tips because their flies were tapping rocks. That may have been true, but sometimes what you think is a rock might actually be the subtle take of a trout. Even if the hesitation is a rock, gently lifting the rod tip allows the flies to move past it without getting stuck.

7. Timing and location. Many anglers fish nymphs or wet flies only out of desperation—as a last resort when there are no rising fish. But just like dry-fly fishing, productive nymphing and wet-fly fishing requires that you fish the proper flies, as dictated by the conditions. One of the best times to nymph is right before a hatch. Nymphs become very active before they hatch into duns, making them prime targets for trout. Wet-fly and nymph fishermen need to have a basic understanding of the hatching characteristics of aquatic insects to be successful with this fly-fishing method. Wet flies work well during many fishing conditions, but your catch rate will greatly improve if you fish flies imitating insects that emerge on the river bottom, such as most caddisflies and all quill Gordons and vitreus mayflies. Wet flies are extremely productive for imitating this behavior.

You won't catch many trout if you're fishing subsurface in the shallow heads of riffles or the still-water sections of pools. Look for dropoff areas in the riffles, where the streambed indents into a mini-pool or where a riffle braids into a pool. Trout also like to hold in front of, beside, and behind large rocks adjacent to deep runs. Focus your subsurface fishing on these areas.

Trout often move upriver from their holding areas in a pool into a riffle slot during a hatch. They can easily intercept emerging insects from this location. A riffle slot is simply an impression in the riverbed that gives the fish a current break. Look for changes in a riffle's color to find these slots. They often appear greener or a darker shade of blue than the rest of the riffle. If you fish the slots, you'll usually find trout that are looking for wet flies or nymphs.

8. Being quiet. Many anglers scare fish because they don't wade through the water carefully and slowly. Gently slide your feet along the river bottom and ease your way toward the fish as you move into casting position. Anglers also scare trout and ruin fly-fishing opportunities by rushing toward the river's center to cast to the far bank. I don't know why, but many anglers seem to believe that there are always more trout near the opposite side of the river. You should always begin by exploring the water closest to you before you move to the middle of the river. You'll often find trout that you would have missed if you had rushed into the river.

9. Strike indicators (nymphs only). The most successful Upper Delaware nymph fishermen all use indicators. The highly pressured wild trout often take nymphs subtlely, and anglers might miss these takes if they wait to feel the strike or see a movement change in the leader. Indicators help you identify subtle takes quickly, and that results in more hookups.

Today's nymph fishermen have lots of strike indicator options. If you've had success with a particular indicator style on other rivers and creeks, then use that style on the Upper Delaware. If you really haven't found a good indicator, you might want to try the ones I use. Deep, heavy nymphing with big flies or a lot of split shot necessitates the use of a very buoyant indicator. I prefer the large yarn indicators called Nymph Trackers, greased with a silicon dry-fly dressing, for this type of nymphing. They attach to the leader with a small hook, just like a bobber, and slide up and down the leader, making it easy to change the fishing depth of your nymphs. I use the foam stick-on indicators for fishing smaller nymphs or when the river is low and clear. Some anglers don't like these indicators because they're difficult to remove from the leader. I like them because they're inexpensive. If I want to remove one, I

Careful, painfully slow wading is vital in low water to get into casting position without scaring the fish. RUTHANN WEAMER

simply use my nippers to cut a slit on the closed edge of the indicator and pull my leader through it.

The color of the strike indicator is important. White indicators may appear to be a good, visible choice, but they're not. The river's white foam and scum lines, well known for holding substantial populations of trout, tend to obscure white indicators. I prefer bright fluorescent orange, red, or pink indicators for most of my fishing. However, if the river's surface is covered with glare from the sun, a black indicator is actually more visible than a bright-colored one.

10. Fishing wet flies dry. One of the best tricks for catching the highly selective surface-feeding Upper Delaware trout is to fish a wet fly dry. Obviously, only unweighted fly patterns can be fished dry, and a wet fly must be dressed with some sort of floatant to ensure that it floats (I dust my wet flies with Frog's Fanny). Wet flies actually sit flush in the surface film, so they aren't really dry—let's call them damp. A damp wet fly looks like a crippled or stunned emerger. It appears to be a helpless insect—very attractive to a trout. One of my favorite wets to fish damp is LaFontaine's Emergent Sparkle Pupa. My friend Ron "Curly" Huber and I jokingly call this damp wet fly the "secret fly" because it has produced so many trout for us. But LaFontaine's fly isn't the only wet that will catch Upper Delaware trout if it's fished damp. I've fished every wet-fly style listed as a damp fly, and I've caught trout on each one of them.

Standard nymph.

Nymph Patterns

Standard Nymphs

All standard nymphs are tied basically the same way. The color of the materials used and the size of the pattern allow them to match specific hatches. Standard nymph patterns can be tied with or without beads or additional weight. The unweighted patterns can be greased and fished in the surface film to imitate an emerging mayfly—similar to the way I use damp wet-fly patterns.

Hook: Daiichi 1560
Thread: 8/0 Uni-Thread
Tail: feather fibers, colored to match the natural
Wing case: turkey or other feathers, colored to match the natural
Body: dubbing to match the natural
Legs: hackle or feather fibers tied as a collar or splayed to the sides, colored to match the natural

Copper John

The Copper John, invented by western fly tier John Barr, has become one of Upper Delaware's most popular nymph patterns. The Copper John is an attractor nymph and doesn't imitate a specific insect. I often use it as a searching pattern.

Hook: Daiichi 1560
Head: gold bead
Thread: 8/0 Uni-Thread
Tail: black goose biots
Abdomen: copper wire
Thorax: peacock herl
Wing case: Wapsi Thin Skin; a strip of Flashabou coated with epoxy
Legs: partridge or hen back feathers

Copper John.

Hare's Ears

The Hare's Ear is a standard pattern for most nymph fishermen. These flies look a little like every mayfly nymph, but not exactly like any of them. Hare's Ear dubbing can be dyed to match the color of any natural nymph, making this one of the most versatile and effective nymphs ever created.

Hook: Daiichi 1560 or 1120 (for curved nymphs)
Head: gold, silver, or copper bead (optional)
Thread: 8/0 Uni-Thread

Hare's Ear.

Tail: brown woodchuck or partridge
Body: hare's ear dubbing
Ribbing: flat gold tinsel
Thorax: hare's ear dubbing
Wing case: dark brown turkey

Pheasant Tails

The Pheasant Tail Nymph, originally created by Great Britain's Frank Sawyer, is probably the most popular nymph pattern in the world. It's similar to a Hare's Ear only because both are attractor patterns—not tied to match a particular hatch. In the insect world, many nymphs darken in color immediately before they emerge into duns, which is when they are most vulnerable and attractive to trout. The dark-colored pheasant tail gives the impression of a nymph ready to emerge.

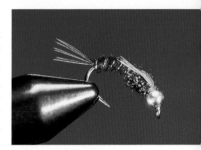
Pheasant Tail Nymph.

  Hook: Daiichi 1560 or 1120 (for curved nymphs)
  Head: gold, silver, or copper bead (optional)
  Thread: 8/0 Uni-Thread
  Tail: pheasant tail fibers
  Abdomen: clump of wrapped pheasant tail fibers
  Thorax: peacock herl
  Wing case: dark brown turkey
  Legs: pheasant tail fibers
  Hackle (optional): brown

Prince

The Prince Nymph, invented by Doug Prince, is also an attractor nymph, but many Upper Delaware anglers use it to match the *Isonychia*. *Isonychia* nymphs have a white stripe in the middle of their backs, which the Prince Nymph's white turkey biot imitates. The Prince should be stripped with short, quick pulls of the fly line to imitate the strong-swimming *Isonychia* nymph. *Isonychia* season isn't the only time to fish the Prince Nymph. Its buggy-looking peacock herl body makes the Prince an effective pattern for imitating many aquatic insects.

Prince Nymph.

  Hook: Daiichi 1710 (for straight hooks) or 1120 (for curved nymphs)
  Head: gold, silver, or copper bead (optional)
  Thread: black 8/0 Uni-Thread
  Tail: brown goose biots
  Rib: gold wire
  Body: peacock herl
  Wing case: white turkey biot
  Hackle: brown

Kyle's Golden Stonefly.

Kyle's Golden Stonefly

This nymph pattern was created by Kyle Giampaoli for western U.S. trout streams, but I consider it the most productive subsurface fly pattern for imitating the Upper Delaware's prolific population of golden stonefly nymphs.

Hook: Daiichi 1720
Head: gold bead
Thread: tan 6/0 Uni-Thread
Tail: brown goose biots
Overback: mottled oak thin skin
Rib: fine gold wire
Body: camel Frog's Hair dubbing (Montana Fly Company)
Wing case: black thin skin
Thorax: yellow Wings-n-Flash dubbing (Montana Fly Company)
Back legs: pumpkin-fleck Silly Legs (Montana Fly Company)
Front legs: tan mallard flank

Bird of Prey Caddis

The Bird of Prey Caddis, invented by Rick Anderson, is one of the most effective caddis larva imitations that I have fished. It also works well as an attractor pattern. I've caught a lot of my winter trout on this fly.

Hook: Daiichi 1120
Head: gold bead
Thread: 8/0 Uni-Thread
Tail: clump of natural Hungarian partridge fibers
Rib: pearl Flashabou accent
Body: dubbing
Hackle: natural Hungarian partridge
Thorax: peacock herl

Bird of Prey Caddis.

Wet-Fly Patterns

Standard Wet Flies

Most standard wet flies are old patterns, and many are no longer fashionable with anglers. The first American dry-fly patterns were actually adapted from these wet flies by adding a stiff dry-fly hackle and erecting their wings. Wet flies, whether fished wet or damp, work as well today as they did in the early days of American fly fishing. Some of my favorite hatches for fishing wet flies are the march browns, sulphurs, quill Gordons, and blue-winged olives.

Standard wet.

Hook: Daiichi 1550
Thread: 8/0 Uni-Thread
Tail: hackle fibers
Body: dubbing, hackle stems, peacock herl stems, or biots—colored to match the natural
Wing: gray duck quill or mottled feather fibers to match the natural
Hackle: hen hackle, colored to match the natural

Soft Hackles

Soft hackles are tied similarly to standard wet flies, but they omit the wings and tails. The flies are quick and easy to tie and are particularly effective for imitating emerging caddisflies, although they can imitate mayflies as well.

Soft hackle.

Hook: Daiichi 1550
Thread: 8/0 Uni-Thread
Body: dubbing or synthetics to match the natural
Ribbing (optional): fine gold or copper wire
Hackle: hen or partridge hackle, colored to match the natural

LaFontaine Emergent Sparkle Pupa

This pattern, created by the brilliant fly tier Gary LaFontaine, is one of the most versatile and effective caddis emergers ever conceived. It can be tied in assorted colors and fished either wet or damp to imitate virtually all caddis species in various stages of development.

LaFontaine Emergent Sparkle Pupa.

Hook: Daiichi 1550
Thread: 8/0 Uni-Thread
Shuck: Antron
Underbody: dubbing
Overbody: Antron
Wing: deer hair
Head: dubbing

Streamer Fishing

Ten Tips for Success

1. **Full-sinking or sinking-tip fly lines.** Many eastern anglers are unfamiliar with sinking fly lines because the narrow, shallow nature of most eastern trout streams limit their use. But if you want to catch Upper Delaware trout on streamers, you need to be familiar with the various types.

Before you purchase a sinking line, you need to decide which rod you're going to use with it. I suggest a 6- or 7-weight rod for Upper Delaware streamer fishing, but you don't have to purchase a rod just for casting streamers. I use the same 6-weight that I use for my dry-fly and nymph fishing.

Sinking fly lines are manufactured in two configurations: full sinking and sinking tip. Full sinking means exactly what its name implies—the entire line sinks. I prefer full-sinking lines because I'm accustomed to using them, the Upper Delaware's pools can be very deep, and I find them easier to cast than sinking-tip lines. The one problem with full-sinking lines for wading anglers is line management. You have to be cognizant of where you are placing the line when you strip in the fly. If you just drop the fly line at your feet, it will tangle on rocks or underwater debris, because it sinks. Some anglers use stripping baskets to correct this problem. I simply wrap the line in loose coils around my stripping hand as I retrieve the fly. It takes some practice to feel comfortable with this technique, but it is effective.

Sinking-tip lines limit how deep the line will sink, based on the length of its head. Most sinking tips for river trout fishing have a 7- to 15-foot sinking section at the head. These lines work as they are intended, and many Upper Delaware anglers use them, but I find that sinking-tip lines tend to hinge when I cast them. The benefit of sinking-tip lines is that most of the line floats. Many anglers find it easier to mend and control a sinking-tip line than a full sinker. I always encourage wading anglers who are unfamiliar with sinking lines to begin with sinking tips because they are easier to manage.

Another characteristic of sinking lines is how fast they sink. Most sinking lines are rated in types or grains. The higher the type or grain number, the faster the line sinks. I prefer my Upper Delaware sinking lines to be type 6, the fastest sink rate, because they get my streamers into the trout's zone very quickly. However, these lines are difficult to use during low-flow conditions because they often catch on the river bottom.

The third sinking-line option, the intermediate line, is useful for low river conditions. These lines fill the gap between sinking and floating lines—they sink just under the water's surface. I'll switch to an intermediate line if I'm constantly snagging the river bottom with my type 6 full-sinking line. If I'm still snagging the bottom with an intermediate line, I'll switch to a floating line and lengthen the leader.

2. Short, heavy leaders. Streamer leader choices are relatively simple compared with those for dry-fly or nymph fishing. I use a short 5-foot leader tapered to a 0X or 1X tippet for all my streamer fishing with sinking lines. I lengthen the streamer leader-tippet combination from $7^1/2$ to 9 feet and reduce the tippet size to 2X or 3X for fishing with floating fly lines or when the river is low and clear. I never use tippets lighter than 3X for Upper Delaware streamer fishing. The size and subsurface nature of streamers make lighter tippets unnecessary.

3. Casting streamers. Casting streamers is similar to casting tandem wet flies or nymphs—you need to use an open casting loop. Many streamer patterns are heavily weighted, which makes them hang below the fly line, just like the trailing tandem fly. Use the same technique for opening your loop that was described earlier for casting tandem flies. Anglers face two additional casting problems when learning to fish streamers. The first is overcastting. Many anglers false-cast too much and have difficulty keeping the heavy flies in the air. They also miss a lot of productive water by constantly false-casting from a drift boat. Backcast your fly line into the air and lay it back into the water immediately. The second problem is getting the streamer from the water into the air to recast. Most anglers who struggle with this are trying to backcast the sinking line when it is still too deep in the river. Begin each backcast by stripping in enough fly line to get it, and the fly, high in the water column. The line will be under much less water tension and will pop out of the water easily.

4. **Stripping and dead-drifting streamers.** Many anglers strip their streamers too slow. It is impossible to strip a streamer faster than a trout can catch it. You want to provoke a predatory response from the fish, and if you strip a streamer too slow, the fish may have time to "rethink" its decision to eat it. If you strip it fast, the fish must decide immediately whether to eat the fly or let it pass. Streamers should be stripped with quick, short strokes to make the fly look like an injured baitfish. Upper Delaware trout want easy meals, so they seldom waste the energy it takes to catch a healthy minnow if they can grab an injured one.

There are a couple of exceptions to the fast stripping method. If the river is low and clear and you are using smaller streamers (which is a good idea under these conditions), it can be more effective to strip the fly slowly. Trout become very wary during low-water conditions, so a large streamer ripped through their holding lies will probably send them swimming away. Small streamers attached to lighter tippets may induce a strike if they are slowly, tantalizingly stripped through pockets of deep water. Use a long strip, and pull the line gently—sometimes even feeding it back and forth—and you may convince a trout to eat your streamer.

Another time when fast stripping may not be productive is when the river is loaded with alewives. Many alewives die when they are flushed into the river, but not all of them die immediately. Trout may feed only on dead or stunned alewives if the river is so full of baitfish that they can afford to feed selectively. The best way to catch these fish is to dead-drift your streamer. Cast it upriver, and follow its downriver progression with the rod tip. If the line stops or hesitates, set the hook. I always begin streamer fishing by stripping fast, regardless of the presence of alewives. But if I'm not catching fish, I slow down and let the fly dead-drift. Sometimes, this trick turns a slow fishing day into a very good one.

5. **Streamer colors.** Always start with a white streamer and then experiment with other colors. The Upper Delaware trout's fondness for alewives is the reason I always begin streamer fishing with a white-colored streamer. More Upper Delaware trout are caught with white streamers than any other color. If the trout aren't interested in a white streamer, I always switch to black. It's the exact opposite of white, and sometimes that's a good enough

reason for the fish to eat it. If I'm not catching fish on either white or black streamers, then I'll try other colors, usually progressing from olive to yellow to brown.

6. Appreciating higher river flows. Many anglers are discouraged—and some don't even try to fish—when the Upper Delaware is running high and off-color, but they miss some of the best streamer fishing opportunities of the year. Upper Delaware trout usually become aggressive during high-flow conditions. Land-born insects are washed into the river, baitfish are displaced from their protected lies, and trout seem to feel more secure when the river is high and dirty. Many trout hold tight to the banks, deep in the submerged grass, and wait to ambush prey. Fishing from a boat is best during high-river conditions, but I've also caught fish while carefully wading. You don't have to wade deep into the river, and you may not have to get into the river at all if you fish along the banks. Don't be discouraged by high water. You may catch more fish than you would during "ideal" conditions.

7. Big flies for high river levels. If a wild trout is going to fight through high river currents to feed, it has to be worth the effort. Use large streamers when the rivers are high or off-color to inspire the fish. I know of several Upper Delaware fly fishermen who have had very large brown trout attack, and sometimes even eat, smaller trout they were playing and about to land. Guide Jim "Coz" Costolnick and a client had one of these experiences in 2003, after the client hooked an 8-inch fish on a dry-fly. The client was bringing the small fish to the boat when a 2-foot brown appeared from nowhere and grabbed the small fish sideways. Coz and his client were able to land both

Upper Delaware brown trout aggressively attack streamers. This one, caught on a white Weamer Streamer, is lying on a submerged weed bed. Trout that are going to be released should never be placed on dry ground for a photograph.

fish, even though the big brown wasn't even hooked—it just wouldn't let go of the smaller fish. It's impossible to fish a streamer that's too large in the Delaware. Use big, flashy streamers when the river is high, and you might catch a 2-foot brown too.

8. Fishing tight to the banks. Upper Delaware trout often hold near the banks during high-flow conditions, so it's vital that your casts land within a few inches of the bank if you want to catch them. Long fly retrieves are unnecessary when the fish are tucked into the grass. Four or five strips are all you need to effectively present your fly. If a trout hasn't taken your streamer by the fourth or fifth strip, cast again. Many anglers spend too much time stripping their streamers all the way to the boat during high river conditions.

9. Early-morning summer streamer fishing. Mark "Striperman" Celebuski is one of the Upper Delaware's best streamer fishermen, and that's because he works at it. Many anglers fish streamers only when the river is blown out, as a last resort when they aren't catching fish on dry flies. Mark *plans* to fish streamers, and that's one of the reasons he's so successful. Some of the most productive times to fish streamers are early summer mornings. Mark begins fishing about half an hour before sunrise, and he's usually done between 10:00 and noon. He generally uses large flies on full-sinking lines, but some of his biggest fish have come during low-light conditions while using Deceivers on a floating fly line. The river is often completely devoid of anglers during Mark's early-morning summer trips—sometimes he catches five or six large browns before most anglers are even out of bed. By the time the sun is high in the sky and the river begins to fill with fishermen, Mark is gone. The trout usually stop eating streamers when they are exposed to the bright, hot summer sun. Upper Delaware anglers who want to catch fish can learn two important lessons from Mark's tactics. First, whenever possible, fish when the trout want to feed. Second, have a plan for your fishing. Dry flies, nymphs, wets, and streamers can all be effective if they are fished at the appropriate times.

10. Short strikes and refusals. Short strikes—when a fish appears to eat your streamer but you don't hook it—and outright refusals tend to occur when the river has been running high for more than a week and many anglers have been fishing streamers, or when the river is low and clear. The fish start to get wary of streamers after a week or two of heavy fishing pressure. There are a couple of ways to combat this problem. First, use a smaller fly. Large streamers are very easy for trout to see, which is a good thing when the water is stained but a potential problem during periods of intense, riverwide streamer fishing or low water. If you use a smaller fly, the trout may not realize that it's a fake until it's too late. Second, reduce the size of your tippet. Most of the time, tippet size is unimportant for streamer fishing. But if the fish have been pressured or the water is clear, dropping a tippet size can produce better results. Last, change the way you strip your fly. Stripping streamers was already discussed in tip 4. If you follow those suggestions, it may also improve your hookup rates.

Streamer Patterns

Clouser Minnow

Clouser Minnow.

Bob Clouser, the great Pennsylvania fly tier, invented this terrific streamer pattern. The Clouser's heavy dumbbell eyes and sparse body make it an excellent choice for high water conditions because it sinks quickly.

Hook: Daiichi 1750
Thread: 6/0 Uni-Thread
Body and Tail: bucktail
Underwing: bucktail
Head: lead dumbbell eyes (painted eyeballs
         are optional)

Double Bunny and Zonker

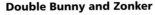

Double Bunny.

It's hard to beat the lifelike effects of a wet rabbit strip for streamers. Both the Double Bunny, created by Scott Sanchez, and the Zonker incorporate rabbit strips into their construction. Double Bunnies and Zonker-style flies have probably caught more Upper Delaware trout than any other streamer pattern.

Hook: Daiichi 2220
Thread: 6/0 Uni-Thread
Head (Double Bunny): lead dumbbell eyes
Body: 2 zonker strips—one on the top and one on
         the bottom of the hook shank—for the Double
         Bunny; Mylar tubing for the Zonker
Fins (Double Bunny): flash material or flank feathers
Wing (Zonker): zonker strip

Lefty's Deceiver

Mark Celebuski was the first person to clue me in to the effectiveness of the Lefty's Deceiver streamer pattern for catching Upper Delaware trout. The versatile Deceiver, created by fly-fishing legend Lefty Kreh, is usually considered a saltwater pattern, but Upper Delaware trout don't know that. Mark believes that the most effective Deceiver pattern for the Upper Delaware is tied with blue and white deer hair. His great success with this pattern, as well as my own, has made me a big believer in the blue and white Deceiver.

Hook: Daiichi 2220
Thread: white monocord
Body: flat silver tinsel

Underwing: 2 saddle hackles
Wing: top—blue bucktail; bottom—white bucktail
Throat: red Krystal Flash
Head: white thread with painted black eyes

Weamer Streamer

I designed the Weamer Streamer as a way to fish
larger streamer patterns. As mentioned in tip 7, large
streamers are often effective for catching Upper
Delaware trout. But how do you tie a 4- to 6-inch
streamer? Long rabbit strips usually tangle around
the hook, and if a trout eats the long fly's tail, you
can't hook it. Weamer Streamers incorporate a non-
traditional snap (the same snap attached to a spin-
fishing snap swivel) into their construction to solve
these problems. The snap is attached to the bend of
the lead hook with heavy monofilament and super-

Weamer Streamer.

glue, just after the marabou tail is tied in. I use the snap to connect two flies by
threading the open snap into the eye of the inverted (upside down) trailing fly.
Make sure that the zonker (rabbit) strip of the lead fly is long enough to extend
beyond the trailing fly's point while the latter is attached to the snap. The trailing hook can then be inserted into the lead hook's zonker strip tail on its
underside (the skin side). The trailing hook should be debarbed so that it can
be pulled in or out of the zonker strip easily, making them interchangeable by
opening the snap and popping them out of the lead fly's zonker strip. The trailing flies can be tied with various colors and flash to produce several patterns
with one fly. This pattern looks incredibly lifelike in the water and has produced a lot of Upper Delaware trout. You seldom miss strikes from trout that
eat the fly's tail, because the tail contains the trailing fly's hook.

Lead hook: Daiichi 2220
Thread: 6/0 Uni-Thread
Snap: attached with heavy monofilament and secured with superglue
Head: gold cone
Tail: marabou
Body: chenille
Palmered hackle: match the color of the body
Wing: zonker strip

Trailing hook: Daiichi 2340 (at least one size larger than the lead hook)
Thread: 6/0 Uni-Thread
Tail: marabou
Body: chenille
Palmered hackle: match the color of the body
Wing: zonker strip

Weamer's Alewife.

Weamer's Alewife

I developed this pattern to imitate the famous West Branch alewives. Most anglers use alewife patterns tied with predominantly white materials, which work well for imitating dead or dying alewives. In contrast, the Weamer's Alewife was designed to imitate alewives that are still very much alive. The pattern is really just a cross between a Woolly Bugger and a Zonker. It has become one of my most productive West Branch streamers.

Hook: Daiichi 2220
Thread: 6/0 Uni-Thread
Head: silver Real Eyes cone
Tail: white marabou
Body: white chenille
Palmered hackle: white saddle
Ribbing: round silver tinsel
Wing: gray zonker strip
Gills: red chenille
Fins: white Antron

Woolly Bugger

Woolly Bugger.

Pennsylvania's Russ Blessing invented the original Woolly Bugger. His pattern has been altered hundreds of times and is probably the world's most popular streamer.

Hook: Daiichi 2220
Head: gold or silver cone
Thread: 6/0 Uni-Thread
Tail: marabou
Body: chenille
Palmered hackle: saddle hackle, colored to match
         the body
Ribbing: fine gold or silver wire

Zuddler

Zuddler.

The Zuddler, created by Joe Emery and John Rode, is a cross between a Muddler Minnow and a Zonker. The pattern was originally designed for steelhead fishing in the Great Lakes region, but it also works well in the Upper Delaware when it's tied with white or black materials (I've also had some success fishing olive Zuddlers). I once caught an 18-inch smallmouth bass and a 21-inch brown trout on back-to-back casts in the Middle Main Stem while fishing a black Zuddler.

Hook: Daiichi 2220
Thread: 6/0 Uni-Thread
Tail: smolt blue Krystal Flash
Body: light gray synthetic with flash
Wing: zonker strip
Legs: medium round rubber
Throat: red Krystal Flash
Head: gold or silver cone on top of spun deer hair

Night Fishing

Many fly fishermen never try fishing at night. Sure, most of us have cast to trout sipping spinners at dusk or even early darkness, but that isn't true night fishing. True night fishermen are beginning their trips while the rest of us are heading home or are already asleep.

Summer is the season for night fishing on the Upper Delaware. Low river flows and higher daytime water temperatures turn many of the largest trout nocturnal. And there's no question that only the largest trout are sought by these anglers. Would you stay up all night to catch little fish? Neither would I.

Upper Delaware night fly fishermen have always been a small group—a secretive cult that seems to take pleasure in being dedicated, tough, or crazy enough to hunt and catch the largest Upper Delaware River trout at the most difficult time of year. And although they do it at some of the most popular access areas, they usually fish in complete solitude.

I'm not a night-fishing expert. In fact, over the years, I had developed a list of excuses to keep me safe at home while my friends were out night fishing. It wasn't until the summer of 2005 that I seriously considered fly fishing after dark. I knew that enough people were fly fishing the Upper Delaware at night to merit its inclusion in this book. My night-fishing friends and fly-shop customers had shown me photos of heavy, hook-jawed browns washed in the glare of camera flash. It didn't hurt that the daytime fishing had been poor that summer and that my friends Walter "Wally" Falkoff and Jack Mynarski were catching large trout at night without me.

Wally and Jack are both hard-core Upper Delaware night fly fishermen. Wally is a retired chef and current Upper Delaware River guide. He's been serious about night fishing the Upper Delaware for only a few years, but he's no rookie. Wally began night fishing in Connecticut as a kid, so it seemed natural to apply those childhood skills to the Upper Delaware River when he retired to Hancock, New York, several years ago. At 72 years old, Jack Mynarski is an Upper Delaware River night-fishing expert. He's been chasing large Upper Delaware brown trout under starlit Catskill skies for over 40 years. Jack has taken night fishing to an art form, and if you invite him to a daytime fly-fishing excursion in the summer, you'll probably get one of his patented responses: "Why would I want to fish with all those people? Who wants to fish in the blazing hot sun with nothing hatching, anyway? All you'll catch is little fish, and that's if you're lucky."

The author's father, Ed Weamer, proves that Upper Delaware night fishing is worth it.

Jack's thoughts on summer fishing may be a little narrow-minded, but he makes a good point. If you enjoy fly fishing in solitude for large trout—fish that few daytime anglers ever see—then night fishing might be for you. Even before my first night-fishing trip, I was sure that it wasn't for me. It was just something that I needed to do for the book.

I met Jack and Wally at 8:30 p.m. for my first night of fly fishing. It was early for my two companions, who are used to fishing much later at night. They had agreed to meet me earlier than normal to answer some of my questions. We talked about tactics, conditions, and where we should fish as we strung our rods, adjusted leaders, and attached our flies under the lights of a Sunoco station.

Jack said that he was glad the air was cool so the "smoke" (Jack's word for fog) wouldn't appear. Apparently, fog ruins night fishing, although Wally doesn't believe that fog is always a bad thing. I began to realize that night fishermen, like most day fishermen, have very different, even divergent views about the best fishing conditions and tactics. Jack told me that the key to catching fish was to get the fly to move and make noise. "Start stripping the fly, as soon as it hits the water," he said. "Always begin working the fly slowly and then quicken the pace." Once again, Wally disagreed. "They want it on the swing. Cast to the far bank and gently twitch the fly as it makes its turn in the current."

One of the few things that night fishermen seem to agree about is fly color. Nearly all of Jack's and Wally's night flies are black. Jack showed me his fly boxes packed full of Harvey Pushers (named for their inventor, Pennsylvania fly-fishing legend George Harvey), large black dry flies with huge wings intended to displace water when stripped, as well as black wets and streamers—flies typically sized for steelhead or salmon.

I watched as Jack tied a massive black wet fly to his leader below a smaller, standard-looking, yellow wet fly. I couldn't understand why he was using the small yellow wet when I had just received a long discourse on the importance of large black flies, so I asked him about it. "I'm fishing a tandem," Jack replied. I told him that I understood the concept of a tandem; I just didn't understand why he was using a small yellow fly instead of another big black one. "I

Harvey Pusher Night Fly (tied by Jack Mynarski).

don't know," he said. "I read about it somewhere—Bashline, I think [a reference to Pennsylvania night-fishing legend James Bashline]. What the hell, sometimes it works." And it did work that night.

We chose our fishing spot and were soon standing on the banks of the Upper East Branch. The river looked different than it does during the day—mysterious and dark, like a simmering cup of black, early-morning coffee. It didn't take long for a trout to appear. I noticed a subtle rise, reflected in starlight, as soon as my feet became wet with river water. I pointed the rise out to Jack, and he cast to it. The fish struck, and Jack quickly landed a beautiful 16-inch brown. "Just a baby," he said, as he gently released it. "Go tell your great-grandmother we're here."

The "small" brown was the only fish we caught that night—not exactly what I had in mind when I agreed to join the adventure. But something happened as we stood there quietly casting our flies to banks we couldn't see. I watched the sky as meteors fell amidst a black field planted with shining stars. It was beautiful. The river was quiet and peaceful, like it must have been centuries ago. I realized that I was really enjoying this night-fishing thing, and I thought I'd like to do it again. And I have.

You won't hear too many night fishermen spouting off Latin names or arguing the best dubbing color for summer sulphurs. I find it refreshing, in a way. It's a relaxed version of fly fishing where the trout sometimes eat your flies just because they want to—no in-depth explanations needed. I'm still making excuses about night fishing, but now I'm giving them to my wife so she'll let me go.

Mynarski's Night Fishing Tips

1. Be familiar with the water you are fishing. Never fish a spot at night that you haven't studied during the day.
2. Go to your night-fishing spot during the day, measure your cast to the bank, and attach a piece of tape on your fly line to mark the distance. You can feel the tape at night and know that your casts are landing near the bank.
3. Fish with a partner whenever possible. If you have to fish alone, tell someone where you are going.
4. Bring a change of clothes so that your night isn't ruined by an unplanned swim.
5. Always carry a few flashlights in case one fails.
6. Slowly shuffle your feet when wading. Avoid wearing noisy, studded wading shoes.
7. Use floating, weight-forward 6- or 7-weight fly lines with heavy, stiff tippets—10-, 12-, or 15-pound test.
8. If trout are rising, try to match what they're eating, just like fishing during the day. If no trout are rising, always begin fishing with a tan-

dem of wet flies—one light and one dark. Prospect with large Harvey Pushers or other night dry flies in the middle of the night; use large black streamers, individually, later at night.

9. Avoid fishing under a full moon—the darker the better.

10. Make flags out of old white cotton T-shirts or paper towels, and use them to mark your path to the river (be sure to remove them when you leave). You'll be surprised how different things look at night.

11. Never shine a flashlight on the water while you're fishing—it scares the fish. But always shine a light on the water before you leave. You'll learn where the fish hold and what, if any, insects are on the water—useful knowledge for future trips.

12. Travel light. Take only items that are absolutely necessary, and leave your fishing vest at home.

13. Fish feed in cycles at night, just like during the day, so be patient if the fishing is slow—it could change in an hour.

Etiquette

All of us are confronted with situations beyond our control when we fish the Upper Delaware River system. Weather, water releases, hatch activity, and trout receptiveness are all things we can't change. The way we interact with one another while we're fishing, however, is one thing we can control—it's called fishing etiquette. This important but often overlooked code of ethics has a tremendous impact on the quality of any Upper Delaware fly-fishing experience.

Boating Etiquette

1. Communicate with other fishermen. If you're not sure which side of the river someone is fishing or where to float through a pool packed with boats and waders, ask the other fishermen how they would like you to proceed around them. You might get an occasional sarcastic reply, but at least you tried. Most anglers will appreciate that.

2. Always float behind wading anglers and other boats. If they are too close to the shore to get behind them, quietly row to the other side of the river. Try not to row, and do not cast, while you are floating past them.

3. Don't be afraid to get out and walk your boat. Sometimes, especially during low water levels, it's the only way to move through a pool or riffle without disturbing everyone else's fishing.

4. Don't choose the peak of the green drake hatch to finally learn how to row a boat. Some outfitters offer rowing courses using guides as teachers, so the guide can take control of the boat during sticky situations. If you want to learn by yourself, practice on a lake or during periods of less intense fishing pressure, such as the fall. Remember, many people plan their vacations or wait all year to fish the Dela-

Boats should be quietly rowed to the far side of the river when it's impossible to float behind a wading angler. Try not to row, and don't cast, as you're floating past.

ware's premier hatches. They shouldn't have to deal with you floating stern first, out of control, over their rising trout.

5. Always give wading anglers plenty of room and the right of way. Never crowd an angler who has walked into a spot. You'll have plenty of opportunities to fish other places when you're drifting, whereas the wader is limited to a much shorter section of the river. If the river is exceptionally crowded or the fishing is poor, it's OK to ask a wader if you can cast to fish rising beyond his or her casting range, as long your casting or boat position doesn't interfere with the wader's fishing. Many waders will say yes, but if not, move on and find another fish.

6. Always ask the intentions of anglers sitting on the bank or anchored in boats. They may be resting a fish. Don't begin fishing in front of or near waders or other boats just because they aren't casting.

7. Row quietly to the takeout after dark. You might be cold, hungry, and ready for a beer, but that doesn't mean that everyone else has stopped fishing. It's difficult to see rising fish after sunset, and the wake and noise from a boat pushing hard to the launch compounds the problem. Judge your time and distance so that you can get off the water without rushing.

8. Release your anchor quietly. Hold the rope and ease it into the water. The splash from an anchor dropped into the water will scare your fish and any one else's nearby.

9. Always be respectful on the water. Don't yell or curse loudly. Don't announce how many fish you caught and then ask a guide with

Stan Gurney and a friend patiently study a trout, rising near the grass, beside an Upper East Branch island. Anglers who aren't casting may be resting a fish, so never begin fishing before you ask their intentions. Patience is one of the most important traits of successful Upper Delaware anglers.

       clients how many they caught. If the guide is having a tough day, neither the guide nor his or her clients will appreciate your bragging.

10. If you screw up—and sooner or later, everyone does—apologize and move on. Try to learn from your mistakes.

Wading Etiquette

1. If you're not sure where an upriver boat is headed, politely reveal where you are fishing and ask the rower to go behind you, if possible. Let your intentions be known—no one can read your mind.

2. Pick one side of the river to fish, and don't switch sides when a boat approaches. Many times, wading anglers cast to one side of the river and then quickly cast in the other direction—too late for an upriver boat to correct its course. Boats are maneuverable, but changing direction quickly in moving water can be very difficult, and sometimes it's impossible.

3. Stop casting when a boat is behind you. Sometimes it's necessary for a boat to float very close to you to avoid spooking your fish. I've seen careless waders unintentionally hook boaters on their backcast because they weren't paying attention.

4. Never stand or cast within at least half a fly line's distance of another angler. If you're lucky enough to be fishing the river on a day when there are few other anglers, then it's proper to give at least half a pool to another fisherman. Solitude is priceless on the Delaware, and it's a great gift to give to yourself or other fishermen whenever possible.

5. Always try to wade as quietly as possible. You'll catch more fish and won't disturb those fishing around you.

6. Cross the river well above or below another angler whenever possible.

7. Anglers fishing downriver have the right of way. If you're fishing upriver and approach another angler, get out of the river or wade as close to the shore as possible. Reenter the river above and well beyond the casting range of the other fisherman. This rule applies specifically to the Upper Delaware River. Throughout fly-fishing history, the angler fishing upriver has always had the right of way. But most seasoned Delaware anglers cast quartering downriver to rising fish. If the traditional rules applied, an upriver wading angler could inadvertently start casting to a trout that another angler was already casting to or approaching.

8. Never stand directly across the river from another fisherman unless you are fishing a large, deep pool. The fisherman across the river may be easing his way out to your fish or may be able to cast farther than you can. It's acceptable to stand across from an angler fishing a big pool only if that angler can't reach the fish you're casting to. If you're not sure whether the other angler can reach the fish, ask.

9. Never trespass across private property, no matter how good the fishing is on the other side.

10. Don't "relieve yourself" within plain sight of someone's house. You wouldn't like someone doing that in your yard. This rule applies to both wading and floating fishermen.

Fishing downriver to rising trout is important in the Upper Delaware system if you want to catch fish.

Parking Area and Boat Launch Etiquette

1. Most of the Upper Delaware's official boat launch sites consist of a parking area, the boat turnaround, and the boat launch. Don't park in the turnaround area just because it's closer to the river than the parking area. I have seen anglers who were unable to launch their drift boats because of parked cars in the turnaround. Occasionally, I've seen boat owners almost hit a parked car while trying to launch their boats. Cars belong in parking lots.

2. Don't block the boat launch areas. Often anglers drive their cars onto the ramp at a boat launch just to get a look at the river. I've done this myself occasionally, but only at appropriate times. It's not OK to park on a boat launch ramp during the river's busy season—from the beginning of May through the end of June.

3. Boating anglers retrieve their vehicles and load their boats in the order they arrive at the boat launch. At the most popular launches during the peak season, it's common to see a line of anglers anchored at a launch, waiting for their turn to remove their boats from the river. Everyone's in a hurry and wants to get home, but you must be patient. I have witnessed near fistfights because anglers tried to go out of turn.

4. When it's your turn to remove your boat at the launch area, get your car, get your boat, and get out. Don't talk with your friends, break down your rods, pack your gear, or have a cigarette. You can do all these things after you're off the launch.

5. Don't shine your headlights toward the river from the boat launch. You will ruin the night vision of any anglers still fishing and blind anyone trying to navigate their way to the launch.

6. Be careful with alcoholic beverages at Pennsylvania boat launches. Although it's legal to have an alcoholic beverage while you're on the river (as long as it's not in a glass container), Pennsylvania has an open container law that prohibits drinking alcohol on any public property.

The two most important fishing etiquette rules are to communicate with others and to treat them with respect. But proper river etiquette is more than just a list of rules to follow; it's a mind-set. If you want to fish the Upper Delaware River system in the twenty-first century, you should expect to be doing it with other people. If you don't communicate with other anglers and consider their right to fish as important as your own, then plan on being upset, and upsetting others, fairly often. But if you follow the rules of river fishing etiquette and politely encourage others to do the same, the Upper Delaware will be a peaceful place for all of us.

CHAPTER 6

Spring Hatches

The hatch charts in this chapter and the next one represent only the most common and most important aquatic insects in the Upper Delaware system. They don't include every hatch that can occur in the rivers. The Upper Delaware is blessed with prolific aquatic insect populations—nearly every mayfly, caddisfly, and stonefly species that exists in the eastern United States lives in the Upper Delaware system. But if you limit your fly patterns to representations of the insects listed here, you'll be prepared for the vast majority of the river's hatches.

Hendricksons are one of the Upper Delaware's best hatches. They often provide some of the first reliable dry-fly fishing of the season, as they did on this day for Upper Delaware guide Steve Taggert.

The charts predict when each hatch will begin and end, but keep in mind that these are only approximate dates. Weather has a tremendous impact on the hatches, but the reservoirs are the real deciding factor. Cold reservoir releases, reservoir spillage, or a lack thereof can all have a huge impact on the timing of the river's hatches. And each year is different. This best way to find out whether a hatch has begun or ended is to contact a local fly shop for the most current information.

The hatch charts don't include the time of day when each hatch will begin. Once again, it's difficult to predict the exact timing of hatches due to the river's variable weather and water-release conditions. The timing of most aquatic hatches relies largely on river temperature, and the unpredictability of Upper Delaware's temperature makes estimating hatch times little more than a guess.

If you are interested in learning more about the mayflies, caddisflies, and stoneflies that hatch in the Upper Delaware system, I suggest that you read the following books: *Caddisflies* by Gary LaFontaine (1981), *Hatches II* by Al Caucci and Bob Nastasi (1986), *Mayflies* by Malcolm Knopp and Robert Cormier (1997), and *Stoneflies for the Angler* by Eric Leiser and Robert H. Boyle (1982). I have used all these books to confirm and advance my own understanding of the Upper Delaware's hatches, and some of the hatch information included in this chapter and chapter 7 is rooted in the research they contain.

For those of you who have neither the time nor the inclination to study the Upper Delaware's aquatic insects, another great book, *The Hatches Made Simple* by Charles Meck (2002), was written just for you. Meck based his book on the premise that all mayflies fall within certain shades of color that vary according to the season. The book guides anglers to create mayfly patterns using only a few colors and sizes that will effectively imitate all mayfly hatches.

Spring Hatches

Insect	Size	Hatch Begins	Hatch Ends
Little black stonefly *(Taeniopteryx navalis)*	14–18	Early March	Mid-April
Little brown stonefly *(Strophopteryx faciata)*	16–18	Early March	Mid-April
Blue-winged olive *(Baetis tricaudatis;* formerly *Baetis vagans)*	18–20	Late March	Mid-May
Little black caddis *(Chimarra aterrima)*	18–20	Early April	Late May
Spring blue quill; aka little mahogany dun *(Paraleptophlebia adoptiva)*	18–20	Early April	Mid-May
Giant stonefly *(Pteronarcys dorsata)*	2–4	Early April	Early June
Quill Gordon *(Epeorus pleuralis)*	12	Mid-April	Mid-May
Hendrickson *(Ephemerella subvaria)*	14	Mid-April	Mid-May

(continued)

Spring Hatches (continued)			
Insect	Size	Hatch Begins	Hatch Ends
Apple caddis; aka shad fly *(Brachycentrus)*	14–16	Mid-May	Late May
Grannom *(Brachycentrus numerosus)*	14–16	Mid-May	Late May
March brown; gray fox *(Maccaffertium vicarium;* formerly separate species known as *Stenonema vicarium* and *Stenonema fuscum,* respectively)	8–14	Mid-May	Early July
Tan caddis; aka spotted sedge *(Hydropsyche* species)	14–16	Mid-May	Late August
Little sister sedge; aka olive caddis *(Cheumatopsyche campyla)*	20–22	Mid-May	Mid-June
Big sulphurs *(Ephemerella invaria;* also includes the species once known as *Ephemerella rotunda)*	14–16	Mid-May	Early June
Big Olive; aka cornuta *(Drunella lata;* formerly *Ephemerella cornuta)*	14	Late May	Mid-June
Dark blue sedge *(Psilotreta labida)*	14–16	Late May	Mid-June
Little summer sulphur; aka pale evening dun *(Ephemerella dorothea dorothea;* formerly *Ephemerella dorothea)*	16–18	Late May	Mid-August
Golden stonefly *(Acroneuria lycorial* and related species)	6–8	Late May	Mid-June
Green drake *(Ephemera guttulata)*	8–12	Late May	Mid-June
Brown drake *(Ephemera simulans)*	8–12	Late May	Mid-June
Slate drake; aka Iso; aka white gloved howdy *(Isonychia bicolor;* also includes species formerly known as *Isonychia sadleri* and *Isonychia harperi)*	8–12	Late May	Late June The hatch continues, to a lesser degree, during the summer months and becomes significant once again in the fall
Pink lady; aka big sulphur; aka vitreus *(Epeorus vitreus)*	12–14	Early June	Late August

Mayflies

Blue-Winged Olive *(Baetis tricaudatis; Drunella lata)*

The Upper Delaware's spring blue-winged olive hatches are sometimes overshadowed by the season's more famous hatches. *Baetis* usually begin emerging before many anglers even begin the fishing season, leaving the olives to appear in rivers that are nearly devoid of anglers. But before you plan a trip to take advantage of the river's solitary condi-

Blue-winged olive.

tions, you should know what to expect from this hatch. *Baetis* often begin hatching in the sometimes snowy and often cold days of early spring. They usually have a difficult time flying because of the weather conditions, which can make the duns very attractive to trout. However, they aren't always eagerly eaten by the fish. In some years, very few trout rise to the earliest *Baetis* hatches because low river temperatures have slowed their metabolism. The *Baetis* that hatch during rainy, overcast days later in the spring are often better received by the trout, and they can provide some fantastic fly-fishing opportunities. But even then, the hatches are sometimes eclipsed by other mayflies that appear simultaneously.

The other spring blue-winged olive, the cornuta, is also underappreciated by many of the river's anglers. But it's not the weather or the trout's receptiveness that stops the cornuta from being a premier hatch. Cornutas usually hatch in the mornings between 9 a.m. and noon, when many anglers are still sleeping off their late-night green and brown drake fishing from the day before. Others are in local diners leisurely planning their fishing around the drakes or maybe even the sulphurs. These more glamorous mayflies usually don't begin hatching until midafternoon or early evening, so many anglers aren't even on the water when the cornutas are. The cornutas are a favorite hatch for some anglers—usually anyone who has fished the hatch before. Trout seem to love these big olives, and some years they provide even better fly-fishing opportunities than their mythical cousins the drakes and big sulphurs. *Drunella cornuta* was recently reclassified as *D. lata*, which recognizes that the mayfly species once known as *cornuta*, *cornutella*, and *lata* are all the same species, differing only by size.

Baetis Nymph

Baetis nymphs are excellent swimmers. They live in riffles but drift or swim to slower river sections to emerge.

> Hook: 16–18 standard length shank
> Thread: dark brown
> Three tails: olive brown
> Body: olive brown
> Wing case: black turkey wing
> Hackle: brown

Baetis Dun

> Hook: 18–20 standard length shank
> Thread: olive
> Shuck (optional): dark brown
> Two tails: light dun Micro Fibetts
> Body: olive brown
> Wing: medium dun
> Hackle: olive

Baetis Spinner

Female spinners return to riverside vegetation to fertilize their eggs and then dive or crawl to the river bottom to lay the fertilized eggs. Wet flies can be used effectively to imitate this behavior. The spinners die after laying their eggs, so fishing a sunken spinner can work very well after the spinner fall has ended.

Hook: 18–20 standard length shank
Thread: rust
Two tails: dark dun Micro Fibetts
Body: rusty brown
Spent wing: clear, light gray, or white

Cornuta Nymph

Cornuta nymphs usually live in riffles and migrate from fast to slow water before they emerge. They are poor swimmers, so they often drift in the river, allowing trout an easy opportunity to eat them. Dead-drifting nymphs to imitate the dislodged *D. lata* nymphs can be deadly before and during these hatches.

Hook: 12–14 standard length shank
Thread: olive
Three tails: olive brown
Body: olive brown
Wing case: black turkey wing
Hackle: olive

Cornuta Dun

Cornuta emergers are very brightly colored when they first hatch. Their color slowly darkens as they are exposed to the air.

Hook: 14 standard length shank
Thread: olive
Shuck (optional): dark brown
Three tails: olive Micro Fibetts
Body: chartreuse or bright olive (emergers) to olive (duns)
Wing: medium dun
Hackle: light olive

Cornuta Spinner

Cornuta spinner falls usually occur at dusk or early morning, depending on weather conditions.

Hook: 14 standard length shank
Thread: olive brown
Three tails: olive Micro Fibetts
Body: dark olive
Spent wing: clear, light gray, or white

Blue Quill, Little Mahogany Dun
(Paraleptophlebia adoptiva)

Blue quills provide one of the first opportunities of the year to fish dry flies to rising trout. The hatch can start in early April in a warm year, but the middle or end of the month is more likely during average spring conditions. Trout sometimes ignore the initial hatches of blue quills due to frigid air and water tem-

Blue quill.

peratures. But as the hatch builds, the fish rise to eat the duns. Warm, overcast spring days can produce incredible numbers of blue quills and some excellent fishing.

The Delaware's Main Stem and both of its branches contain excellent populations of blue quills, but I spend most of my time pursuing the hatch on the West and Upper East Branches. The long, flat pools on these rivers provide excellent opportunities to find trout actively eating blue quill duns. Main Stem and Lower East flows are usually high at this time due to melting snow and spring rain. Anglers searching for blue quill hatches in either of these larger rivers may find productive fishing from a drift boat or with careful wading near the shore. Larger flies such as Hendricksons, *Baetis,* and quill Gordons often accompany the blue quills, especially in May. You may need to change fly patterns more than once when individual trout are keying on a particular species.

Nymph

Dark brown *P. adoptiva* nymphs migrate out of the current into slower sections of the river before emergence. They are poor swimmers and often drift with the current. Blue quill nymph patterns should be fished on a dead drift along the edges of any slack water adjacent to a current seam.

    Hook: 16–18 standard length shank
    Thread: dark brown
    Tail: dark brown mallard flank feather fibers
    Body: dark brown
    Wing case: black turkey wing
    Hackle: dark brown

Dun

The blue quill's common name is actually a misnomer—the flies aren't really blue. Summer blue quill species such as *P. mollis* do have a bluish gray body color, so they must be responsible for *P. adoptiva*'s moniker.

    Hook: 16–18 standard length shank
    Thread: rust
    Shuck (optional): dark brown
    Three tails: rust Micro Fibetts
    Body: mahogany
    Wing: medium gray
    Hackle: reddish brown

Spinner

Blue quill spinners aren't blue either—both male and female duns molt into a rusty brown body color. Spinner falls often occur in mid to late afternoon but may appear in the evening or early morning during periods of especially warm weather.

    Hook: 16–18 standard length shank
    Thread: rust
    Three tails: rust Micro Fibetts
    Body: rust
    Spent wing: clear, light gray, or white

Quill Gordon *(Epeorus pleuralis)*

Quill Gordon mayflies require extremely clean and well-oxygenated water, so they are a good indicator of the health of a river system. Quill Gordons usually begin hatching in the Upper Delaware watershed in mid to late April and often coincide with hatches of *Baetis,* blue quills, and early Hendricksons. The hatch lasts approximately two weeks, but it can be accelerated, shortened, and intensified by periods of unusually warm weather.

Quill Gordon.

    The Delaware Main Stem and both of its branches have fishable quill Gordon hatches. However, the Upper and Lower East Branch provide the best fishing opportunities because of their exceptionally large insect populations. The Upper East in particular showcases one of the heaviest quill Gordon hatches I've encountered on any trout stream.

Nymph

Olive-brown colored, quill Gordon nymphs live in well-oxygenated riffles. They are poor swimmers and relocate by drifting to slower water before emerging in the warmest part of the day, usually early afternoon. Quill Gordons emerge on the stream bottom and swim to the surface as duns, and it's vital to imitate this trait for successful subsurface fishing. Size 10 and 12 quill Gordon wet flies are especially effective during the hatch.

    Hook: 12 standard length shank
    Thread: brown
    Tail: mallard flank dyed olive
    Body: dark brown mixed with olive
    Wing case: mottled brown turkey wing
    Hackle: dark olive

Dun

The quill Gordon dun's underside is noticeably lighter than its back, which is similar in coloration to a dark greenish gray stripped peacock quill. I tie some of my quill Gordon drys with trailing shucks, although the duns, emerging on the stream bottom, are usually free of their nymphal shucks when they reach the surface. Shucks are a triggering mechanism for Upper Delaware trout, indicating an easy meal of trapped, stationary flies. They may induce even a lethargic fish to strike.

Hook: 12 standard length shank
Thread: iron gray
Shuck (optional): dark brown
Two tails: dark dun Micro Fibetts
Body: olive gray
Wing: medium gray
Hackle: medium dun

Spinner

Quill Gordon spinners mate and lay eggs in the warmest part of the day, usually early afternoon. I have found that trout often ignore quill Gordon spinners, and in some years, I never even attach a quill Gordon spinner imitation to my tippet. But an uncharacteristically warm spring can create exceptions to this rule. It's better to be prepared for the spinner fall than to be left standing on the shore watching rising trout.

Hook: 12 standard length shank
Thread: rust
Two tails: rust Micro Fibetts
Body: rust
Spent wing: clear, light gray, or white

Male Hendrickson.

Hendrickson *(Ephemerella subvaria)*

Ephemerella subvaria, the Hendrickson, is probably the Catskill's most famous mayfly species due to its long and well-documented fishing-related history in the region. Hendricksons remain one of the Catskill's premier hatches today, and I view the hatch as the official beginning of the Upper Delaware's dry-fly season. When the Hendricksons begin, I can leave my nymphs, wets, and streamers at home and expect to find rising fish. I'm not the only one who feels this way. The hatch is widely followed by Upper Delaware regulars, and once word gets out that the Hendricksons are on, anglers flock to the river.

You might think that a hatch this popular would be widely understood by most anglers, yet I find that there's a great deal of confusion concerning the common names for this fly. An angler visiting the Upper Delaware in early spring will probably overhear lengthy conversations about red quills, light Hendricksons, dark Hendricksons, Hendrickson spinners, male Hendricksons, and female Hendricksons. More than once, springtime customers in my fly shop have informed me that they saw no Hendricksons hatching, only red quills. Yet red quills, dark Hendricksons, and male Hendricksons are all the same fly. I believe that these names developed to explain the color variations in the male dun's body, which can range from deep red to pinkish gray with a hint of olive. Female or light Hendrickson duns also have varying shades, with tan, yellow, olive, and pink predominating. These color variations are probably the result of diet or habitat during their nymphal stage.

The Delaware Main Stem and both its branches all have fantastic Hendrickson hatches. Hendricksons often appear first on the Upper East Branch and are seen last on the upper sections of the West Branch; hatches on the Lower East Branch, middle to lower sections of the West Branch, and the Main Stem fall somewhere in between. Hendricksons are a prolific and long-lasting hatch. Never be caught streamside without a few Hendrickson patterns any time from the beginning of April until the end of May.

Nymph

Hendrickson nymphs should be fished on a dead drift or swung and stripped like wet flies. The nymphs usually undulate just under the river's surface as they try to break free of their shucks. Pause at the end of a nymph or wet-fly swing to allow the fly to pulse just below the surface film to imitate this behavior.

    Hook: 14 standard length shank
    Thread: dark brown
    Tail: mallard flank dyed dark brown
    Body: dark brown
    Wing case: dark brown mottled turkey wing
    Hackle: brown

Male Dun

Hendricksons are often referred to as the "gentleman's hatch" because they often do so during the warmest part of the day—usually late morning into the afternoon.

    Hook: 14 standard length shank
    Thread: red
    Shuck (optional): dark brown
    Three tails: red or rust Micro Fibetts
    Body: reddish gray
    Wing: dark dun
    Hackle: reddish brown

Female Dun

    Hook: 14 standard length shank
    Thread: olive
    Shuck (optional): dark brown
    Three tails: olive Micro Fibetts
    Body: pinkish olive
    Wing: dark dun
    Hackle: light olive

Female Hendrickson.

Spinner

Hendrickson spinner bodies, both male and female, turn a rusty red color (some anglers mistakenly call the spinners red quills). The females carry a yellow egg sac that can be imitated with a small ball of yellow dubbing tied at the tail of the fly.

> Hook: 14 standard length shank
> Thread: rust
> Three tails: rust Micro Fibetts
> Egg sac (females only): yellow dubbing
> Body: rust
> Spent wing: clear, light gray, or white

Big sulphur.

Big Sulphur *(Ephemerella invaria)*

Sulphurs are one of the Upper Delaware's most important hatches. The first sulphurs of the year are much bigger than those found later in the season. These big sulphurs were formerly classified as two separate species: *E. invaria* and *E. rotunda*. Recent entomological studies have found that both insects are identical, resulting in one classification: *E. invaria.*

The big sulphurs often appear near the end of the Hendrickson hatch, and the yellowish tint of the Hendrickson female's body causes some anglers to confuse the two insects. All the Upper Delaware branches have excellent populations of big sulphurs. They are a fairly long-lasting hatch and often provide some of the first good evening fishing opportunities of the season.

Nymph

E. invaria nymphs swim to the river's surface, where they emerge into duns just in or below the surface film. They drift in the river's current, making them an easy target for trout. Nymph patterns and wet flies should be fished on a dead drift, with a swing at the end of the drift to imitate this behavior. Allow the flies to pulse just under the surface before retrieving them, to imitate nymphs trying to escape their shucks.

> Hook: 14–16 standard length shank
> Thread: dark brown
> Tail: mallard flank dyed dark brown
> Body: dark brown
> Wing case: black turkey wing
> Hackle: coachman brown

Dun

Big sulphur duns usually become airborne very quickly after they emerge, but the Upper Delaware's cold, bottom-released water sometimes keeps them on the water longer they would be on other rivers. This tendency, combined with the river's excellent population of big sulphurs, makes this a premier hatch.

      Hook: 14–16 standard length shank
      Thread: yellow
      Shuck (optional): dark brown
      Three tails: cream Micro Fibetts
      Body: yellow with an orange to olive cast
      Wing: medium gray
      Hackle: cream

Spinner

After mating, female *E. invaria* spinners return to the banks to allow their eggs to ripen. They then return to the river to deposit their eggs and fall, spent. Anglers need to remain patient when they see the male and female spinners undulating over the riffles. The insects will get onto the water, but not until the females return.

      Hook: 14–16 standard length shank
      Thread: tan
      Three tails: tan Micro Fibetts
      Body: yellowish tan
      Spent wing: clear, light gray, or white

March Brown, Gray Fox
(*Maccaffertium vicarium*)

March brown.

It has been two decades since entomologists dumbfounded anglers by reclassifying the well-known *Stenonema fuscum* (gray fox) hatch into *Stenonema vicarium* (march brown), officially dismissing the mayfly known throughout the fly-fishing world as the gray fox. A few years ago, they threw us another curve by changing the genus from *Stenonema* to *Maccaffertium*. Each of these changes involved the discovery of small, angler-insignificant physical differences—or a lack thereof—between species. I still believe that there are obvious differences between a march brown and a gray fox, but I'll defer to the experts.

    The march brown hatch doesn't usually produce large numbers of flies that blanket the river's surface. Rather, the hatch is more like a trickle throughout the day, usually beginning in late morning and lasting through the afternoon and evening. The lack of significant numbers of insects often frustrates anglers, who see only a few bugs. But this hatching characteristic provides some of the most enjoyable spring fishing for Upper Delaware River anglers—blind-casting large dry flies. The trout's fondness for march browns provides the opportunity to fish the water by covering promising riffles with a dry-fly. Blind casting is an often fruitless tactic on the Upper Delaware due to the vast amounts of subsurface food, but it will produce during the march brown hatch.

March brown dry-fly patterns should be fished without drag most of the time. However, an occasional twitch may provoke a violent strike when trout are feeding selectively on duns trying to dry their wings. March browns tied Catskill style work especially well for blind-casting the large riffles of the Lower East Branch and the Main Stem. These high-riding flies are visible and less likely to sink when cast into fast, riffled water.

The Upper Delaware's Main Stem and both its branches have excellent populations of march browns. My personal preference for pursuing the hatch is the Main Stem and the Lower East, because their long riffles present a lot of opportunities for blind-casting dry flies.

Nymph

March brown nymphs begin to migrate into shallow areas about a week before their emergence, giving the nymph angler extended opportunities to fish them. Nymphs should be fished on a dead drift or down and across, wet-fly style. Anticipate strikes when swinging flies have straightened below you and are moving toward the shore.

    Hook: 8–12, 2XL shank
    Thread: dark brown
    Tail: mallard flank dyed dark brown
    Body: orangish brown
    Wing case: dark brown turkey wing
    Hackle: brown

March Brown Dun

The earliest march brown hatches produce large flies, size 8 to 12. They have wide bodies and heavily mottled, swept-back wings, which are unique to the species. This accounts for only the original march brown hatch, before it was combined with the gray fox.

    Hook: 8–12, 2XL shank
    Thread: tan
    Shuck (optional): dark brown
    Two tails: brown Micro Fibetts
    Body: creamy tan
    Wing: tannish brown with black venations
    Hackle: tan

Gray Fox Dun

The mayfly once called the gray fox dominates the march brown hatches occurring from early June through July. These flies are smaller, size 12 and 14, and have a lighter pale wing with light brown venations. The brown markings ribbing their backs and femurs are also less prominent than on the early march browns. They retain the beefy, wide body of the early flies but look like shrunken, sun-bleached versions.

Hook: 12–14, 2XL shank
Thread: cream
Shuck (optional): dark brown
Two tails: brown Micro Fibetts
Body: cream
Wing: yellowish tan (with light gray venations)
Hackle: cream

March Brown and Gray Fox Spinner

March brown spinners, both the early and late types, have rusty brown bodies with clear wings and black venations. Although march brown duns seldom appear in large numbers, this isn't the case for the spinners. March brown spinners are an infamous tease for many anglers. It's common to have massive numbers of them suddenly collect over riffles, only to disappear without ever touching the water. However, great fishing is possible when the spinners do decide to mate and then fall, spent.

Hook: 8–12, 2XL shank
Thread: rust
Two tails: rust Micro Fibetts
Body: rust
Spent wing: clear, light gray, or white

Little Summer Sulphur, Pale Evening Dun (*Ephemerella dorothea dorothea*)

Little summer sulphur.

The little summer sulphurs are, as the name implies, considered a summertime hatch. However, these prolific little yellow mayflies actually begin to emerge in the Upper Delaware system well before spring gives way to summer. The importance of these mayflies only continues to build throughout their duration, which is one of the longest in the Upper Delaware system. The little summer sulphurs are the dominant reason for the river's very good summer fly-fishing opportunities, when the hatch often occurs during the day, predominantly in sections near reservoirs. In both the Upper East Branch and the West Branch, the cold reservoir releases instigate the little sulphurs. These mayflies continue to provide excellent daytime dry-fly fishing opportunities long after most eastern trout streams are too dry and hot to fish.

Nymph

E. dorothea dorothea nymphs are poor swimmers. They usually swim haphazardly to the surface and hold in the surface film to emerge, making them prime targets for trout.

Hook: 16–18 standard length shank
Thread: camel
Tail: tan wood duck flank fibers
Body: light brown
Wing case: brown turkey wing
Hackle: tan

Dun

Male duns have very large red eyes, so substitute red thread for the fly pattern's head to imitate this trait. The cold, reservoir-released water that encourages the little summer sulphur hatch can also retard its progression. Low water temperatures create a lot of cripples and ensure that even the healthy mayflies are unable to leave the river's surface. This keeps them on the water for extended periods and allows the trout ample time to eat them.

Hook: 16–18 standard length shank
Thread: yellow
Shuck (optional): dark brown
Three tails: yellow Micro Fibetts
Body: pale yellow; some flies also have an orange or light olive cast
Wing: light dun
Hackle: cream

Spinner

E. dorothea dorothea spinners behave similarly to the larger *E. invaria* species. They should be fished in the same manner described in that section.

Hook: 16–18 standard length shank
Thread: orange
Three tails: cream Micro Fibetts
Body: pale orange
Spent wing: clear, light gray, or white

Green drake.

Green Drake *(Ephemera guttalata)*

Green drakes are either the most eagerly anticipated or the most overhyped Upper Delaware mayfly hatch, depending on who you're talking to. There are several problems with the drakes: there are often too many of them, the fish don't always eat the duns, the hatch often appears at dark, and the bugs are huge. Some Upper Delaware green drakes can easily fill a size 8, 2XL dry-fly hook. But the vast majority of the flies are a size 10, 2XL, which isn't too bad either. The drakes are well known for bringing some of the river's largest fish from their deep holding lies to the surface to feed. But they are equally infamous for producing frustrating dry-fly conditions when the trout key on the emergers. In spite of the unpredictable fishing associated with the hatch, the green drake is one of my favorites—not only for the excellent fly-fishing opportunities it can provide but also for its spectacle.

Green drake hatches are often difficult to time, and anglers with flexible schedules have a better chance of hitting the drake hatch at its peak. Stay in contact with local fly shops near the end of May through the middle of June. Then, when the drakes begin, drop everything and head to the river.

Some sections of the Upper Delaware's branches are warming up beyond trout preferences by the time the drakes begin their emergence. Because of the warm water, hatching conditions are often most favorable in the evening hours—creating a small window of opportunity to fish the hatch. But cold-water releases or a colder than normal weather pattern can instigate the drakes to hatch in the middle of the day. The shaded geography of the Upper East Branch also encourages daytime drake hatches in its watershed.

All the Upper Delaware branches have very good green drake hatches, but the Upper East Branch and the Main Stem have some of the most prolific hatches in the eastern United States.

Nymph

Green drake nymphs tend to wiggle just under the water's surface while they emerge. Try swinging and twitching nymph and wet-fly patterns, allowing the flies to dangle in the surface film at the end of the cast, to imitate this behavior. It can also be effective to strip green drake nymph patterns like streamers.

Hook: 8–12, 2XL shank
Thread: olive
Three tails: olive
Gills: medium dun ostrich herl
Body: olive brown
Wing case: dark brown mottled turkey wing
Hackle: olive brown

Dun

Green drake duns are hard to imitate because they're so big. Trout can easily scrutinize any drake dry-fly pattern because they don't have to look very closely to do it. Sometimes, especially near the end of the hatch, trout feed selectively on drakes that move; they won't eat a pattern fished on a dead drift no matter how well it's presented. During these conditions, dry-fly patterns should be cast about a foot ahead of the fish so that they can be gently twitched, signifying life, before reaching the trout.

Hook: 8–12, 2XL shank
Thread: pale yellow
Shuck (optional): dark brown
Three tails: black Micro Fibetts
Body: pale yellow or cream
Wing: grizzly dyed olive (olive with black venations)
Hackle: grizzly dyed olive

Coffin fly.

Spinner

Green drake spinners are commonly called coffin flies—a name coined by Catskill legends Walt Dette and Ted Townsend during a tying session after a funeral. Many anglers believe that the spinners provide the best dry-fly fishing opportunities for this hatch—and sometimes they're correct. Green drake spinners often fall in incredible numbers—so many that you can actually hear their wings flapping as they emerge from the hemlocks to gather over the river's riffles. I use coffin fly imitations as large as a size 6, tied Catskill style, when the river is covered with the flies. The big pattern makes the fly stand out to me and to the trout.

> Hook: 8–12, 2XL shank
> Thread: white
> Three tails: black Micro Fibetts
> Body: white
> Spent wing: clear, light gray, or white

Brown drake *(Ephemera simulans)*

Brown drakes are the often overlooked cousin of the green drake. The history, myth, and legend of the green drake just seem to get all the attention. Most eastern anglers, even those who have fished during an intense brown drake emergence, know little about the bugs. It's easy to confuse brown and green drakes from a distance. They prefer similar habitat, their hatches often overlap, and both are huge.

Brown drake.

Brown drake hatches are a good indicator of how long the green drakes have been hatching in the Upper Delaware system. The brown drakes usually begin their emergence as the green drake hatch is subsiding. The brown drake hatch has a shorter duration than the green drake, so it signifies the beginning of the end for the season's drakes.

All the Upper Delaware branches have good populations of brown drakes. But once again, the hatch is heaviest on the Upper East Branch and the Main Stem.

Nymph

Brown drake nymphs should be fished in the same manner as green drake nymphs.

> Hook: 8–12, 2XL shank
> Thread: tan
> Three tails: olive brown

Gills: light dun ostrich herl
Body: tan
Wing case: dark brown mottled turkey wing
Hackle: light brown

Dun

Brown drake duns should be fished the same way as green drake duns.

Hook: 8–12, 2XL shank
Thread: brown
Shuck (optional): dark brown
Three tails: black Micro Fibetts
Body: tannish olive
Wing: grizzly dyed brown (with black venations)
Hackle: grizzly dyed olive

Spinner

Brown drake spinners often keep their wings erect even after they've mated and laid their eggs. Upper Delaware trout sometimes key on this behavior and selectively feed on the upright-winged spinners. Anglers can effectively mimic this behavior by fishing dun patterns even during the spinner falls. I usually tie oversized brown drake patterns, the same size as I tie for the green drakes, to get the trout's attention and to make the fly pattern more visible as daylight fades.

Brown drake spinner.

Hook: 8–12, 2XL shank
Thread: brown
Three tails: black Micro Fibetts
Body: dark brown, ribbed with heavy yellow thread
Spent wing: clear, light gray, or white

Slate Drake, Iso, White Gloved Howdy (*Isonychia bicolor*)

Slate drakes, often called Isos by Upper Delaware anglers, are one of the most important hatches in the Upper Delaware system. The hatch is significant not because of its intensity but rather because it's long lasting and because the trout love it. The first good Iso hatches occur in the spring, but these hatches can sometimes be overshadowed by the many other

Isonychia.

mayflies that occur simultaneously. The Iso's importance is more obvious in the summer and fall. Slate drakes are a summer staple for the Upper Delaware's trout. Summer *Isonychias* tend to trickle during rainy, overcast days, much like blue-winged olives. But they can hatch in the middle of a sunny day during heavy water releases from the Cannonsville Reservoir. In fact, the heaviest summer Iso hatches that I've encountered have been during periods of increased reservoir releases. Upper Delaware trout respond to Iso hatches like they do to march browns. It's effective to blind-cast Iso dry-fly patterns, especially in the summer and fall.

Isos often emerge outside of the river on exposed rocks, but they can also emerge in the river where habitat precludes them from reaching dry areas. It's important to locate sections where the flies hatch in the river to find productive Iso dry-fly fishing. All the Upper Delaware branches contain very good populations of *Isonychia*, although they tend to be more populous in river sections that are not immediately adjacent to the dams.

Isonychia used to be divided into separate species, but entomologists have now classified them all as *I. bicolor*. One of the reasons for the original division was body color differences. Some Upper Delaware *Isonychias* are bright green when they first emerge. They eventually change into their typical reddish purple to grayish pink color as they are exposed to the air. But it's vital to have a few Iso emergers tied bright green if you want to catch fish.

Nymph

Isonychia nymphs are excellent swimmers. Fly patterns should be aggressively stripped toward the shore with short, quick pulls on the fly line to imitate their behavior.

> Hook: 8–12, 2XL shank
> Thread: red
> Three tails: reddish brown
> Body: reddish brown with white strip down the back of the abdomen
> Wing case: black turkey wing
> Hackle: grizzly dyed yellow

Dun

This is the most common Iso pattern.

> Hook: 8–12, 2XL shank
> Thread: red
> Shuck (optional): dark brown
> Two tails: dark dun Micro Fibetts
> Body: reddish purple to pinkish gray with an olive cast
> Wing: dark dun
> Hackle: reddish brown

Dun-Emerger

Use this recipe to imitate *Isonychia* that are bright green when they emerge.

> Hook: 12–14, 2XL shank
> Thread: olive
> Shuck (optional): dark brown

Upper Delaware trout love **Isonychias.** *The author's wife, Ruthann Weamer, caught this big brown with an* **Isonychia** *imitation.*

Two tails: dark dun Micro Fibetts
Body: bright green
Wing: dark dun
Hackle: light olive

Spinner

Like march brown spinners, it's fairly common for thousands of Iso spinners to collect over riffles before dark, even though anglers have not seen significant numbers of hatching *Isonychia*. The Iso spinners can also be temperamental, choosing to return to riverside brush and trees if conditions are not ideal for mating. Sudden rainstorms or windy weather can send the spinners back to the trees, frustrating anglers who have been waiting for them to get on the water.

Hook: 8–12, 2XL shank
Thread: red
Two tails: dark dun Micro Fibetts
Body: dark reddish brown
Spent wing: clear, light gray, or white

Male vitreus.

Pink Lady, Big Sulphur, Vitreus (*Epeorus vitreus*)

Epeorus vitreus, called the big sulphur by some Delaware fly fishermen and the pink lady by others, isn't related to any of the other mayflies commonly called sulphurs. Its *Epeorus* genus classifies the vitreus with quill Gordons and several other mayflies that look nothing like sulphurs. The vitreus is a good example of the lack of importance placed on mayfly coloration by the scientific community—just because two mayflies look similar doesn't mean that they are. *E. vitreus* doesn't really have one standard angling name, so most Delaware River guides simply call this hatch the vitreus.

The Upper Delaware's Main Stem and both its branches all have fishable populations of vitreus. Vitreus hatches are often found in the same river sections that provided good springtime hatches of quill Gordons. Vitreus duns also emerge on the river bottom (just like quill Gordons) and swim to the surface as duns, so it's important to imitate this trait.

Nymph

E. vitreus nymphs are poor swimmers and relocate by drifting to slower water before emerging. They share physical features with quill Gordons, as well as the need for clean, oxygenated water. Wet flies work well for the vitreus hatch. Nymphs should be fished on a dead drift along current seams and areas of slow water adjacent to riffles.

> Hook: 12–14 standard length shank
> Thread: olive
> Tail: mallard flank dyed olive brown
> Body: olive brown
> Wing case: brown mottled turkey wing
> Hackle: medium olive

Female vitreus.

Female Dun

Female vitreus duns can be strikingly colorful. They share the same body features and wing and thorax coloration of the males, but their abdomens are bright red to pink to deep orange. Because of this coloration, some anglers confuse this mayfly with the large *E. invaria* sulphurs.

> Hook: 12–14 standard length shank
> Thread: olive
> Shuck (optional): olive brown
> Two tails: olive Micro Fibetts
> Body: thorax—olive; abdomen—pink to deep orange
> Wing: light dun
> Hackle: olive

Male Dun

The predominantly olive male vitreus duns are relatively bland creatures compared with their female counterparts. I usually tie all my vitreus dun patterns in two-tone colors—olive for the thorax and hackle, and orange for the abdomen—intended to imitate the females. This usually works even if the fish are also eating the males. If the trout are keying only on the males and refuse the two-toned patterns, then a size 14 Blue-Winged Olive with a light-colored wing is a good choice. I tie some of my vitreus drys with trailing shucks, although the duns, which emerge on the stream bottom, are usually free of their nymphal shucks by the time they reach the surface. The shuck provides the same triggering effect discussed in the quill Gordon section.

Hook: 12–14 standard length shank
Thread: light olive
Shuck (optional): olive brown
Two tails: olive Micro Fibetts
Body: light olive and orange
Wing: light dun
Hackle: light olive

Spinner

Male and female vitreus spinners also differ in their coloration. Male spinners become a deeper shade of olive, and the orange-red female coloration also intensifies. The wings of both sexes become clear as spinners. Most vitreus spinner falls occur in the early evening, but they can appear in the morning if the air temperatures are unusually high.

I tie my vitreus spinners with dark orange bodies, neglecting the two-tone effect used for the female dun and the male's olive coloration. The trout don't seem to mind.

Hook: 12–14 standard length shank
Thread: pink
Two tails: cream Micro Fibetts
Body: orangish red or dark olive (for males)
Spent wing: clear, light gray, or white

Caddisflies

Little Black Caddis *(Chimarra aterrima)*

Chimarra caddisflies usually make their initial appearance in the Upper Delaware River system before the Hendrickson mayfly hatches begin. But as the *Chimarra* hatch progresses, it usually overlaps with the Hendricksons. Trout often feed selectively on the caddis, frustrating anglers who want to fish the legendary mayfly hatch. Anglers should study a trout's riseform closely if they aren't catching fish with their

Chimarra caddis.

Hendrickson patterns. If a trout is aggressively splashing when it feeds, rather than delicately dimpling the surface, it may be feeding on the caddis, not the Hendricksons. The *Chimarra* hatch can be prolific, providing good fly-fishing opportunities.

Larva

Chimarra caddis larvae are net spinners. They construct their nets on the underside of rocks, where they spend most of their lives. But they do travel to the top of the rocks to emerge. Larva patterns should be fished very slowly along the river bottom at the beginning of the hatch to imitate this behavior.

    Hook: 18–20 standard length shank; 16–18 curved shank
    Thread: yellow to orange
    Body: yellow to orange

Pupa or Adult

Egg-laying *Chimarra* caddisflies often fall helplessly to the water, providing an easy meal for trout. Dry-fly patterns should be fished on a dead drift to imitate this behavior.

    Hook: 18–20 standard length shank
    Thread: black
    Body: very dark brown
    Hackle: dark brown
    Wing: black

Brachycentrus **caddis.**

Grannom and Apple Caddis *(Brachycentrus)*

The Grannom and the apple caddis are two of the Upper Delaware's most prolific hatches. They are amazing to witness but often frustrating to fish. The bugs are sometimes so thick that motorists on New York Route 17 have to pull off the road to clean the bugs from their windshields. But for all the biomass that the rivers produce with these caddisflies, the trout often ignore the newly hatched adults on the surface, opting to feed subsurface on the larvae and pupae. Egg-laying *Brachycentrus* caddisflies are more readily eaten on the surface. They provide an easy meal for trout when the river bottom isn't full of larvae and pupae. The females often fall helplessly to the river's surface as they try to rid themselves of their egg balls. Anglers can effectively imitate this behavior by either dead-drifting or gently twitching dry-fly patterns.

Larva

Grannom and apple caddis larvae live in little brown, cone-shaped tubes. Thousands of these cases may be visible on rocks at the bottom of the river in the spring. The larvae leave these cases and swim to the surface to emerge in the film. This behavior is best imitated by swinging wet flies.

Hook: 14–16 standard length shank; 12–14 curved shank
Thread: brown
Body: brown head; bright green body

Pupa or Adult Grannom

Grannom pupa and adult dry-fly patterns are most productive when the hatches are just beginning or near their end. There are just too many larvae and pupae in the water during the hatch's peak for most Upper Delaware trout to surface feed. It's also productive to imitate the egg-laying flies described earlier.

Hook: 14–16 standard length shank
Thread: black
Body: greenish black
Hackle: black
Wing: light brown

Pupa or Adult Apple Caddis

Apple caddis adults look very strange with their light-colored wings and bright, two-toned bodies. Anglers should fish adult apple caddis flies during the same conditions and with the same methods described for the Grannom.

Apple caddis.

Hook: 14–16 standard length shank
Thread: chartreuse
Abdomen: apple green
Thorax: medium ginger
Hackle: medium ginger
Wing: cream or very light tan

Tan Caddis, Spotted Sedge
(*Hydropsyche* species)

The *Hydropsyche* caddis species are some of the most important for Upper Delaware anglers. Collectively, they form a long-lasting group of insects that begin hatching in midspring and continue throughout the summer and sometimes into the early fall. But it's not just the hatch's duration that makes it important for

Spotted sedge.

anglers. Upper Delaware trout seem to love this caddis, and unlike the *Brachycentrus* species, they often eat the adults, creating dry-fly fishing opportunities.

Larva

Hydropsyche larvae anchor themselves to the river bottom with a silk anchoring line. They are very difficult to imitate with artificial flies because of the way they dangle in the current. Gary LaFontaine proposed several ideas in his book *Caddisflies* (1981) to imitate this behavior, including coloring tippets white to suggest the anchoring line. *Hydropsyche* larvae often float with the river's current before they molt into pupae. This trait allows anglers extended opportunities to fish larva fly patterns. I've found that dead-drifted larva imitations often produce trout in the early stages of this hatch.

Hook: 14–16 standard length shank; 12–14 curved shank
Thread: olive
Body: brown head and back; olive belly

Pupa or Adult

Upper Delaware anglers have two good opportunities to fish *Hydropsyche* dry-fly patterns—when they first molt into adults and when they return to lay eggs. The adults often remain on the surface for extended periods after they hatch as they try to recover from molting. Egg-laying adults dive to the river bottom to lay their eggs and then float to the surface, where they often lie spent in the film. Wet-fly patterns can be swung to imitate the diving egg layers, and dry-fly patterns should be fished flush with the surface film on a dead drift to imitate the pupae and spent caddis.

Hook: 14–16 standard length shank
Thread: tan
Body: creamish tan
Hackle: ginger
Wing: light brown

Little sister sedge.
JOHN MILLER

Little Sister Sedge, Olive Caddis (*Cheumatopsyche campyla*)

This species' common name of little sister sedge derives from its close physical resemblance to the spotted sedge and their similar hatching characteristics. Anglers can apply the larva, pupa, and adult descriptions of the *Hydropsyche* species to the *Cheumatopsyche* species as well. The only significant differences between these caddisflies are their size and body color and the fact that *Cheumatopsyche* hatches usually end by mid-June.

Larva

Hook: 20–22 standard length shank; 18–20 curved shank
Thread: olive
Body: brown head; olive body

Pupa or Adult

Hook: 20–22 standard length shank
Thread: olive
Body: greenish brown
Hackle: olive
Wing: light brown

Dark Blue Sedge *(Psilotreta labida)*

Dark blue sedge.

Gary LaFontaine (1981) referred to this hatch as the "Slap-in-the-Face-Caddis" because it often interfered with his "beloved green drake hatch." The *Psilotreta* caddisflies do emerge in the Upper Delaware system at the same times as the green drakes, which can complicate the sometimes difficult drake hatch. It might seem logical to assume that if the trout are rising subtly, you should try a drake pattern, and if they're splashing when they rise, you should try a *Psilotreta*. But that approach doesn't work. I've seen too many trout splash at emerging drake nymphs, and even duns, to assume that fish are eating caddis if they splash when they rise. My only advice is to closely study feeding trout and make an educated guess at what they're eating. If you guess that they're eating drakes but they won't eat your fly pattern, try fishing a *Psilotreta* caddis pattern—it might just solve the riddle.

Larva

Psilotreta larvae build little tube-shaped cases out of bits of sand and gravel. I've turned over many rocks in the Upper Delaware system that were covered with dozens of empty cases after the *Psilotreta* emerged. The larvae tend to migrate to common areas to pupate, so it's a good idea to look for river sections with large numbers of these cases to fish pupa imitations.

> Hook: 14–16 standard length shank; 12–14 curved shank
> Thread: green
> Body: gray head; green body

Pupa or Adult

Psilotreta pupae and adults tend to jostle and struggle as they attempt to escape the river's surface film. The adults are especially rambunctious when they return to the river to lay their eggs. The movement associated with the *Psilotreta* species provides some enjoyable fly-fishing opportunities. The best way to imitate these behaviors is to skitter a caddis dry-fly pattern across the river's surface. You shouldn't mend the fly line if you want the fly pattern to skitter. Cast slightly upriver, and allow the river's current to pull the leader, dragging or skittering the fly. Occasionally, I feed line into my cast to ease the river's tension on the line and then allow it to drag again. This creates a very lifelike effect, causing the dry-fly to skitter, pause, and then skitter again. And can sometimes inspire a spirited strike from a trout.

> Hook: 14–16 standard length shank
> Thread: iron gray
> Body: dark gray with green reflections
> Hackle: dark blue dun
> Wing: dark bluish gray

Stoneflies

Little black stonefly.

Little Black Stonefly *(Taeniopteryx navalis),* Little Brown Stonefly *(Strophopteryx faciata)*

Early black and brown stoneflies are two of the first aquatic insects to hatch in the Upper Delaware system. They usually begin in late February or early March, after the less important *Allocapnia* stonefly emergence. It's well known that all stonefly species crawl to riverside rocks to emerge. This hatching characteristic reduces the importance of dry-fly imitations because the adults aren't always available to the trout. But I have found trout eating little black and brown stonefly adults during several early-spring outings in the Upper Delaware system, probably because some of the little black stones hatch in-river—breaking the stonefly emergence rule. Most of the Delaware branches are still closed to fishing when the little black and brown stoneflies begin hatching, leaving only the bottom of the West Branch and the Main Stem as possible fly-fishing destinations. The West Branch is the best destination for anglers searching for productive fishing during these hatches. Main Stem flows are usually very cold and exaggerated in the early spring from snowmelt runoff. These conditions often preclude Main Stem trout from rising to adult stoneflies, and nymphing is difficult in the deeper water.

Nymph

More trout will probably be caught with flies imitating little black and brown stonefly nymphs than with those imitating adults. Nymphs should be fished very slowly, on a dead drift, because the cold water at this time of year reduces the trout's metabolism, making them feed sluggishly.

Hook: 14–18 standard length shank
Thread: black or brown
Two tails: black or brown goose biots
Body: black or brown
Wing case: black turkey wing
Hackle: black or dark brown

Little brown stonefly.

Adult

Stonefly adults often buzz and skitter across the surface if they manage to get onto the river. It's often effective to skitter a small black Elk Hair Caddis dry fly to imitate this behavior. Early spring days with warm sunshine and a steady breeze are prime times to find Upper Delaware trout rising to the adults. The sunshine warms the water, encouraging the hatch, and the breeze helps blow some of the stonefly adults onto the water's surface, making them available to the trout.

Hook: 14–18 standard length shank
Thread: black or brown
Two tails: black or brown goose biots
Body: black or brown
Hackle: black or dark brown
Wing: white or clear Antron, or light dun deer hair

Giant Stonefly (*Pteronarcys dorsata*)

Giant stonefly.

Pteronarcys dorsata is the largest stonefly species in North America. Giant stoneflies are a relatively long hatch in the Upper Delaware system, but they seldom emerge in significant numbers. Giant stoneflies mate and lay their eggs on the shore, so mating flights are generally unimportant for anglers. All the Upper Delaware branches maintain fishable populations of giant stoneflies, but the best fishing is usually found in the Main Stem.

Nymph

The giant stonefly has a three-year life cycle, so its substantial nymphs are always available, in various sizes, to the river's trout. I fish giant stonefly nymphs on a dead drift throughout the year in tandem with other nymphs designed to imitate whatever is hatching at the time. It can also be effective to slowly strip giant stonefly nymph patterns toward the banks during the hatch's peak from late April to early June. This imitates nymphs that are moving toward riverside rocks to emerge.

Hook: 2–4, 2XL shank
Thread: black
Two tails: black goose biots
Body: black
Wing case: black turkey wing
Hackle: black

Adult

Giant stonefly adults aren't always available to trout because of the emergence characteristics described earlier. But giant stoneflies are very clumsy fliers, however, and fishing during windy days or in river sections with overhanging vegetation will increase your chances of finding Upper Delaware trout eating giant stonefly adults that have blown or fallen into the river. Blind-casting large stimulators can be a very effective method of fishing at this time. Use heavy tippet, and prepare yourself for violent strikes if you skitter your fly across a riffle. Fishing adult giant stonefly dry-fly patterns is especially effective in the Lower East Branch and the middle and lower sections of the Main Stem.

Hook: 2–4, 2XL shank
Thread: orange
Two tails: black goose biots
Body: orange mottled with black
Wing: white or clear Antron, or light dun deer hair
Hackle: black

Golden stonefly.

Golden stonefly (various members of the Perlidae family, including *Acroneuria lycorial, Paragnetina media,* and *Paragnetina immarginata*)

Golden stoneflies may not be the largest stonefly in North America, but they aren't a family of small flies either. Many of them easily reach a size 6, and smaller specimens won't be less than a size 12. The importance of golden stoneflies to the Delaware River system greatly overshadows that of their larger cousin, the giant stonefly. It's common for the rocks and vegetation along the shoreline, particularly on the West Branch, Lower East Branch, and Main Stem, to be covered with so many golden stoneflies that you can actually scoop up handfuls of them. All the Upper Delaware branches hold amazing numbers of these large insects.

Nymph

Members of the Perlidae family of stoneflies have a two- to three-year life cycle, depending on the species. I fish these nymphs the same way I fish the giant stonefly nymphs.

Hook: 6–12, 2XL shank
Thread: yellow
Two tails: yellow goose biots
Body: yellow with olive and brown reflections
Wing case: brown mottled turkey wing dyed yellow
Hackle: grizzly dyed yellow

Adult

Use the same tactics for fishing Perlidae adults as described in the giant stonefly section.

Hook: 6–12, 2XL shank
Thread: yellow
Two tails: yellow goose biots
Body: yellow
Wing: white or clear Antron; or light dun deer hair
Hackle: yellow

CHAPTER 7

Summer Hatches, Fall Hatches, and Winter Fly Fishing

Summer Hatches

Insect	Size	Hatch Begins	Hatch Ends
Tan caddis; aka spotted sedge (*Hydropsyche* species)	14–16	Mid-May	Late August
Little summer sulphur; aka pale evening dun (*Ephemerella dorothea dorothea;* formerly *Ephemerella dorothea*)	16–18	Late May	Mid-August
Pink lady; aka big sulphur; aka vitreus (*Epeorus vitreus*)	12–14	Early June	Early September
Little chocolate dun *(Ephemerella needhami)*	16–18	Mid-June	Late July
Dark blue-winged olive (*Sarratella deficiens;* formerly *Ephemerella deficiens*)	18–20	Mid-June	Mid-September
Little blue-winged olive (*Acentrella turbida;* formerly *Pseudocleons*)	22–26	Mid-June	Late October
Light blue-winged olive (*Attenella atenuata;* formerly *Ephemerella atenuata*)	16–18	Mid-June	Mid-July
Blue-winged olive (*Drunella lata;* formerly *Drunella cornutella*)	14–16	Mid-June	Mid-August
Green sedge (*Rhyacophila* species)	14–16	Mid-June	Late August
Slate drake; aka Iso; aka white gloved howdy (*Isonychia bicolor;* also includes species formerly known as *Isonychia sadleri* and *Isonychia harperi*)	12–14	Hatches sporadically throughout the summer	

(continued)

Summer Hatches (continued)			
Insect	Size	Hatch Begins	Hatch Ends
Yellow drake (*Ephemera varia*)	8–10	Late June	Late July
Golden drake (*Anthopotamus distinctus;* formerly *Potamanthus distinctus*)	10	Late June	Mid-August
Light cahill (*Maccaffertium ithaca;* formerly *Stenonema ithaca*)	14	Late June	Late August
Orange cahill; aka summer steno (*Stenacron interpunctatum;* formerly *Stenonema heterotarsale* and *Stenonema canadense*)	12–14	Late June	Mid-September
Trico (*Tricorythodes stygiatus*)	24	Early July	Mid-October
Blue-winged olive (*Drunella lata;* formerly *Ephemerella lata*)	16–18	Mid-July	Late October
Hebe (*Leucrocuta hebe;* formerly *Heptagenia hebe*)	18–20	Mid-July	Mid-October
Whitefly (*Ephoron leukon*)	14–16	Mid-August	Early September

Summer Mayflies

For descriptions of the little summer sulphur *(Ephemerella dorothea dorothea);* the pink lady, big sulphur, and vitreus *(Epeorus vitreus);* the blue-winged olive *(Drunella lata);* and the slate drake *(Isonychia bicolor),* see chapter 6.

Little Chocolate Dun *(Ephemerella needhami)* and Dark Blue-Winged Olive *(Sarratella deficiens)*

These two mayfly species are very similar in physical appearance, hatching characteristics, and preferred habitat. They are often found hatching together in the late morning or early afternoon in weedy river sections. All the Upper Delaware branches maintain populations of these mayflies, but the populations in the West Branch and Upper East Branch are particularly prolific due to their weed beds.

Nymph

Dead-drifting nymph patterns in and around weed beds and then allowing them to swing at the end of the drift can be very effective during hatches. Try to use as little weight as possible to keep the flies from entangling in the weeds.

>   Hook: 18–20 standard length shank
>   Thread: dark brown
>   Three tails: brown
>   Body: dark brown
>   Wing case: black turkey wing
>   Hackle: dark brown

August whitefly hatches can provide good trout fishing opportunities in the Middle and Lower Main Stem, as long as summer water temperatures remain cool. This Middle Main Stem brown was caught by the author during a whitefly hatch at Bouchouxville.

Dun

The duns of both these species often remain on the river's surface for long periods because they prefer to live in the aforementioned weed beds, which are often located near the reservoirs and their cold-water releases. The cold water stuns the flies and keeps them on the water even longer.

    Hook: 18–20 standard length shank
    Thread: dark brown
    Three tails: medium dun Micro Fibetts
    Shuck (optional): dark brown
    Body: chocolate
    Wing: dark dun
    Hackle: tan

Spinner

Spinner falls usually occur in the evening, but the effects of reservoir releases can sometimes instigate daytime spinner falls. Generally, imitating the spinner stage of these two mayfly species is not as important for catching Upper Delaware trout as imitating the nymph and dun stages.

    Hook: 18–20 standard length shank
    Thread: brown
    Three tails: medium dun Micro Fibetts
    Body: rusty brown
    Spent wing: clear, light gray, or white

Upper Delaware blue-winged olive hatches can be prolific, especially during rainy or overcast weather. Bruce Miller caught this rainbow on a Blue-Winged Olive dry fly in Junction Pool.

Little Blue-Winged Olive *(Acentrella turbida)*

These mayflies were formerly in the genus known as *Pseudocleons* before they were reclassified, and in spite of the scientific name change, most Upper Delaware anglers still refer to this hatch as the pseudos. Pseudos have three broods (a brood is a complete life cycle from egg to spinner) that are usually heaviest in June, August, and October. However, pseudo hatches can be very prolific in the Upper Delaware system during any day with cool overcast, or rainy, conditions throughout the summer and fall months.

Nymph

Most Upper Delaware anglers don't bother trying to imitate *A. turbida* nymphs, probably because the nymphs are so small and because most anglers associate this hatch with dry-fly fishing. But anglers who want to fish nymphs before the hatch begins or before the trout begin to surface feed can be successful by dead-drifting nymphs near weed beds and allowing the flies to swing at the end of the drift. Nymphs tied without weight and greased to float in the surface film can also be effective for catching trout—even those that appear to be eating duns.

Hook: 22–26 standard length shank
Thread: olive
Two tails: olive
Body: medium olive
Wing case: brown turkey wing
Hackle: light olive

Dun

Upper Delaware trout are particularly found of these little mayflies, and they often feed on them all day if the sky is overcast or even if a light rain is falling. However, a steady, driving rain or a heavy downpour can curtail surface feeding activity—probably because the trout have a difficult time seeing the tiny insects on the rain-disturbed surface. The extremely small size of *A. turbida* duns, combined with the trout's tendency to eat them in slow-moving pools, sometimes necessitates the use of 7X tippet. I always begin fishing with 6X, but if I'm not catching fish, it's often beneficial to drop down one tippet size.

Hook: 22–26 standard length shank
Thread: light olive
Shuck (optional): olive brown
Two tails: light olive Micro Fibetts
Wing: very light dun
Body: light olive mixed with yellow
Hackle: light olive

Spinner

Spinner falls usually occur in the evening, but the cold water from reservoir releases can sometimes instigate daytime falls.

Hook: 22–26 standard length shank
Thread: light olive
Two tails: tan Micro Fibetts
Body: brownish olive
Spent wing: clear, light gray, or white

Light Blue-Winged Olive *(Attenella atenuata)*

Attenella atenuata hatches are often confused with the cornuta hatches described in chapter 6. Both insects usually hatch in the morning, but they can also be found throughout the day in river sections near the reservoirs.

Nymph

A. atenuata nymphs migrate from riffles to slower river sections to molt into duns. Dead-drifting nymphs on the edges of riffles adjacent to back eddies can produce excellent results. The nymphs emerge into duns on the river bottom and swim to the surface. Imitate this behavior by swinging wet flies through slow pools.

    Hook: 16–18 standard length shank
    Thread: brown
    Three tails: tan
    Body: olive brown
    Wing case: black turkey wing
    Hackle: dark ginger

Dun

The body and wing color of *A. atenuata* duns darkens when they are exposed to the air. This transformation begins very quickly after the duns hatch, and the longer they are on the river's surface, the darker they become. Emergers should therefore be tied with light dun-colored wings and a yellowish olive body. To imitate "older" insects, use dark dun wings and dark olive bodies. *A. atenuata* duns often take a long time to try their wings. This tendency makes them very attractive to surface-feeding trout, and it can be exacerbated in sections near the reservoirs, where cold water temperatures and fog often stun the flies, keeping them on the water for extended periods.

    Hook: 16–18 standard length shank
    Thread: olive
    Shuck (optional): dark brown
    Three tails: medium olive Micro Fibetts
    Body: yellowish olive to medium olive
    Wing: medium dun
    Hackle: light olive

Wild trout want easy meals, and spent mayfly spinners often provide one. Upper Delaware guide Pat Schuler caught this twilight brown with an Antron spinner imitation.

Spinner

Spinner falls often occur at dusk, but they may be seen even on a hot summer afternoon in the sections near the reservoirs.

    Hook: 16–18 standard length shank
    Thread: dark brown
    Three tails: olive Micro Fibetts
    Body: olive brown
    Spent wing: clear, light gray, or white

Yellow Drake (*Ephemera varia*)

Yellow drakes aren't nearly as famous as their green and brown cousins. In fact, in some years, they are relatively unimportant for catching Upper Delaware trout. Yellow drake emergences are usually sparse, and they often overlap with flashier hatches such as those of the green and brown drakes, sulphurs, and cahills. The one yellow drake characteristic that merits its inclusion in this book is the long duration of the hatch. I've found yellow drakes in the Upper Delaware system from the middle of June until early

Yellow drake.

August. One year, they were particularly evident in the Upper East Branch, where I encountered spinners at the lights of the Route 30 Sunoco station almost every night for two months. Yellow drakes prefer warm, slow-moving water, making the Upper Delaware's Main Stem or the bottom end of the Upper East Branch the best sections to fish the hatch.

Nymph

Yellow drake nymphs are active swimmers. They tend to wiggle just under the water's surface as they emerge. Try swinging and twitching nymph and wet-fly patterns, allowing the flies to dangle in the surface film at the end of the cast, to imitate this behavior. It can also be effective to fish yellow drake nymph patterns like streamers, slowly stripping them through slow, silty pools at dusk and into the night.

    Hook: 8–10, 2XL shank
    Thread: tan
    Three tails: cream
    Gills: light brown ostrich herl
    Body: yellowish tan
    Wing case: dark brown turkey wing
    Hackle: cream

Dun

Some Upper Delaware anglers confuse yellow drake duns with green drake duns, which may have a yellow tint. The easiest way to differentiate the two species is to look at their hind wings (the smaller wings to the rear of the larger forewings). Green drake hind wings are mottled with venations like their forewings. Yellow drake hind wings have no venations. Yellow drake duns usually emerge near dark and often vigorously flap their wings to dry them for flight. Dry-fly patterns should be fished with a dead drift or with a twitch to imitate the dun drying its wings.

> Hook: 8–10, 2XL shank
> Thread: pale yellow
> Shuck (optional): tan
> Three tails: pale yellow Micro Fibetts
> Body: pale yellow
> Wing: pale yellow
> Hackle: pale yellow

Spinner

Yellow drake spinner and dun bodies look exactly alike. The only physical difference between the two stages is that the spinner's forewing becomes clear. Spinner falls usually begin in the late evening or at dusk and continue into the night.

> Hook: 8–10, 2XL shank
> Thread: pale yellow
> Three tails: yellow Micro Fibetts
> Body: pale yellow to cream
> Spent wing: clear, light gray, or white

Golden drake. JOHN MILLER

Golden Drake *(Anthopotamus distinctus)*

The golden drake can be an unreliable Upper Delaware hatch, similar to the yellow drake. Sometimes, however, it can be a very important hatch for catching fish. Golden drake hatches, and the trout's reaction to them, differ from year to year. Some years, the bugs barely show themselves, and the trout seem to ignore the few flies that do hatch. Other years, the trout seem to look for these large mayflies and eat every one of them that floats within range. Golden drakes can be found throughout the Upper Delaware system, but they are similar to yellow drakes in their preference for warmer, slow-moving pools. This habitat preference usually means that the Upper Delaware's Main Stem or the bottom ends of the Upper East and West Branches are the best sections to fish the hatch.

Nymph

Golden drake nymphs swim to the river's surface to emerge into duns in the film. The same fishing tactics described in the yellow and green drake sections also apply to fishing golden drake nymph patterns.

Hook: 8–10, 2XL shank
Thread: brown
Three tails: dark ginger
Gills: reddish brown ostrich herl
Body: reddish brown
Wing case: brown turkey wing
Hackle: ginger

Dun

Golden drake duns have unique tails—the middle tail is approximately one-third shorter than the two outer tails—making it easy to identify them. Dry-fly patterns should usually be fished without drag.

Hook: 10, 2XL shank
Thread: gold
Shuck (optional): reddish brown
Three tails: yellow Micro Fibetts—middle tail one-third shorter
         than outer tails
Body: deep golden yellow to pale yellow
Wing: yellow
Hackle: yellow

Spinner

Golden drake spinner falls usually begin at dusk, but they are seldom numerous or intense. The trout do seem to like this large insect, however, making golden drake spinner falls a productive time to fish.

Hook: 10, 2XL shank
Thread: cream
Three tails: cream Micro Fibetts—middle tail one-third shorter
         than outer tails
Body: pale yellow
Spent wing: clear, light gray, or white

Light Cahill *(Maccaffertium ithaca)*

Light cahills are one of the most important summer mayfly hatches in the Upper Delaware system. They are especially important to the Main Stem and the bottom sections of the West and Upper East Branches—river sections that don't benefit from the daytime summer sulphur hatches initiated by cold reservoir releases. Light cahills often provide excellent dry-fly opportunities in the last hour before dark.

Light cahill.

Slow daytime fishing can erupt into an evening feeding frenzy when the light cahills are emerging or their spinners are falling. It's common for the hatches and spinner falls to overlap. Some of the trout may be feeding selectively on either the duns and emergers or the spinners, requiring anglers to switch back and forth between patterns to catch individual trout.

Nymph

Light cahill nymphs should be fished with a dead drift, particularly in sections of braided water adjacent to slow-moving pools.

> Hook: 14 standard length shank
> Thread: cream
> Two tails: dark amber
> Body: amber
> Wing case: dark brown turkey wing
> Hackle: dark ginger

Dun

Light cahill dun dry-fly patterns should usually be fished without drag. However, some of the duns occasionally flutter their wings to dry them. Dry-fly patterns can also be twitched to imitate this behavior.

> Hook: 14 standard length shank
> Thread: cream
> Shuck (optional): amber
> Two tails: cream Micro Fibetts
> Body: cream
> Wing: very light blue dun
> Hackle: cream

Spinner

Light cahill spinner falls usually occur in the evenings, generally in the last hour before dark. They can be very prolific and usually attract pods of surface-feeding trout.

> Hook: 14 standard length shank
> Thread: cream
> Two tails: cream Micro Fibetts
> Body: cream
> Spent wing: clear, light gray, or white

Summer steno.

Orange Cahill, Summer Steno (*Stenacron interpunctatum*)

The summer stenos formerly encompassed several species that have now been grouped together into *Stenacron interpunctatum*. They are extremely important to all the Upper Delaware branches because they have a long hatch duration and because they appear in the summer and fall—seasons with fewer aquatic insect hatches. The summer stenos can provide very good action for blind-casting dry flies. Upper Delaware trout seem to get used to seeing them and will often eat a dry-fly imitation even if there are no naturals hatching.

Nymph

Summer steno nymphs usually emerge behind rocks or other current obstructions in the river. They drift or swim to the surface to emerge, making them very attractive to trout. Nymph fly patterns should be fished with a dead drift, along any structure adjacent to faster water.

> Hook: 12–14 standard length shank
> Thread: light brown
> Three tails: light ginger
> Body: yellowish brown
> Wing case: dark brown turkey wing
> Hackle: light ginger

Dun

Summer stenos often hatch in the evenings, just like light cahills, in warmer sections of the system. But it's also common to find them hatching sporadically throughout the day, particularly in colder river sections adjacent to the reservoirs.

> Hook: 12–14 standard length shank
> Thread: yellow
> Shuck (optional): amber
> Two tails: cream Micro Fibetts
> Body: yellow with an orange cast to cream
> Wing: pale yellow with brown venations or cream
>   with brown venations
> Hackle: ginger

Spinner

The orange cast to the summer steno spinner imitates eggs in the female's lower abdomen.

> Hook: 12–14 standard length shank
> Thread: yellow
> Two tails: cream Micro Fibetts
> Body: cream to pale yellow with an orange cast
> Spent wing: clear, light gray, or white

Trico *(Tricorythodes stygiatus)*

In my opinion, Tricos may be the Upper Delaware's most overrated mayfly hatch. Perhaps I feel this way because I began my love affair with fly fishing amidst the legendary Pennsylvania limestone streams, where the Trico is the unrivaled mayfly king of summer. Tricos are consistent in limestone streams—you can set your watch and calendar according to their emergence—and the trout love them. This just isn't

Trico.

the case in the Upper Delaware system. Upper Delaware Tricos are an often strange, inconsistent hatch. Some days, they appear in mating funnel clouds that rival the most prolific hatches I've seen anywhere in the East. Other days, they don't appear at all. Often, the majority of Upper Delaware trout seem to ignore Tricos even when they are on the water in significant numbers, and the fish that do eat them are usually small. Then there are those days when the stars align and large Upper Delaware trout are ready to feed during an intense Trico hatch or spinner fall. These days should be treasured, because they are relatively rare. All the Upper Delaware branches exhibit Tricos, but the best hatches I've found have been in the West Branch's mudflats and Game Land Pool, the Main Stem's Junction and Stockport Pools, and the pools in the bottom section of the Upper East Branch.

Nymph

The most effective use for tiny Trico nymph patterns is to grease them and fish them in the surface film like emergers. Trico spinners can also be tied with a microbead at their head to make them sink like nymphs. Trico spinners are often washed below the river's surface after they float through riffles. Fish these sunken, beadhead Trico spinner patterns with a dead drift, just like standard nymphs. Another effective tactic, taught by Charlie Meck, is to tie a sunken Trico spinner as a dropper, in tandem with a dry fly. I usually use *Isonychia* patterns for the dry fly. And sometimes, the trout eat the Iso pattern instead of the Trico.

> Hook: 22–24 standard length shank
> Thread: black
> Tail: dark brown hackle fibers
> Body: dark brownish black
> Wing case: black turkey wing
> Hackle: coachman brown

Male Dun

Male Tricos emerge the night before they mate with the females. Occasionally, you'll find Upper Delaware trout gingerly sipping at the water's surface during a summer evening when no hatch or spinner fall is visible. It often looks as if these fish aren't eating anything at all, but they might be eating emerging male Tricos. Try fishing a male dun pattern, and you may be pleasantly surprised by the result.

> Hook: 24 standard length shank
> Thread: dark brown
> Three tails: cream Micro Fibetts (twice the length of the body)
> Body: dark brown
> Wing: light blue dun
> Hackle: dark brown

Female Dun

Female Trico duns emerge in the morning. They usually molt into spinners very quickly and then mate and die. It can be productive to fish the female Trico hatch before the spinner fall, but you'll probably have to be on the river very early to do it.

    Hook: 24 standard length shank
    Thread: olive
    Three tails: cream Micro Fibetts
    Body: olive
    Wing: light blue dun
    Hackle: olive

Spinner

Trico spinners are often much more important than the emergers or duns. In fact, when most anglers talk about fishing a Trico hatch, they are usually referring only to the spinner fall. Trico spinner falls usually occur between 9 a.m. and noon, but they may be found at dawn in warmer river sections during especially hot, summer conditions. Conversely, the beginning of the spinner fall can be delayed until late morning or even early afternoon during cold, rainy weather—conditions that are usually found in the fall.

    Hook: 24 standard length shank
    Bead (optional): black microbead
    Thread: black
    Three tails: black Micro Fibetts
    Body: black
    Spent wing: clear, light gray, or white

Hebe (*Leucrocuta hebe*)

Upper Delaware anglers haven't given this hatch a common angling name. Most of the time, they simply call it the hebe (pronounced He-Be). Hebes are an extremely important, long-lasting hatch, yet they are largely misunderstood. Many anglers confuse them with little summer sulphurs or even blue-winged olives, but they are actually a separate species that looks like a cross between the two. The easiest way to differentiate hebes from olives or sulphurs is to look

Hebe.

at their wings. Hebe wings are mottled with dark gray venations, whereas olive or sulphur wings are a solid dun color. All the Upper Delaware branches have excellent populations of hebes, but I spend a great deal of time pursuing this hatch in the Upper East Branch (summer and fall), Lower East Branch (fall only), and West Branch (summer and fall).

Nymph

Hebe nymphs live in riffles but migrate to slow-moving river sections to emerge. They emerge just below surface, making them difficult to imitate with standard nymphing techniques. The best way to represent an emerging hebe nymph is in tandem with a dry fly, just like fishing the sunken spinners described in the Trico nymph section. Attach the hebe nymph pattern, with a separate piece of tippet, to the bend of a large dry fly's hook (once again, I often use an *Isonychia* for the dry fly). The nymph will sink a few inches under the surface and remain suspended, just like the natural nymphs. Standard nymph patterns can also be fished with a dead drift in riffles to imitate nymphs that haven't yet migrated to the slower river sections.

> Hook: 18–20 standard length shank
> Thread: olive
> Three tails: light dun
> Body: olive brown
> Wing case: brown turkey wing
> Hackle: brown

Dun

Hebe duns often provide some of the Upper Delaware's last good dry-fly fishing of the year. Look for trout eating them in slow pools.

> Hook: 18–20 standard length shank
> Thread: light olive or yellow
> Shuck (optional): olive
> Two tails: light dun Micro Fibetts
> Body: bright yellow with olive cast (almost chartreuse)
> Wing: light dun with pale yellow highlights and dark gray venations
> Hackle: medium ginger

Spinner

Hebe spinner falls usually occur right before dark during the summer months, but they may commence earlier in the afternoon in sections near the reservoirs or in the fall.

> Hook: 18–20 standard length shank
> Thread: yellow
> Two tails: light dun Micro Fibetts
> Body: yellowish brown
> Spent wing: clear, light gray, or white

Whitefly *(Ephoron leukon)*

Whiteflies are a warm-water mayfly species. Their preference for warm, silty habitat in slow-moving pools ensures that they aren't prolific or very important in most of the Upper Delaware branches. The Main Stem, particularly its middle and lower sections, is the best place to find this hatch. You will also

find whiteflies upriver from the Main Stem's Buckingham boat launch, and maybe even a few trout eating them. Whiteflies aren't a factor in the West and
Upper East Branches.

Whitefly.

Whiteflies usually begin their emergence right
before dark. Anglers who are unfamiliar with the
hatch often leave the river too early when they fail to
find mayflies and rising trout. Many times, the river
can appear completely dead, without rising fish or
aquatic insects, until sunset. Then, suddenly, the
river comes alive with whiteflies in proportions that
can only be described as blizzardlike, especially since the bugs are white.
Whiteflies emerge in incredible numbers in the Middle and Lower Main
Stem, where they can provide just as much insect biomass—and as many
good fishing opportunities—as the famous whitefly hatches in Pennsylvania's Yellow Breeches Creek and Susquehanna River. The Upper Delaware
trout's receptiveness to this hatch really depends on the river's temperature
in June and July, well before the hatch begins. If the Cannonsville Reservoir
has released little water in these months, and if the Main Stem is especially
warm, few trout may occupy the sections with whitefly populations. But if
the river has been cool, either from unusually cold and wet weather or from
significant reservoir releases, the whitefly hatch can provide terrific fly-fishing action.

Nymph

Whitefly nymphs are good swimmers. Nymph fly patterns can be effective if
they are stripped like streamers to imitate the swimming nymphs before the
hatch begins. The nymphs emerge into duns just below the river's surface.
Tandem techniques like those described in the hebe nymph section can also be
very effective for imitating the emerging whiteflies—substitute a size 14 White
Wulff dry fly and a whitefly nymph for the flies mentioned in the hebe section.

> Hook: 12–14 standard length shank
> Thread: white
> Three tails: light dun mallard flank
> Body: cream
> Wing case: gray mallard quill
> Hackle: very light dun

Dun

Whitefly duns are unusual mayflies. Their legs are atrophied, so they don't
often land. Male whiteflies have three tails and often molt into spinners while
they are flying. Female whiteflies have two tails and don't molt into spinners
at all. The females also carry two large eggs sacs in their abdomens, which
gives them a slight yellowish cast until they drop the eggs to the surface and
fall spent to the river.

Hook: 14–16 standard length shank
Thread: white
Shuck (optional): male only—white
Three tails (females have only two): light dun Micro Fibetts
Body: very pale yellow (females) to chalky white (males)
Wing: very light dun or white
Hackle: white

Male Spinner

Hook: 14–16 standard length shank
Thread: white
Three tails: light dun Micro Fibetts
Body: white
Spent wing: white

Summer Caddisflies

Green sedge. JOHN MILLER

Green Sedge (*Rhyacophila* species)

The *Rhyacophila* caddis species are especially plentiful and important in the Upper Delaware system. They live in riffled or swift-flowing sections in all the branches, and they hatch in significant numbers. I'll never forget an intense *Rhyacophila* egg-laying session that took place in the riffle below the West Branch's Balls Eddy access in 1999. Trout were eagerly thrashing at hundreds of these caddisflies that were hatching and laying eggs. I caught several nice trout that day, but it's the caddisflies that I remember best. I broke a nice rainbow off and was tying some new tippet into my leader when I noticed hordes of caddisflies laying eggs on my waders—the insects were so thick that I couldn't even see my waders. Those waders are long gone, but I'll never forget the egg sacs sticking to the fabric or how eagerly the trout pursued those caddisflies. *Rhyacophila* egg layers attaching themselves to anglers' waders must be fairly common. In his book *Caddisflies*, Gary LaFontaine (1981) recounts a story by Pennsylvania fly-fishing legend Charles Wetzel that is almost exactly like mine.

Pupa

Rhyacophila pupae do not construct cases. They freely wander the rocks underneath riffles, anchored to the river bottom only by a light brown silk line. Trout have ample opportunity to eat the pupae as they dangle from their anchor lines and when they are swept into the current. The pupae are strong swimmers and are best imitated by swinging fly patterns wet-fly style.

Hook: 14–16 standard length shank; 12–14 curved shank
Thread: green
Body   brown head; bright green body

Adult

Standard Elk Hair Caddis imitations fished on a dead drift or skittered in riffled sections can accurately imitate the adults. *Rhyacophila* caddisflies lay their eggs on the bottom of the river and then slowly drift to the surface. It can also be effective to sink dry-fly patterns and allow them to drift under and in the surface film to imitate the spent egg layers.

> Hook: 14–16 standard length shank
> Thread: green
> Body: medium olive green
> Hackle: dark ginger
> Wing: light brown

Spotted Sedge (*Hydropsyche* species)

See the description in chapter 6.

Summer Terrestrials

Ants and Flying Ants

Upper Delaware trout seem to love ants. The trees, shrubs, Japanese knotweed, and other vegetation that overhang the Upper Delaware branches provide homes and travel routes for ants. Their precarious search for food amidst the vegetation ensures that a steady supply of black and cinnamon ants is available to the Upper Delaware's trout.

Ants are often overlooked by anglers who expect trout to be feeding on aquatic insects. An ant's dark coloration hides it from predators but also makes it difficult for anglers to distinguish in the surface glare. I once spent a fruitless afternoon on the Upper Delaware's Main Stem, even though every trout in the river seemed to be rising. I must have tied a dozen mayfly patterns to my tippet, without a glance from the trout, before frustration made me step back and watch the riseforms. The fish weren't splashing; they weren't dimpling. They were eagerly sucking large mouthfuls of something off the surface, but it wasn't the blue-winged olives that were sailing down the river unmolested. I bent down to get a better look. I could see thousands of black specks that looked like grains of pepper floating past me. I didn't realize that these "pepper grains" were size 22 ants until I dipped my hand into the river and studied them against my light skin. I switched to a small ant pattern and reconciled with a few of the trout before diminishing daylight chased me from the river.

The trout's fondness for ants makes them a vital component in any Upper Delaware angler's fly box. Wet, parachute, foam, standard, and an array of other ant patterns will catch fish. I sometimes try an ant during long-lasting hatches, such as the Upper West Branch's sulphur, when the fish ignore my hatch-matching fly patterns. Trout that have seen every known sulphur pattern variation for two months will often ignore artificial sulphurs but sometimes take an ant.

It's impossible to know whether the trout will be eating land-bound ants before you get to the river. But near the end of August you can be reasonably sure that they'll be eating flying ants. In his terrific book *Pennsylvania Trout Streams and Their Hatches,* Charlie Meck (1993) states that flying ants will appear on the waters of the Northeast within one or two days of August 25. I've found his prediction to be accurate in the Upper Delaware system 99 percent of the time.

Flying ants seem to prefer dry, sunny days. You can reasonably expect to find them on the water anytime these conditions occur, after their initial flight. A little wind is a good thing, because it seems to force more of the bugs onto the water. Flying ants are also black or cinnamon colored and vary in size from 24 to 14. I always begin fishing with a size 14 because they are easier to see and because the trout sometimes prefer the larger ones. But trout can be selective when it comes to ant size, so it's prudent to carry ant patterns in a range of sizes.

Harry Steeves Beetle.

Beetles

Beetles are another terrestrial favored by Upper Delaware trout. My friend, the gifted southern fly tier Harrison Steeves, does very well fishing his wonderfully imitative foam beetles along the Japanese knotweed–shrouded banks on the West Branch's no-kill section. However, standard deer-hair, or crow, beetles also produce fish. Beetles should be fished near the banks with a gentle "plop" when they hit the water.

Moths

The uncharacteristically hot, dry summer of 2005 led to my discovery of Upper Delaware moth fishing. The extreme weather created poor daytime and evening fishing conditions that year, so I decided to try to visit the river at the coolest part of the day—sunrise.

I really didn't expect much that first day. My alarm cried out at 5:30 A.M., and after getting dressed and drinking several cups of coffee, I left, unhurried, for the Upper East Branch, hoping to find some Tricos and a few trout eating them. The river valley was tucked into a thick blanket of fog as I navigated the short drive from my house to the river. Fog is a normal condition when the cold, bottom-released reservoir water meets the hot summer air, but that day, the fog was thicker than normal—a good sign of a nice water release. I noticed that there were no cars parked at the access areas I passed on the way to my fishing spot, meaning that there was no one else on the river that early. I parked my car and decided to walk down to the river to have a look, but I couldn't see anything because the fog was too thick. I could certainly hear something, though—the loud slurping sounds a large trout makes when it's gleefully sucking green drakes off the surface under the cover of darkness, not daintily eating Tricos during the day.

Then the first moth hit me in the face. I had been seeing these big moths all week. They congregated under the lights of the East Branch Sunoco station at night—hundreds of them. Bob Laubauch, a retired forester and a good friend, would later tell me that they were the adult form of the forest tent caterpillar, but I didn't know that then, and I really didn't care. I was more concerned about whether I had any patterns in my fly box that looked like a big moth.

I returned to the car and prepared my gear. I found three ratty-looking size 8 Elk Hair Caddis flies buried in the recesses of my box, which I didn't even know I had. They were simple flies with a natural deer-hair wing, a creamy tan body, and brown palmered hackle. Because of their large size, I think they were intended to be October caddis patterns, but today, they would have to impersonate moths. I noticed that the fog was beginning to lift from Route 30 as I strung my rod, and I could see more moths flying up and down the road. They appeared sluggish and lethargic, as if the cool fog had stunned them.

The river, unlike Route 30, was still buried deep in fog when I returned. I noticed fewer of the moths in the air, but the sounds of feeding trout remained. I got my first real look at the water as I began inching my way into

One of the big browns the author caught during the moth hatch.

casting position toward the sound of the closest fish. Every foot of river had an anesthetized moth riding on its surface. The few moths that were flying were moving up and down erratically, like baby birds that still didn't believe they could fly.

My initial cast, over what appeared to be a very large brown trout, was about a foot short. I was waiting for my fly to float below the trout before I picked it up to recast, but the big fish turned, followed the fly for a few inches, and then inhaled it with a loud slurping sound just like the ones I had heard on shore. I set the hook, and the big fish burrowed deep into the hole. I wrestled with it for five minutes before I could gently place it in my net—most of it, anyway. The large female was almost 22 inches long. I caught five more fish that first morning, all over 15 inches, and broke off several more before I came to my senses and trimmed the leader back to 3X. This pattern of large trout feeding without caution continued for the duration of the moths. I don't believe I had even one fly refused when there were moths on the water.

I fished the moth hatch for the next four days, both with my wife and by myself, and then I realized that there were no more moths under the Sunoco station lights at night. I still went to the river the next morning, but I knew it was over. The moths disappeared just as quietly as they had arrived. The moth fishing lasted a little over a week. I still wonder what I missed those first few nights when I saw the moths but didn't fish the next morning. Next summer, I'll be ready.

Moths are cyclical, so there are no guarantees. But if you notice a lot of moths under the lights on a summer night, and if enough cold water is being released to create fog, you should be standing on an Upper Delaware riverbank at sunrise. You may discover some unbelievable fishing.

Grasshoppers and Crickets

Although large grasshopper and cricket patterns provide excellent, highly visible fishing opportunities on many western trout rivers, as well as most of the revered northeastern limestone streams, they fail to inspire Upper Delaware trout, and geography is to blame. Wind is required on most western rivers to push grasshoppers onto the water. Wind sweeps across the wide, grassy valleys and throws the bugs from the fields onto the water. The Upper Delaware's valleys are narrow in comparison and predominantly tree-lined, not grassy. The physical nature of the rivers, usually wending east to west, also contributes to the lack of hopper and cricket availability. Rather than blowing across, the wind usually blows up- or downriver, keeping the insects tucked safely in their few grassy hideaways.

Another factor in the lack of hopper and cricket productivity is the health of the Upper Delaware system and the reluctance of most of its wild trout to feed opportunistically—they simply don't have to. There is too much food on the bottom of the Upper Delaware branches for the trout to surface feed unless a steady supply of insects is floating past their lies.

Fall Hatches

Fall Hatches			
Insect	Size	Hatch Begins	Hatch Ends
Dark blue-winged olive (*Sarratella deficiens;* formerly *Ephemerella deficiens*)	22–24	Mid-June	Mid-September
Little blue-winged olive (*Acentrella turbida;* formerly *Pseudocleons*)	22–26	Mid-June	Late October
Orange cahill; aka summer stenos (*Stenacron interpunctatum;* formerly *Stenacron heterotarsale* and *Stenacron canadense*)	12–14	Late June	Mid-September
Trico (*Tricorythodes stygiatus*)	24	Early July	Mid-October
Hebe (*Leucrocuta hebe;* formerly *Heptagenia hebe*)	18–20	Mid-July	Mid-October
Blue-winged olive (*Drunella lata;* formerly *Ephemerella lata*)	16–18	Mid-July	Late October
Slate drake; aka Iso; aka white gloved howdy (*Isonychia bicolor;* also includes species formerly known as *Isonychia sadleri* and *Isonychia harperi*)	12–14	The hatch usually increases in intensity in mid to late September	Mid to late October
October caddis; aka great brown autumn sedge (*Pycnopsyche*)	10	Late September	Late October

Fall Mayflies

See the descriptions in the summer mayflies section for blue-winged olives orange cahills, tricos, and hebes. The fall *Isonychia* hatches are especially important and often provide the best dry-fly fishing opportunities for the season. The fall Isos are usually one to two sizes smaller than the spring insects because they have less time to grow.

October Caddis, or Great Brown Autumn Sedge *(Pycnopsyche)*

October caddisflies do not emerge in large numbers in the Upper Delaware. In fact, large portions of the system have very few of them. However, October caddisflies do hatch in large enough numbers on the Lower East Branch and Main Stem to make blind-casting a large caddis dry-fly pattern in the riffles worthwhile. October caddis are important not because of their numbers but because they are a large

October caddis.

insect that begins hatching after most of the other aquatic insect hatches have ended for the year. Some of my final dry-fly-caught fish of the season have been taken with October caddis patterns.

Fall is a great time to fish the Upper Delaware. Air and water temperatures are cool, trout want to feed, and fishermen are few.

Larva

October caddisflies construct cases from pieces of sticks and other plant debris. The larvae often emerge into pupae at night, so many anglers don't have the opportunity to imitate them. However, it can be productive to swing an October caddis larva through riffles even during the day.

    Hook: 8–10, 2XL shank; 8 curved shank
    Thread: yellow
    Body: brown head; ginger body

Pupa or Adult

October caddis adults should be blind-cast in riffles. Twitching and skittering the dry-fly patterns can sometimes elicit aggressive strikes from trout.

    Hook: 10 standard length shank
    Thread: rust
    Body: tannish orange
    Hackle: reddish brown
    Wing: orange

Winter Fly Fishing

The Upper Delaware's winter fly-fishing opportunities are limited to the Pennsylvania and New York border water—most of the Lower West Branch, and all of the Main Stem. By far, the more consistent of the two rivers for productive winter fly fishing is the Lower West Branch. There are fewer trout in the Main Stem, and they are more difficult to isolate because the river is so big.

The best time of day to fish in the winter is usually from 11:00 A.M. to 3:00 P.M.—the warmest part of the day. Some anglers believe that trout will feed aggressively only when the water temperature is their ideal range of 55 to 65 degrees. But a trout's metabolism actually increases, inducing it to feed, when water temperatures are moving toward that ideal range. I've had some very good winter fly-fishing trips when the thermometer showed that the river temperature had increased only a couple of degrees and remained well below 55.

At this time of the year, fly pattern selection is relatively simple. Forget dry flies. I have never found significant numbers of Upper Delaware trout rising to winter midge hatches on either the Lower West Branch or the Main Stem. Nymphs are the fly patterns of choice, although I've also had some success fishing streamers very slowly along the river bottom. The same nymph-

Winter can be a great time to find solitude and good fishing in the West Branch and Main Stem. Here, two anglers are fly fishing below the West Branch's Route 191 Bridge after a dusting of late winter snow.

ing techniques and fly patterns described in chapter 5 work well during the winter. I strongly suggest trying stonefly nymphs, which provide a substantial meal to a hungry winter trout. And stoneflies are always in the river due to their two- to three-year life cycle.

The best Upper Delaware winter fly fishing usually occurs when the river is low, as long as the water remains open and not completely encased in ice. If West Branch flows are at or below 300 cfs, the fishing will probably be very good. I seldom fish during flows over 500 cfs. Low flows concentrate the trout, and you'll find them holding in any area with deeper water. It's also much easier to get your flies into the trout's strike zone, without using a lot of weight, if the river is low. I prefer to use as little weight as possible, just because it's much more pleasant to cast and fish without it.

Most of the river's access areas and many of its dirt roads are not maintained during the winter. It's common for them to be completely unplowed and clogged with snow. It's a good idea to use four-wheel drive vehicles for winter fly-fishing trips. They allow you to park much closer to the river than you could with conventional vehicles—a good idea in case of an emergency.

A great deal of consideration should be given to your own safety before you plan a winter fly-fishing trip to the Upper Delaware. Hypothermia can be deadly, and it can quickly overcome you if you aren't dressed properly or if you fall into the river. Always bring towels and an extra change of clothes, just in case, and keep them in the car. Don't wade as aggressively as you would during the spring or summer. Stay out of water that is more than knee deep, and don't try to cross the river anywhere but at its shallowest sections. You should also be very wary of the ice shelves that often form near the shore. They usually extend into the river, making them attractive perches for fishermen who are trying to get a good drift on the river's far side, but the ice is often thin and can break under an angler's weight.

CHAPTER 8

Understanding the Resource

Management of the Upper Delaware's reservoirs and branches is always changing. Future management practices could alter the validity of some of the information provided in this chapter. It now appears that, for the first time, flood mitigation will become an important function for the Delaware River system's reservoirs. This new mandate is sure to impact the timing and availability of released water for the trout fishery. But no one can predict with certainty what effect this change will have on the fishery. In spite of this and other potential management changes, I believe that the information in this chapter is important. It provides a historical overview of practices that have advanced and limited the Upper Delaware's trout fishery until the time the writing of this book was completed in the autumn of 2006. Understanding present and past water management practices and their consequences will be essential for anglers who want to protect the Upper Delaware's trout in the future. Concerned anglers who want to find the most current information for Delaware River and reservoir management should contact Friends of the Upper Delaware River (FUDR) and the New York DEC, Region 4.

Commonly Asked Questions

What is cfs?

Cubic feet per second (cfs) is the unit of measurement for the amount of water flowing past a given point. For instance, if the flow at the West Branch's Hale Eddy gauge is 600 cfs, it means that 600 cubic foot–size boxes of water are moving past the gauge each second.

What is the difference between water flow and water release?

Water flow is simply the amount of water moving past a gauging station at a given time. The water could be from dam releases, rain, tributaries, or spillage over the top of a dam. This water can vary in temperature from very cold in the winter and early spring to lethally warm, for trout, during an unusually hot spring or summer.

Water release is the amount of water coming out of the bottom of a dam. Water release is much more important to the health of the Upper Delaware River system than water flow, especially during periods of warm weather. Water released from the dams is cold—usually somewhere between the upper 40s and the lower 50s, depending on reservoir levels. Therefore, more water being released from the dams means colder river temperatures and better trout and insect habitat.

What is the difference between the New York City DEP and the New York State DEC?

The Department of Environmental Protection (DEP) is the New York City agency that is directly responsible for the operation, maintenance, and protection of the city's water and sewer systems. One of its primary functions is to procure, protect, and advance the city's water supply. The DEP's power and influence branch out from the city to all parts of New York State that have an influence on the city's water supply, including the Delaware River system. Because of its charter, the DEP controls nearly all the water management decisions for the Upper Delaware's trout fishery.

The Department of Environmental Conservation (DEC) is a New York State agency that exists to conserve, improve, and protect the state's natural resources and environment and to control water, land, and air pollution. The DEC's jurisdiction overlaps and occasionally even conflicts with the DEP's when it comes to shared natural resources such as the Delaware River system. But historically, the DEP's authority has rendered the DEC almost powerless to manage the Upper Delaware's trout water. One way the DEC can influence water conditions in the Upper Delaware system is through the use and management of the habitat bank (see next question). But the relatively small amount of water allotted to the bank severely limits the DEC's ability to provide trout-sustaining flows and releases.

What is the habitat bank, and how does it work?

The habitat bank was created to maintain the Upper Delaware and Neversink trout fisheries during periods of low river flows and elevated water temperatures. The size of the habitat bank has been expanded in recent years, and it could be expanded, reduced, or eliminated in the future. Currently, the bank is a preconditioned volume of 20,000 cfs-days—combined for the Cannonsville, Pepacton, and Neversink Reservoirs. For example, 1,000 cfs of water could be released for 20 days before the bank would be depleted. Water in the bank can be released in any increment that the New York State DEC deems necessary. The habitat bank can also be reduced in times of drought (discussed later).

At first blush, the habitat bank seems like a good thing, and sometimes it is. But it is not the answer for maintaining the Upper Delaware as a trout fishery. The DEC seldom uses the habitat bank as aggressively as the river's anglers would like it to be used. If the rivers become low and warm early in season, the DEC may decide not to use the bank at all, even if the river temperatures are potentially lethal to trout. DEC officials believe that very little habitat bank water should be used early in the season—the rationale being that if they drain the bank in May, they won't have any water left for the typically dry, hot month of August.

This reasoning demonstrates one of the greatest flaws of the habitat bank: it isn't large enough to protect the fishery. The size of the bank is arbitrary and lacks any scientific basis. The DEC is also at fault for not taking a more active stance in safeguarding the river system. As I have told DEC representatives many times, having a lot of water in the habitat bank in August is of little use if all the trout died in May. My point is that the DEC needs to be more aggressive in its management of the Upper Delaware trout fishery. One DEC representative informed me in 2003 that the bank has never run out of water by the end of the year. What are they saving it for?

What is the Montague target, and how does it affect the Upper Delaware trout fishery?

The Montague target was created by a 1954 Supreme Court decision involving the states of Pennsylvania, New Jersey, and Delaware, which had sued New York State over the proposed Catskill reservoirs. The three plaintiff

Upper Delaware rainbows average about 15 inches. An evening hatch in the Lower Main provided this average-sized rainbow.

states were concerned that New York City would dewater the Delaware River after the dams were completed. This would have had a catastrophic effect on the downriver states, which need adequate Delaware River flows for drinking water, shipping, sewage transfer, and oyster farms. The Supreme Court decreed that a minimum river flow had to be maintained by New York City at the Delaware River's Montague, New Jersey, gauging station to protect the needs of all the states. The minimum flow has changed over time, but it is currently set at 1,750 cfs.

The 1,750-cfs target has a huge impact on the Upper Delaware summer trout fishery. Low river flows occur often, but not always, in the summer as rainfall diminishes. These low flows require New York City's DEP to call for additional water releases from the reservoirs to maintain the flow at Montague. The water can come from any of the reservoirs above the Montague target, but historically, the majority has been released from Cannonsville. The released water cools the West Branch and Upper Main Stem and allows their trout to survive. It also induces mayfly hatches that provide excellent summer dry-fly fishing while other eastern trout streams are stressed from low flows and higher water temperatures. Much of the Upper Delaware is largely a spring and fall fishery without significant summertime Montague water releases.

Why is more water released from the Cannonsville Dam than other Catskill reservoirs? What impact does this have on the Upper Delaware trout fishery?

The West Branch above the Cannonsville Dam meanders through farmland and small towns. It receives inflows of phosphorus, silt, and other pollutants along its course. These pollutants are then deposited into the Cannonsville Reservoir, creating algae blooms and, ultimately, a degraded water source for New York City. The water is potable but is considered more expendable than the relatively pure water in the other Delaware reservoirs (Pepacton, Neversink, and Rondout).

Cannonsville water is usually withheld for release down the West Branch of the Delaware, eventually meeting the mandated flow at Montague, New Jersey. The decision to release water predominantly from Cannonsville has created the fantastic wild rainbow and brown trout fishery in the Main Stem that we have today.

Released water is constantly warming as it travels downriver. Water released from Pepacton Reservoir, on the East Branch, travels approximately 34 miles before it reaches the Main Stem—by which time it has warmed considerably. Cannonsville water travels a much shorter distance of approximately 17.5 miles to the Main Stem and remains significantly colder. This cold water from Cannonsville creates a thermal refuge in the West Branch and upper portion of the Main Stem and allows the wild trout in these rivers to survive, even during hot summer weather.

Do New York City residents drink the water from Cannonsville Reservoir?

Many knowledgeable Delaware River anglers believe that New York City dwellers don't drink any of the water in Cannonsville Reservoir, but this is a misconception. They do drink Cannonsville water, especially in the spring.

All the water found in the Delaware reservoir system can be diverted into Rondout Reservoir through the series of intricate underground portals described in chapter 1. It's common for the DEP to divert water from Cannonsville into Rondout throughout the year, but it happens most often in the spring, when Cannonsville begins to spill and pollutants are diluted by the increased water volume. The DEP considers any water that spills over the top of its reservoirs as waste. So if water levels are high enough that spillage is possible, and if Rondout isn't full, the DEP will divert water.

The main reason that so many people believe that Cannonsville water isn't used for drinking is because the DEP is constantly bemoaning the quality of the water, even though it has improved greatly in recent years. DEP officials use Cannonsville's water quality as an excuse to hoard water in the Pepacton and Neversink Reservoirs and as a reason to withhold water from the East Branch and Neversink Rivers.

Drift boats provide access to parts of the Upper Delaware system that are surrounded by private property. The boats are extremely stable and very popular due to their fishing-friendly features.

Why do West Branch water releases usually increase on summer weekends? Is it for the benefit of fishermen and boaters?

On weekends throughout the summer, it's common to have a large water release from Cannonsville Reservoir that begins on Friday and ends on Sunday. Many anglers believe that these releases are a gift from the New York City DEP to the many fishermen and boaters who take weekend getaways to the Catskills. They are not. The increased water release is usually due to the cessation of power production at the Pennsylvania Power and Light (PP&L) plant on Lake Wallenpaupack.

PP&L uses water from Lake Wallenpaupack to generate electricity. The used water is released into the Lackawaxen River, which empties into the Delaware River above the Montague gauging station. This water increases the Delaware's volume and helps maintain the Court-mandated 1,750-cfs flow—reducing the need for Delaware River water to fulfill the Montague target. PP&L does not generate electricity on weekends, so extra water is needed from the Delaware to maintain the Montague requirement.

The most important facet to understanding Upper Delaware flow management is the realization that the DEP places little importance on the health of the river or its trout when determining flows. The DEP's only obligation is to New York City, and if it weren't for the Supreme Court, the DEP might have been happy to turn the Delaware River into a dry riverbed.

Why wouldn't water be released to protect the river, especially if the reservoirs are full?

Anglers often ask this question when the Upper Delaware's flows are very low during unusually hot, dry periods, particularly when rainfall occurring downriver of Callicoon is maintaining the Montague target. It's typical for the Upper Delaware and its branches to be low and warm at these times, even though the reservoirs are comparatively full. DEP officials are fond of saying that the drought of the century could begin tomorrow, and they won't release any more water than they have to because of this fear. There is some validity to this argument. New York City built its reservoirs to provide drinking water, not for fishing. No one would argue that the needs of the Upper Delaware trout fishery should outweigh the needs of America's most important city or the lives of its millions of residents. However, a closer look at the issue reveals that it's not so clear-cut.

New York City's DEP has 19 reservoirs and 3 controlled lakes at its disposal. It could also draw water from the Hudson River. Could the relatively small amount of water it would take to maintain the fisheries each year actually save the city during a severe drought? Some risks are so minimal compared to the potential benefits that they are worthwhile. If the DEP is willing to live with the real risks involved with its leaking aqueducts—water that could also be used for the city in a time of crisis—then I don't think for a little water for the trout fishery is too much to ask. The answer to the original question is that the DEP doesn't release enough water to protect the fishery because it doesn't have to and because it doesn't want to.

What happens to the Upper Delaware's flows if a drought is declared?

New York City's DEP developed a series of drought curves to track reservoir water volumes and to warn of potential droughts. These drought curves have a tremendous impact on the management of the Delaware River system, and they are one of the key ingredients to any long-term solution for the river's flow issues.

The drought curves initiate a series of actions and reactions that wreak havoc throughout the river system when a drought is declared. But an actual drought is not declared without warning. The drought curves instigate drought awareness in three distinct stages: drought watch, drought warning, and drought. The stages are determined by the total combined water volumes in the three Delaware River basin reservoirs (Cannonsville, Pepacton, and Neversink). Even though water is often diverted underground from each of these reservoirs into Rondout, Rondout's volume is not factored into the drought curves. Once water leaves the Delaware system and goes into Rondout, it's like it never existed.

A declared drought limits how much water is legally available for use by New York City, the river's bordering communities, and the fishery. The fear of the reservoir system falling into a declared drought is the DEP's primary reason for not providing more water for the protection and enhancement of the Upper Delaware's trout fishery. However, many conservationists believe that the DEP has never provided enough concrete scientific evidence to substantiate its drought curves. The drought curves appear to be just as arbitrary as the habitat bank—like the numbers were just picked out of the air.

The accompanying table shows the Upper Delaware branches' minimum flows according to stage of drought. If a drought is declared, the minimum river flows are maintained only at the discretion of the border states—that is, minimum flows could be reduced even further than those shown in the table.

Minimum Upper Delaware Flows by Drought Stage

River Gauge Location	Minimum Flows during Normal Conditions (cfs)	Minimum Flows during Drought Watch (cfs)	Minimum Flows during Drought Warning (cfs)	Minimum Flows during Declared Drought (cfs)
West Branch at Hale Eddy	225	190	160	145
Upper East Branch at Harvard	175	150	120	115
Neversink at Bridgeville	115	100	80	75

The drought curves are one more way that the DEP treats Catskills residents like second-class citizens. Water restrictions initiated by a declared drought do not end equitably for all water users. Reservoir levels have to be higher, and have to stay that way for a longer time, for a drought to end in the Catskills than they do for a drought to end in New York City. So, while the city's residents are washing their sidewalks and their children are dancing in open fire hydrants, Catskills residents remain under water restrictions—interesting, since all the water began as rainfall in the Catskills.

Is there a way to predict river levels when planning a trip to the Upper Delaware?

Anglers often call my fly shop to get river flow information for their upcoming fishing trips, which are sometimes weeks away. I give these anglers current river conditions and try to make educated guesses about the future, but they are only guesses. Ron "Curly" Huber, one of my fly-shop employees and a good friend, once told such an angler that he would have a better chance of guessing the color of God's eyes than predicting future river flows. I don't think I can say it any better than that.

Is the current experimental flow-based plan (often referred to as Revision 7) good for the Upper Delaware system?

There are few absolutes in the world, and the answer to this question isn't one of them. It's impossible to say that the current experimental flow plan is entirely good or entirely bad—it really depends on which river is involved and what time of year it is.

A rare rainbow caught in the Upper East Branch.

The current flow plan has been good for the Upper East Branch. Upper East Branch flows at the Harvard gauging station in 2005 were nearly double their recorded levels before the experimental flow plan was enacted in 2002: 100 cfs before, and 175 cfs after. The plan kept the Upper East Branch's daytime water temperature, downriver of Harvard, at or below 70 degrees for much of the summer. It obviously would have been better if more water had been released so that the entire Upper East Branch could have had better habitat and fishable water temperatures. And one could argue that the only reason that Upper East flows are improved now is because they were so poor before the flow plan was enacted. But 2005 was an improvement nonetheless.

The experimental flow plan is also an improvement for all the Delaware branches during the winter—some of the time. Cannonsville and Pepacton minimum winter releases were a pathetic 45 and 23 cfs, respectively, before the current flow plan was enacted. These paltry releases created flows that jeopardized both trout and insects as pools froze solid and anchor ice formed. Winter flows have been higher since the plan was enacted, unless you count the many times the gauges froze and the releases were returned to 45 and 23 cfs. Supposedly, the New York State DEC and the city's DEP have begun to calculate winter flows and no longer have to rely on frozen gauges in the winter. But only time will tell if the Upper Delaware's wintertime river flows can actually be maintained by these calculations.

The most glaring failure of the current flow plan is what it has done to the Lower West Branch (below Hale Eddy) and the Upper Delaware's Main Stem. The summer of 2005 created water temperatures in the upper 70s to mid-80s throughout the Lower West Branch and Main Stem. The New York State DEC publicly stated that there wasn't enough water in the plan to protect the Main Stem and officially abandoned all trout-protecting temperature and flow targets because half the habitat bank had been depleted—even though the reservoirs were almost full. There is no reason to believe that the Lower West Branch and Main Stem will be protected in the future as long as governmental agencies can hide behind the fact that there is too little water in their own arbitrary plans.

There is hope, however. A new plan, called Revision 8, is supposed to be in place when Revision 7 expires in April 2007. This plan will have the power to change the management of the Delaware trout fishery from target-driven releases to a more stable system of minimum releases, to keep the river's management exactly as it is now, or to do something in between.

What happens when the DEP and DEC violate the current flow plan?

The answer is simple—nothing happens. The DEP and DEC often violate their Upper Delaware River fishery agreements because there is no outside agency willing to enforce them. The DEP's and DEC's positions are that Upper Delaware flow and temperature agreements are just "targets," nothing more. If they miss a target, they know that there will be no consequences other than the whining of a few fly fishermen.

These targets are heavily based on weather predictions. Most of us know that weather predictions aren't a good way to plan a picnic, let alone manage the Upper Delaware trout fishery. The river master often curtails water releases when rainfall is predicted, the idea being that runoff will provide the extra water needed to maintain minimum flows and the Montague target, and that any additional water releases would be a "waste." But as we all know, weather forecasting is not an exact science; predictions are often inaccurate or just plain wrong. So, if the 225-cfs flow at the West Branch's Hale Eddy gauge is reduced to 150 cfs and a predicted thunderstorm misses the Catskills, the river and trout have to suffer. If it happens on a weekend, the flows may not be corrected until Monday. A concerned angler can't even call the DEC or DEP to complain—their offices are closed on the weekends.

If there are so many flow problems hindering the Upper Delaware trout fishery, why is the fishing still so good?

I'm asked this question several times a year, usually by anglers who want to know why they should spend their time worrying about river flows and water releases when they just enjoyed some of the best trout fishing of their lives. The point really isn't about what the river is now. It's about what the river *could be* if it were managed properly.

The Upper Delaware has a short fishing season. Anglers can expect reasonably good trout fishing from about the middle of April to the middle of June. All late-spring and summer fishing varies with the inconsistent ebbs and flows of reservoir releases and weather patterns. This puts a tremendous strain on the fishery. The Upper Delaware has a lot of fans, and most of them don't live locally. Most anglers don't want to travel to the river unless they are reasonably sure they'll find opportunities to catch some fish. So they come during the two months they can expect to catch trout, resulting in crowded conditions throughout the system in April, May, and June. If the river had steady releases throughout the summer, the system could remain highly productive for six months. Anglers wouldn't feel pressured to fish the Upper Delaware only in the spring, and they could plan their trips throughout the year.

Another strain placed on the fishery is the elevated water temperatures that have now become common on the Upper Delaware. This adds to the physical wear and tear on trout that have already been stressed from high angling pressure; it forces them into shallow riffles, the bottoms of deep pools, and near areas with groundwater infiltration—making them targets for predators and disease. It's reasonable to assume that a significant number of Upper Delaware trout succumb to angling and water temperature pressures during the summer, leaving a reduced trout population at the end of each year. Most biologists agree that the river system has never reached its trout-holding capacity due to insufficient water releases and the temperature problems they create.

If these problems were corrected, we would have a longer fishing season, possibly diluting angling pressure, and more consistently productive fishing because there would be more trout to catch. Some might say that angling pressure would actually increase over a greater part of the year if river conditions were improved, and that may be true. But at least there would be more trout to survive the onslaught. And more river areas would fish well because they would hold more fish. Fishing pressure could be distributed throughout the river system, instead of intense fishing pressure directed at only a few of the river's hotspots. How could more trout be a bad thing?

Navigable Public Highways and the High-Water Mark

The parts of the Upper Delaware system that form the border between New York and Pennsylvania—the West Branch and the entire Main Stem—are considered navigable public highways. This designation means that the public has certain rights associated with these rivers, and it assures every angler the right to travel and fish along these river sections as long as they stay within the high-water mark. But what exactly is the high-water mark?

The high-water mark in the Upper Delaware system is usually well defined. It doesn't include the highest point to which the rivers have flooded. If that were true, we would be able to fish inside some people's houses. The high-water mark is the area along the riverbanks where the river normally flows throughout the year. This area is usually defined by tree growth, since trees can't grow within a river's channel. If you stay between the tree line and the river, you will probably be within the high-water mark. And it is your right to be there.

The entire East Branch flows within New York State. Since it is not interstate border water, the public's right to traverse and fish within its high-water mark is murky at best. A March 1992 New York State DEC study by D. Kay Sanford, former senior aquatic biologist of the Region 4 Fisheries Office, cites New York State legislation that appears to address the question of East Branch navigability and the public's right to traverse its banks:

> Chapter CXCV
> An Act declaring the Delaware River and its Branches, Public Highways.
> Passed April 12, 1822.
>
> I. Be it enacted by the People of the State of New York, represented in the Senate and Assembly, That all that part of the Delaware River, from Carpenter's point, near the north boundary of the State of New Jersey, to the northerly boundary of the town of Delhi, in the county of Delaware, and also all that part of the east branch of the said river, from the forks where it forms a junction with the west branch in the town of Hancock, to the farm of Frederick Kittle, in the town of Middletown, in said county; and all that part of the Beaver kill (a stream tributary to the said east branch) which is within the said county of Delaware, be and the same are hereby declared each to be a public highway: Provided, That nothing herein contained shall

be construed to prevent any person or persons from erecting, keeping, and maintaining, over, on, or across the said west and east branches of said river, and the said Beaver Kill, any bridges, mill dams, water fences, or eel weirs, to be erected or construed in such manner as in no wise to interrupt or materially injure the free navigation of the waters of the said streams, with rafts or lumber, in time of an ordinary freshet, for running lumber.

II. And be it further enacted, That it shall be lawful for any person or persons, by and under the authority of the State of Pennsylvania, to improve the navigation of the said river, so far as the same, or the westerly shore thereof, is a boundary line between this state and the state of Pennsylvania: Provided, That nothing contained in this section shall be constructed to affect the rights of any person or body corporate, nor the jurisdiction of this state.

Regrettably, Sanford's study doesn't definitively state that the public has the right to wade within the high-water mark on the East Branch. I called the New York State DEC in the spring of 2006 to try to achieve some clarity on the issue, but it was unable to give me a satisfactory answer. Basically, no one is sure of the legal status of the East Branch, and the issue may ultimately have to be decided in court. The question is intriguing and important, and the public deserves an answer.

Most Upper Delaware trout are wild. This fish's perfect fins, bright red spots, and colorful blue dot behind its eye signify that it has never eaten a hatchery pellet.

Catch-and-Release

The Upper Delaware has only one state-mandated catch-and-release section, near the top of the West Branch. Anglers are allowed to catch and kill trout throughout the rest of the system. So, the choice whether to kill wild Upper Delaware trout or to set them free is usually your own. But the Upper Delaware hosts too many anglers each year to believe that even a single fish is insignificant. All the legally harvestable Upper Delaware trout you catch have attained their size by surviving floods, droughts, thermal stress, predation from other animals, and an onslaught of anglers. They are the reason you traveled to the Upper Delaware fishery. Put them back in the river so that you'll have a reason to come back too.

Thermal Stress

The Upper Delaware relies on cold-water releases from its reservoirs to maintain the trout fishery. But, as noted throughout this book, these releases aren't always adequate to protect the fishery. There are times when warm river temperatures should discourage catch-and-release fly fishermen from fishing some parts of the system, but the entire system is seldom unfishable due to high water temperatures. Anglers can fish close to the dams or in one of the river's icy feeder creeks if the temperatures in their preferred sections are above 70 degrees.

One year, it was distressing to watch fly anglers harassing thermally stressed trout in the Beaverkill, Main Stem, and Lower East Branch, whose water temperatures were all over 75 degrees. Many Upper Delaware guides canceled trips that year due to unfit river conditions, which was the proper thing to do. But other guides ignored the dire conditions and worked the thermally stressed rivers, which was unfair to both their clients and the river's wild trout. I realize that many anglers travel great distances to fish the Upper Delaware system and that they are often bound by vacation schedules and can't always plan their trips around ideal fishing conditions. But there is no excuse for, and no glory in, catching and releasing a wild trout in a river with temperatures that are destined to kill it—especially when other parts of the system could be fished without jeopardizing the trout.

The Future of the Fishery

The Upper Delaware trout fishery is man-made—enhanced with nonnative fish and artificial cold-water releases from New York City's reservoirs. But is the fishery less valuable simply because humans created it? Marc Lee, one of my fly-shop customers and a New York City resident, phrased it best: "New York City's Central Park is man-made, but I don't think anyone wants to get rid of it." People need wild places, even if these places had more civilized beginnings. The Upper Delaware's wild brown and rainbow trout have lived in the river for over 100 years. Like most Americans, they were forced from their homes abroad and eventually thrived in a new world. They have earned the right to exist.

Formed in 2003, Friends of the Upper Delaware River (FUDR) is a non-profit organization comprising concerned anglers and businesspeople dedicated to protecting and enhancing the Upper Delaware trout fishery. Every angler who currently fishes the Upper Delaware River system or cares about wild trout should consider joining FUDR (PO Box 69, Minoa, NY 13116; 866-230-3767, ext. 7466; www.fudr.org).

FUDR Mission Statement

To improve the flows and protect the habitat of the famous Upper Delaware wild trout fishery through consistent coldwater releases from the Cannonsville dam.

FUDR's Release-Based Plan

To protect both the wild trout and the coldwater ecosystems (of the West Branch and Upper Main Stem), we seek a minimum release (from Cannonsville Reservoir) of 600 cfs, from May 15th to September 15—a rate of release that not only protects the fishery, but readily accommodates both drifting and wading fishermen and, in doing so, stabilizes local fishing related economies. During the less critical winter months, we are seeking a 300 cfs flow; adequate for preventing anchor ice and similar threats. To eliminate the now common and dangerous (to trout and insects) practice of sudden, abrupt release rates, we maintain that releases should be "ramped," that is, changed gradually. We have called for the development of a mutually agreed plan for proportional water releases during times of declared drought, and for locating and correcting the problem of silt entering the river from long-neglected feeder streams. We maintain that warm water spillage from overflowing reservoirs be offset with coldwater bottom release—a net loss of nothing to the system—and that water temperatures should not exceed 70 degrees at Lordville, a village located about midpoint on the River's Main Stem. And we maintain that the new electrical power generating releases from Pennsylvania's PP&L power plant—located below the fishery—should not be a determining factor in how much overall water is released.

APPENDIX: RESOURCES

Hotels and Motels

Capra Inn-Motel
103 W. Main St.
Hancock, NY 13783
607-637-1600

Delaware River Club
  Flyfishing Resort
1093 Winterdale Rd.
Starlight, PA 18461
570-635-5880
drc@hancock.net
www.mayfly.com

Deposit Motel
Route 17
Deposit, NY 13754
607-467-2998

Downsville Motel
State Highway 30
Downsville, NY 13755
607-363-7575

East Branch Motel
Old Route 17
East Branch, NY 13756
607-363-2959

Green Acres Motel
Route 17
Deposit, NY 13754
607-467-3620

Hankins House
6628 Route 97
PO Box 115
Hankins, NY 12741
845-887-4423

Hill's Twin Spruce Lodge
PO Box 212
Equinunk, PA 18417
570-224-4191

Laurel Bank Motel
Oak St.
Deposit, NY 13754
607-467-2427

Long Eddy Hotel & Saloon
7 Depot St.
Long Eddy, NY 12760
845-887-4554

Rolling Marble Guest House
PO Box 33
Long Eddy, NY 12760
845-887-6016

Scott's Oquaga Lake House
Oquaga Lake
Deposit, NY 13754
607-467-3094

Smith's Colonial Motel
23085 Route 97
Hancock, NY 13783
607-637-2989

Bed-and-Breakfasts

Adam's Farm House B&B
Main St.
Downsville, NY 13755
607-363-2757

Alexander's Inn
770 Oquaga Lake Rd.
Deposit, NY 13754
607-467-6023

Beagle B&B
Silver Lake Rd.
Hancock, NY 13783
607-467-5115

Becky's Bed and Breakfast
2406 State Highway 268
Hancock, NY 13783
607-637-5499

Chestnut Inn
498 Oquaga Lake Rd.
Deposit, NY 13754
607-467-2500
866-467-0002

Cranberry Inn
38 W. Main
Hancock, NY 13783
607-637-2788

Point Mountain Lodge B&B
186 Yendes
Hancock, NY 13783
607-637-2629

Sandercock House B&B
Grocery Hill & Kellam Rd.
Equinunk, PA 18417
570-224-8302 or 224-4551
www.sandercockhouse.com

Victoria Rose B&B
Main St.
Downsville, NY 13755
607-363-7838

Cabin Rentals

Bass Cabins
Route 97
Hancock, NY 13783
607-637-1800

Dream Catcher Lodge
Deposit, NY 13754
877-275-1165
607-637-4296 (Border
  Water Outfitters—
  booking agent)

Indian Springs Flyfishing
Camp
Lee Hartman
RR 1 Box 200 AA
Hancock, NY 13783
215-679-5022 (office)
570-224-2708 (camp)
215-679-4536 (fax)
leehrtmn@erols.com
www.indianspringsflyfish
.com

Peaceful Valley Cabin
Rentals
Shinhopple, NY 13837
607-363-2211

Pepacton Cabins
River Rd.
Downsville, NY 13755
607-363-2094
pepacton@catskill.net
www.pepactoncabins.com

West Branch Angler's
Resort
PO Box 102
Deposit, NY 13754
607-467-5525
607-467-2215 (fax)
wbangler@tds.net
www.westbranchangler.com

Campgrounds

Beaver Del Campgrounds
Old Route 17
East Branch, NY 13765
607-363-7443

Catskill Mountain
Campground
State Highway 30
Downsville, NY 13755
607-363-2599

Delaware River Club
Flyfishing Resort
*See listing under Hotels
and Motels.*

Oxbow Campsites
3026 State Highway 30
Downsville, NY 13755
607-363-7141

Peaceful Valley Campsites
Shinhopple, NY 13838
607-363-2211

Red Barn Campground
PO Box 50, Route 97
Hankins, NY 12741
845-887-4253
JHab@warwick.net
www.catskillmountain
canoerentals.com

Soaring Eagle Campground
Kellams Bridge, RR 1
Box 300
Equinunk, PA 18417
570-224-4666
soaringeagle@ezaccess.net

Terry's Shinhopple
Campground
HC 68 Box 38
East Branch, NY 13756
607-363-2536

Fast Food,
Restaurants, and
Specialty Foods

Bluestone Grill
62 West Main St.
Hancock, NY 13783
607-637-2600

Chestnut Inn
498 Oquaga Lake Rd.
Deposit, NY 13754
607-467-2500
866-467-0002

Circle E Diner
E. Front St.
Hancock, NY 13783
607-637-9905

Cornerstone Café
5 State Route 41
Deposit, NY 13754
607-467-1111

Crane's Restaurant
68 Second St.
Deposit, NY 13754
607-467-2406

Delaware Delicacies
Smokehouse
Ray Turner
Green Flats Rd.
Hancock, NY 13783
607-637-4443

Delaware Inn
70 W. Front St.
Hancock, NY 13783
607-637-2749

Katie's Café
121 Front St.
Deposit, NY 13754
607-467-3206

La Salette Restaurant
490 Golf Course Rd.
Hancock, NY 13783
607-637-2505

Little Italy II
15 W. Main St.
Hancock, NY 13783
607-637-2855

Lydia's Crosstown Tavern
Route 191
Starlight, PA 18461
570-635-5926

Maclean's Scottish Pub
23 E. Main St.
Hancock, NY 13783
607-637-9917

Martin's Village Barn
Route 191
Equinunk, PA 18417
570-224-2772

McDonald's
86 W. Main St.
Hancock, NY 13783
607-637-2333

Ming Moon
32 E. Front St.
Hancock, NY 13783
607-637-3528

1906 Restaurant and
Steakhouse
Callicoon, NY 12723
845-887-1906

Panda Restaurant
114 Front St.
Deposit, NY 13754
607-467-4926

Red Barn
18 Kelsey Rd.
Deposit, NY 13754
670-467-3789

River Run Restaurant
*See West Branch Angler's
Resort listing under Cabin
Rentals.*

Riverside Bar and
Restaurant
Route 17 (exit 92)
Horton, NY 12776
607-498-5305

Schoolhouse Inn and
Restaurant
Main St.
Downsville, NY 13755
607-363-7814

Scott's Oquaga Lake House
Oquaga Lake
Deposit, NY 13754
607-467-3094

Subway
494 W. Main St.
Hancock, NY 13783
607-637-4800

Teddy's Road House Bar
& Grill
21 Sands Creek Rd.
Hancock, NY 13783
607-637-4500

The Timber
42 Oak St.
Deposit, NY 13754
607-467-5500

Wendy's
390 Route 10
Deposit, NY 13754
607-467-4299

Fly Shops

Border Water Outfitters
159 E. Front St.
Hancock, NY 13783
607-637-4296
607-637-3296 (fax)
bwo@hancock.net
www.borderwateroutfitters
.com

Delaware River Club
Flyfishing Resort
*See listing under Hotels and
Motels.*

West Branch Angler's
Resort
*See listing under Cabin
Rentals.*

Wild Rainbow Outfitters
HC 1 Box 1061
Starlight, PA 18461-9504
570-635-5983
www.wildrainbowoutfitters
.com

Fishing Licenses

New York

Marino's Outdoor World
95 East Front St.
Hancock, NY 13783
607-637-3573

New York City reservoir
fishing permits
http://www.nyc.gov/
html/dep/watershed/
html/wsrecreation.html

New York City Reservoir
Office
800-575-LAND (5263)

West Branch Angler's
Resort
*See listing under Cabin
Rentals.*

Pennsylvania

There are no shops near the
river that sell Pennsylvania
fishing licenses, but you can
purchase one online from
the Pennsylvania Fish and
Boat Commission at
https://www.theoutdoor
shop.state.pa.us/FBG/
fish_secured/FishLicenses
.asp?ShopperID=1CED
3054D58E480090D54BF4B76
6262E.

Guide Services

Ackerman Guide Service
Walt Ackerman
PO Box 181
Roscoe, NY 12776
732-693-3738
bluemoon@pocketmail.com

Angling Adventures
Chuck Swartz
570-296-2823
570-905-4141

Baxter House Bed &
Breakfast
Ken Tutalo
PO Box 751
Roscoe, NY 12776
607-498-5811

Border Water Outfitters
See listing under Fly Shops.

Scot K. Brown
2030 Camp Swartara Rd.
Myerstown, PA 17067
717-933-8974
www.indianspringsflyfish
.com

Bud's Fly Box
Buddy Sherry
91 Last Rd.
Middletown, NY 10941
914-954-2427

Captain Adrian LaSorte
Guide Service
33 Riverside Dr.
Binghamton, NY 13905
607-722-2482
570-635-5968
tightlines@fishadrian.com
www.fishadrian.com

Al Caucci Flyfishing Guide
Service
1 Chestnut Ridge
Tannersville, PA 18372
570-629-2962
ancfbn@1acc.com
www.mayfly.com

Cross Currents Guide
Service
Joseph Demalderis
100 Laurel Acres Rd.
Milford, PA 18337
570-296-6919
crosscurrent@optonline.net
www.crosscurrentguide
service.com

Curly's Guide Service
Roland "Curly" Huber
RR 1 Box 1708
Starrucca, PA 18462
570-798-5151

Patricia "Sam" Decker
530 Prospect Hill Rd.
Cuddybackville, NY 12729
845-754-8226

John Endreson
6448 CR 27
Canton, NY 13617
sledhead162@aol.com

Walter H. Falkoff
Lake Rd.
Starrucca, PA
570-727-2747
860-575-1123

Gone Fishing Guide Service
Anthony Ritter
PO Box 230
Lake St.
Narrowsburg, NY 12764
845-252-3657
riverguide@gonefishing-
gs.com
www.gonefishing-gs.com

Gray Ghost Guides & Flies
Jim Serio and Patty
McGinnis
PO Box 675
Hancock, NY 13783
607-637-3474
570-224-6969
607-637-5484 (fax)
jimserio@hancock.net
www.grayghostguides.com

Jerry Hadden's Guide
Service
33 East River St.
Susquehanna, PA 18847
570-853-4048
fly@jerryhadden.com
www.jerryhadden.com

Gary Henderson
HC 1 Box 1061
Starlight, PA 18461
607-743-0793

Joe Hendrick
1053 Easton Ave.
Schenectady, NY 12308
518-381-8835

Hooks and Brooks Guide
Service
Mark Malenovsky
10 Sterling Pl.
Sayville, NY 11782
631-589-0065
mmalenovsky@yahoo.com
www.ny-fishingguide.com

Indian Springs Flyfishing
Camp
*See listing under Cabin
Rentals.*

Chris Jensen
PO Box 340
Hope, NJ 07844
908-459-4005

Allan Johnson's School
of Fly Casting
PO Box 363
Allamuchy, NJ 07820
908-850-5771
ajflycasting@aol.com
www.ajflycasting.com

Knee Deep Guide Service
Michael Lane
3288 Pioneer Rd.
LaFayette, NY 13084
315-469-6417
Weedrift@aol.com

Bob Lewis
9605 Mallory Rd.
New Hartford, NY 13413
315-737-7841
robertlewis05@yahoo.com

John Miller
231-519-1222
jgm56@hvi.net
www.mayflyphotos.com

Ray Ottulich
3270 Route 28
Shokan, NY 12481
845-657-9522

Outback Outfitters
Robert Sauer-Jones
345 New Turnpike Rd.
Cochecton, NY 12726
845-932-8598
suhn@catskill.net
www.outbackoutfitter.com

Outdoor Adventures
Jim Costolnick
HC 1 Box 1835
Starlight, PA 18461
570-635-5935

Ben Rinker
Hancock, NY 13783
267-221-4383

Darren Rist
6 Hill Terrace
Fredon, NJ 07860
973-300-5726

River of Life Outdoor
Adventures
Wayne Aldridge
19 Latham Rd.
Deposit, NY 13754
607-467-4215
riveroflife@outdrs.net
www.river-of-life.com

Pat Schuler
Callicoon, NY 12723
845-887-5917

Stefan Spoerri
62 Fifth St.
Narrowsburg, NY 12764
845-252-3961

Roger "Moose" Stewart
105 North St.
Saratoga Springs, NY 12866
315-778-1229

Streams of Dreams Inc.
Harry Huff
324 Route 17 North
Upper Saddle River, NJ
07458
201-934-1138

Sweetwater Guide Service
Michael Padua
RR 1 Box 1503
Beach Lake, PA 18405
570-729-0715
sweeth20@ptd.net
www.sweetwaterguide.com

Steven J. Taggert Jr.
29 Euclid Ave.
Middletown, NY 10940
845-342-1670

Trailwater Troutfitters
Timothy Oliphant
2301 Ruddiman Dr.
North Muskegon, MI 49445
231-744-5899

JW Trout
John Warakomski
39 Edgewood Dr.
Baldwinsville, NY 13027
315-638-8230

Two Dog Outfitters
John Dembeck
1522 City Route 3
Hannibal, NY 13074
315-564-6366

Upper Delaware Outfitters
William Fraser
PO Box 1
Hankins, NY 12741
845-887-4853
wfraser1@hvc.rr.com
www.upperdelaware
  outfitters.com

Paul Weamer
607-267-6404
prweamer@frontiernet.net

Judd S. Weisberg
Route 42, Box 177
Lexington, NY 12452
518-989-6583
518-989-6583 (fax)
aware@mhonline.net

West Branch Angler's
  Resort
*See listing under
Cabin Rentals.*

West Branch Gillie
Stan Stavish
60 Lincoln Ave.
Johnson City, NY
  13790-3044
607-729-0885

James Zervos
74 Woodland Ave.
Binghamton, NY 13903
607-723-8082
607-777-4009 (fax)
jimmy@uflyfish.com
www.uflyfish.com

Mike Zukovich
750 Stockport Rd.
Hancock, NY 13783
607-637-2924

Drift Boat and Canoe Rentals

Al's Sports Store
Routes 30 and 206, Box L
Downsville, NY 13755
607-363-7740
(canoes only)

West Branch Angler's
  Resort
*See listing under Cabin
Rentals.*

Wild Rainbow Outfitters
See listing under Fly Shops.

Shuttle Services

Border Water Outfitters
See listing under Fly Shops.

Frank and Bob's Apple
  Shuttle Service
607-768-2059

River Flow Information

Hotline for Delaware
  water releases
845-295-1006

National Park Service
  24-Hour River Hotline
  (April–October)
845-252-7100

Real-time data for Delaware
  River flows
http://waterdata.usgs
  .gov/ny/nwis/current/
  ?type=flow

Reservoir storage and
  capacities
http://www.ci.nyc.ny.us
  /html/dep/html/
  current.html
http://www.state.nj.us/
  drbc/data.htm

Local Split Bamboo Fly-Rod Builders

Little River Rods
Dennis Menscer
PO Box 843
Hancock, NY 13783
607-637-3984

Delaware River Legislation

1954 Supreme Court decree
http://water.usgs.gov/
  orh/ nrwww/odrm/
  decree.html

Regulation 671
http://www.dec.state.ny
  .us/website/regs/
  part671.html

Current "experimental"
  flow agreement
  (Revision 7)
http://www.state.nj.us/
  drbc/Res2004-3.pdf

REFERENCES

Bruno, Greg, and Jessica Gardner. 2006. Phony dam reports. *Middletown (NY) Times Herald-Record,* January 17.

Caucci, Al, and Bob Nastasi. 1986. *Hatches II.* Piscataway, NJ: Winchester Press.

Francis, Austin M. 1996. *Catskill Rivers: Birthplace of American Fly Fishing.* New York: Lyons & Burford.

Galusha, Diane. 1999. *Liquid Assets: A History of New York City's Water System.* Fleischmanns, NY: Purple Mountain Press.

Karas, Nick. 1997. *Brook Trout.* New York: Lyons Press.

Kennedy, Robert F. Jr., Odefey Wegner, and Marc A. Yaggi. 2001. *Finger in the Dike, Head in the Sand: DEP's Crumbling Water Supply Infrastructure.* New York: Riverkeeper.

Knopp, Malcolm, and Robert Cormier. 1997. *Mayflies: An Angler's Study of Trout Water Ephemeroptera.* Helena, MT: Greycliff.

LaFontaine, Gary. 1981. *Caddisflies.* Guilford, CT: Lyons Press.

Leiser, Eric, and Robert H. Boyle. 1982. *Stoneflies for the Angler.* New York: Knopf.

McBride, Norman. 2002. *Radiotelemetry Study of Trout Movements in the Delaware Tailwaters and the Beaverkill: 1995–1997.* Stamford: New York State DEC.

McDonald, John, ed. 1995. *The Complete Fly Fisherman: The Notes and Letters of Theodore Gordon.* Norwalk, CT: Easton Press.

Meck, Charles. 1993. *Pennsylvania Trout Streams and Their Hatches.* Woodstock, NY: Backcountry Publications.

———. 2002. *The Hatches Made Simple.* Woodstock, NY: Countryman Press.

Peper, Eric, and Gary LaFontaine. 1999. *Fly Fishing the Beaverkill.* Helena, MT: Greycliff.

Sanford, D. Kay. 1992. *A Fishery Management Plan for the Upper Delaware Tailwaters.* Stamford: New York State DEC.

Van Put, Ed. 1996. *The Beaverkill: The History of a River and Its People.* New York: Lyons & Burford.

INDEX